The Jaundiced Eye

The Jaundiced Eye

Forty Years of Writing, Reporting and
Ranting from *AutoWeek*'s Publisher Emeritus
Leon Mandel

Edited by
Kevin A. Wilson

"The car enthusiast world loved Leon Mandel. He brought class and authority to the auto industry, in particular motor sports. As a journalist, he was very direct and sometimes feared, but always fair. And for that, he was respected. I am very happy to have called him a friend and to have enjoyed and appreciated his work."

—Mario Andretti

"Leon was a great friend and a credit to the automotive journalism profession. He certainly had a great passion for life and cars. His wit and insight will be sorely missed. I'll always remember one funny story about Leon. Many years ago, he 'rescued' me along Jefferson Avenue in Detroit after the 'gray market' Range Rover I was driving broke down. Imagine my surprise when he pulled over to help. We both laughed about it then, but he never, ever let me forget that day."

—Edsel B. Ford II

"For decades Leon was a lion in the automobile and motor racing world. Back when the print industry had enormous clout he was able to roar and when he did we paid attention. He brought integrity, passion, knowledge and a critical eye to every subject he wrote about. We miss him."

—Dan Gurney

"Through the years, Leon and I shared a passion for the auto industry, in general, and auto racing, in particular. He was a dedicated, intellectual journalist who really understood the business. A tireless researcher, Leon would patiently wait until the appropriate moment to discuss the subject at hand. I always looked forward to seeing him and reading his work. He was a consummate professional and a good friend."

—Roger Penske

"One of my most prized possessions was my friendship with Leon Mandel. He was the heart and soul of *AutoWeek* throughout the years, as the publication went from childhood to adulthood."

—Carroll Shelby

"Leon's words are more than just insight to the auto industry and to the business of racing. He had an extraordinarily keen understanding of life and the world around him. He shared his friendship and his counsel with me, and for that I'm forever grateful."

—Danny Sullivan

"Talk about inspiring, 20 profanity-laced minutes in his office and I chucked a high-paying engineering job to follow him in a life of journalistic poverty. And I'd do it again."

—Patrick Bedard, formerly of *Car and Driver*

"At his knee, a couple of generations of journalists learned to revere—and strive for—great writing. For those of us he mentored, this long-overdue anthology is definitive proof that he clearly taught by extraordinary example."

—David Abrahamson

"Anyone whose major decision in life was whether to become a rabbi or a race car driver has the right priorities."

—Tom Cotter, author of *Cobra in the Barn*

"In the landscape of automotive journalism, Leon Mandel was a force of nature. Direct, acerbic, informed and eminently entertaining, Leon had a unique style, which cut through the hype and hyperbole surrounding new car launches, auto shows and races. Whenever we met, Leon would always ask me to tell him what he should think, when, in fact, it was vice versa."

—Matt DeLorenzo, *Road & Track*

"Leon Mandel was the master craftsman of our trade, the writing of stories about the automobile and those passionate about what we drove. We who were his apprentices could only imagine how Leon could tell those stories so vividly—and with a vocabulary that frequently had us going to the dictionary."

—Larry Edsall, author

"Leon Mandel changed car magazines from sleazy product brochures into first-class literary publications with wide influence. There was a time when the editors of all the major car magazines were all his guys. It was all about the Leon Mandel Code of Behavior."

—Michael Jordan, *Edmunds.com*

"Flaming arrows. That's what I remember about conversations with Leon. One weekend we came together at a race I was writing about for his magazine, and I must have confessed to feeling a barrenness of creativity. His eyes brightened. He started talking. Into my mind came an image: a hillside covered with dry brush, and Leon's words were shooting into it like firebrands, kindling ideas. Our chat left me invigorated, motivated, my brain nicely alight. He gave me a good weekend."

—Pete Lyons, author

"Leon Mandel, a writer whose subject happens to be cars, always rewards anyone interested in either writing or cars."

—Denise McCluggage, *AutoWeek*

"I worked with Leon at a formative time in my career, and he taught me some foundational journalistic principles. Most memorably: "You always have to answer the big, 'So What?'"

—Kevin Smith, *Edmunds.com*

Edition 1.0, April 2010

ISBN-10: 0-9821733-5-0
ISBN-13: 978-0-9821733-5-0

On the Cover
Main image of Leon Mandel: *AutoWeek Archives*
Overlaid image of car competing in Copperstate 1000. *Rhea Dods*, *Ray Eher*, and *Terry Larson*

Book design by Tom Heffron
671 Press logo design by Micah Edel
Copy edit by Leah Noel
Proofread by Wendy Keebler

www.671press.com

Printed in the United States of America

For Leon's grandchildren:
Jake, Alex, Matt, Clay and Maddie

Contents

Contents

Foreword

I WAS LUCKY ENOUGH TO KNOW LEON MANDEL for quite a while. Our friendship covered several decades, and we worked together for much of that time.

Leon was a very special person. He and I logged more than a few frequent-flier miles together, and we never stopped having a good time, something that we both needed on some of our trips. Almost all of our trips were about cars and car companies, and we both seemed to have the same sense of humor when others around us were trying to be serious.

Leon's been gone a while, but I still think about him and feel very fortunate that his wit and wisdom live on in his writings.

I always enjoyed what Leon wrote. I remember when we first met, it was on a Ford press trip to San Diego to test the new Mustang II. We were assigned to bunk together, and we hit it off right away.

The press-trip guidelines suggested that we test-drive a prototype Mustang II, come back and swap with someone for another model, and drive and swap till we got a chance to try out all the various models.

Troublemakers that we were, Leon and I decided that it would be far more interesting and we'd learn a lot more about the new Mustang II if we headed for Mexico.

In those days, it didn't matter much whether or not you had a passport or registration or anything, so we headed into the border town on a mission to see if we could get a new Mexican interior installed that afternoon.

We both chickened out but had a wonderful afternoon together and headed back to the hotel, breezing through U.S. customs without a peep from the border cops. I think we were both hoping to be arrested to make our adventure more exciting.

The PR folks from Ford were outraged. But they couldn't do anything except stew.

Leon wrote a great piece about it, and that was the beginning of a long friendship.

Leon was a great writer, and I've enjoyed the chance to reread these words of his once again.

He was a true treasure among automotive journalists, and anyone who enjoys great writing and cars will enjoy these pages.

—Keith Crain
Detroit, Mich.
January 2010

Introduction

"History ain't history until it's writ."

LONGTIME *AUTOWEEK* contributing editor Kevin Wilson plopped down in a chair in my office and, after letting out a deep cleansing breath, said, "This is *not* the book Leon would have chosen or wanted."

Precisely because Kevin could make that observation is the reason he is overseeing this compilation project. He spent 16 years working with and for Leon, and through passionate pencil edits, laser gazes from over reading glasses, and top-of-lung rants and rails, Kevin got to know whether Leon did or didn't approve of something.

Kevin had often seen the blank look I now gave him—a look I learned at the knee of my old man. I was waiting for the rest of the story and not giving "the tell" of curiosity. "Leon absolutely *hated* stories where the writer put himself into the piece, but some of his best stuff did that." Kevin was right; nothing frosted Leon more than reading not about the subject but about the writer. He said the reader cares not about the author but about the experience. He was also right in that many of the stories chosen here include Leon front and center, and they are some of his best work.

Automotive journalism is about the experience. It delivers a fantasy. It puts a reader behind the wheel—whether it's in a high-horsepower sports car slicing through a mountain pass or in the coddling embrace of a family minivan. Few were better than Leon at transporting the reader in words. He explained the intricate dealings of the automotive business, the sociology and psychology of collectors, the history of the car, profiles of racers, scoundrels and ne'er-do-wells, and did it with the right number of the correct words. He did this because he was a writer first and a keen observer second.

And Leon did not suffer fools. His craft was writing; not a day went by that he didn't consume a book or correct someone's grammatical execution. He did this not to show a superior comfort with the language but because he loved words.

Imagine, then, growing up in a household with someone as passionate about cars and words as Leon. It was fun and precise, agonizing and challenging. But the wonder of the cars he brought home, the people he collected—and who collected him—and the places he went was intoxicating to the point where I knew it was the best job in the world.

Cars became central to his life. The first date he went on with my mother, Olivia Eskridge, was to a race at Watkins Glen when they were in college at Cornell. It was she who invited him. They later gathered their worldly goods and moved across the country in a Porsche. He sold British cars in Northern California. He became an active member of the Sports Car Club of America and started writing. In 1963, Leon joined a San Francisco-based automotive newspaper called *Competition Press*. He found his calling.

This collection should be enjoyed for the quality of writing first and for the historical significance and relevance of the automobile second. That might be difficult, because this collection hits the sweet spot of how the automobile affected the last half of the last century. The pieces describe the car as a societal tool, they share stories about those who profited from their sale and competed at the highest levels, they retell scandal and woe, joy and riches. Central to nearly all of these stories is the car—the lens through which Leon looked—and we look—at life.

And because it shows Leon's love of the language, there's even a fishing story in here, too. By the way, fishing was a pastime he absolutely loathed.

But writing he loved.

—Dutch Mandel
Grosse Pointe, Mich.
January 2010

Editor's Note

ONE THING I'VE KNOWN FOR CERTAIN about this compilation of Leon's writing: My selections from his vast body of work, some guided by his son Dutch's advice, would not coincide with Leon's own.

But that's OK. Intentional, even.

This was never meant to a "best of" Leon Mandel collection so much as it is one compiled for and by people who knew, admired and, all in our own ways, loved him, including most of all his many readers. We've included stories and columns that make us say, "That's Leon, that's his voice, these are the topics that intrigued and motivated him, here are the people who engaged his interest, the places and activities that made his a full and well-lived life."

Leon's six books do not include a memoir, which is no surprise at all to those writers who worked for him over the years. None of us will ever forget his distinctive gravelly voice commanding: "We do not write about ourselves." By this he meant to focus us on the readers and their concerns, not our own.

But of course we all do write about ourselves—and he did, too, probably more frequently than he'd have recognized, though almost always in the context of trying to convey a universal experience. His readers connected with what he wrote. They reacted and communicated in ways that made *Competition Press* and its successor, *AutoWeek*, "interactive" publications long before the Internet and Web pages made that word commonplace.

He delighted, disappointed or even infuriated readers with his views, which typically did not coincide with those of the mainstream. But his readers stuck with him, following him from *Competition Press* to *Car and Driver* in 1968 and '69, to his books about William Harrah and Peter Revson in the early '70s, even to *Motor Trend* later that decade, and always when he returned to *AutoWeek* (he left three times and returned as many). Readers stayed with him even when he was irritating and when they thought he was wrong-headed. His work made it clear that he cared deeply about the same things his readers cared about. The cold, dispassionate objectivity of the itinerant reporter of news was not for Leon—he was one of us before he was a journalist, and he stayed one of us even as he stood up for the highest standards of journalism in the automotive arena.

This book won't substitute for a memoir or autobiography, not least because he never chose to tell his readers anything much about himself before age 25 or so (those who were close to him didn't hear much more than the readers did). But I do hope that this compilation will remind us all of who Leon Mandel was and of the important contributions he made to automotive journalism, motorsports and the auto industry. I've left out nearly as much excellent work as I've chosen to include, so if you don't find your favorite Leon Mandel piece in this book, I apologize and encourage you—as Leon always did—to communicate that to the folks at *AutoWeek*.

—Kevin A. Wilson
Waterford, Mich.
January 2010

Chapter One

The Journalist's Eye

66 **Where, I wonder,** are the concerned thinkers among you? Don't you see the evils of motor racing; don't you see its shining virtues? Or don't you care? Or can't you write? Or would you rather whine to your wife and slink away into a corner of your garage when you are raped by the likes of Douglas Toms or William Haddon or Shirley Povich? You can be passive if you wish, my friends. I will not. **99**

Leon insisted that automotive journalists should be just that—journalists first, with all the ethical standards that implies. In the late '80s, at an editorial-staff retreat, he distributed a summation of this ethic that I kept pinned to a wall for decades. Some excerpts:

GOALS, HOPES AND EXPECTATIONS

1. Best weekly in the country. By the way, the subject is motoring . . .
SOME POLICY ABSOLUTES and some not quite so.

- AutoWeek is part of a profit-making entity. One of its principal functions is to make money, but not at the cost of integrity. Money is made through excellence, liveliness, innovation.
- AutoWeek edit does not tolerate conflict of interest. This is the absolute among absolutes.
- AutoWeek is the reader's ambassador to the industry and to the racing community. It has entre everywhere. It keeps no secrets. It does not, for example, suppress or bend facts "for the good of the sport."
- AutoWeek is written in the English language. Offenses against the language are forms of self-abuse, masochism. They will not be tolerated. This is the second absolute among absolutes.
- AutoWeek's inventory goes down the elevator each night and comes back in the morning. Only the best and brightest will do.

Not all of that "inventory" stayed at AutoWeek, of course, so for a long while the majority of automotive journalists in America could include reference to the publication on their résumés, and that meant they'd all been exposed to Leon's approach (including the ones he'd fired, who for a while seemed to outnumber those who'd left of their own volition). Those who worked with and for him heard a lot of this kind of talk, while readers, appropriately, were better served by the application of these high standards rather than discussion of them. Sometimes, though, Leon found it worthwhile to lift the veil and talk about the journalist's role in the interest of providing readers with context. This chapter compiles a few of those examples.

Objectivity Be Damned

June 17, 1972

It's been nearly 40 years since Leon penned this statement of purpose and intent, so some topical references might elude the understanding of younger readers. If Formula B or Brett Lunger means nothing to you, you won't miss the point as a consequence. Where explanation seems essential, you'll find footnotes clarifying a point.

MIKE HANSEN, AT LEAST, HAS BEEN PAYING ATTENTION. He not only read the race report on the Formula B event at Laguna Seca, he objected to it and went so far as to write a complaining letter to us.

It was not objective, he said. It was overly critical. How could we, who have gone on record as favoring the Formula B series, actually presume to rush into public print with the criticism that "outsiders" might read and believe? It was shocking, he implied, it was the act of a turncoat, it was . . . unAmerican.

Right, Hansen. Absolutely right.

Because, you see, the race was dreadful. It was boring. It was an endless parade of witless driving. It lacked drama, suspense and artistry. It was quite the opposite of what Formula B racing can and should be—and we, more properly, I, had the temerity to say so.

You had better know, if reading that piece and a Sebring race report some weeks ago had not already given you a clue, that I am no believer in objective journalism. Objectivity (as I wrote Hansen and am now telling you) is the province of the *Christian Science Monitor* and *Consumer Reports*. It has long been discredited as a realistic goal of modern journalists; even journalism schools, those citadels of contemporary William Jennings Bryanism, have abandoned it as a precept. You might get it from Knepper and his minions (who vastly outnumber me in both manpower and influence as well they should, he is the editor after all), but you'll never get it from me.

(As an aside, the British motoring press is the great exponent of objectivity in racing journalism. I will content myself with quoting Raymond Chandler: "The English," he said in *The Simple Art of Murder*, "may not be the best writers in the world, but they are incomparably the best dull writers.")

The point to all this being I tend to think rather more highly of most of you than to be objective. *AutoWeek* readers (to whom I have been addressing myself, on and off, for now about eight years) are not your average strokes. They—you—are participants and competitors and car owners and other motorsports writers. In sum, the people who not only know the sport but have an investment in it. And they—you—are brave enough to be told the truth. Moreover, your faith is firm enough to withstand it. Even more than that, you deserve to know.

So if the town of Sebring is an execration, you will hear that from me, in addition to the race report, of course. You will even find out if the Florida heat is beating up on spectators again this year. On the other hand, if the L&M Continental 5000 is the best road racing ever, which it surely is, you will be so informed. And if Brett Lunger is the Hope of Heaven—which after his performance in Monterey is not out of the question—don't be shocked if you read it here. To go even further, I am sufficiently unawed by shibboleths that if I see Benny Scott almost stuff a couple of other drivers into the cactus through sheer ineptitude, I'll mention it—even if he is black.

Well, that's what you're going to get from me.

What I want from you is something other than apathy. At least Mike Hansen is not guilty of that. It seems to me that you—collectively—have two problems in your attitudes about motorsports and your willingness to express them. Either you're willing to accept too many horrors attendant upon the sport: foul johns, rude officials, corrupt writers, avaricious promoters, indifferent sanctioning bodies, etc., because you're afraid the hold that motorsports has on life is too tenuous to jeopardize by criticism; or your vested interest as an F/B freak or an Indy worshipper precludes the very thought of committing the sacrilege of questioning your values.

This Ken Dallison illustration of Leon was used as his portrait for columns.

So the letters that come flooding into *AutoWeek's* offices are filled with platitudes or they carp about something so arcane that it simply doesn't matter to any but about one percent of the motorsports world or they are semi-illiterate flattery. Where, I wonder, are the concerned thinkers among you? Don't you see the evils of motor racing; don't you see its shining virtues? Or don't you care? Or can't you write? Or would you rather whine to your wife and slink away into a corner of your garage when you are raped by the likes of Douglas Toms[1] or William Haddon[2] or Shirley Povich?[3] You can be passive if you wish, my friends. I will not.

---

1. *Toms was NHTSA administrator when Mandel wrote this piece.*
2. *Haddon was Toms's predecessor, the first federal traffic safety chief.*
3. *Povich was a sports columnist for the* Washington Post, *a stick-and-ball guy often critical of auto racing, and also father of Maury.*

25

So I am grateful to Mike Hansen. And to the bizarre lady who wrote in to say she thought it was a shocking violation of the Bill of Rights that I should presume to mention religion in a race report and to Sam Posey who defended his right to the lion's share of the purse in the Continental with an unabashedly elitist argument and to John Timanus[4] whose dry and convincing replies to the macho freaks among you who want to do away with safety precautions in motor racing are welcome whiffs of sanity.

I am on record as saying you will get no Crunchy Granola from me. Kindly do the same for us.

Only an ongoing dialogue by knowledgeable and concerned people can hope to influence the direction of motorsports in this country. It must be passionate and reasoned, mild and outrageous, relevant and peripheral. But most of all it must be. *AutoWeek* is your forum (as it is my platform and you do not notice me being diffident about using it as such); through the pages of this paper you can expect to be heard by the feudal lords of the industry and the sport. If you decline to do so, you are abdicating your right to be heard and you deserve whatever you get. You may even subject me to criticism if you choose. I have no desire to be enshrined in the *Reader's Digest* as the kindliest character you have ever met—which seems to be the ambition of the majority of my fellow motorsports writers.

But I will do this for you. You have a right to know if something you read in *AutoWeek* has been contaminated by exposure to my typewriter. So I will petition Knepper to consider using a byline or initials on my submissions. If you're going to have a bout of hydrophobia about something that appears in these pages—and I sincerely hope you do—you at least ought to know over whom to spew the foam.

I'll be here.

---

4. Timanus was SCCA's technical chief for more than 20 years.

Pony Express Rides Again!

Sept. 22, 1973

This short piece resulted from Keith Crain and Leon teaming up to test the new Ford Mustang II by skipping out on the canned press introduction plan and driving the car from San Diego to Mexico.

SECURITY ON THE MUSTANG II has been about as leak-proof as Watergate, admitted Ben Bidwell, general manager of Ford Division, at the car's introduction on Coronado Island near San Diego.

And its reviews have been about as favorable, he might have added but didn't. The *Detroit News*, whose auto editor is considered the single giant in a population of journalistic pygmies, ran without further comment excerpts from the buff books. *Road & Track*, *Car and Driver* and *Car Craft*. They were bad, almost without exception.

But what the hardcore porno enthusiast wants and needs is not necessarily what the public wants and needs. From a four-hour drive in the Mustang II, every impression is that it will be a car the public will want as much as its beloved uncle, the Mustang I.

The new car is not startling, but it is attractive. There are only two models, but between them they offer some 50 options, including a new U.S.-made 2.8-liter V-6 engine (the 2.3-liter, also made in the United States, is standard), steel-belted radials, velour seats and sunroof.

Ford has upped its production figures for the Mustang II from 300,000 to 400,000 for the coming year. If they have trouble selling all 400,000 in San Diego, they might try crossing the border. One comely lady in Tijuana, riding in the back of a pickup, spent four blocks looking at the front of the new Mustang, coming out of her reverie only when she realized it was something new in her experience. For the whole distance of Block Five she laughed and applauded.

And the hard-bitten customs and immigration agent at the crossing dropped her bored expression at the sight of the red fastback,

AutoWeek used this photo to accompany Leon's column for those instances he defined as "viewing with alarm."
AutoWeek Archives

hitched her regulation .38 a little further over toward her right buttock so she could exit her cubby box, squealed in delight and engaged the publisher of *Automotive News* in intimate conversation about the car.

He thought about it all the way back to Charger Stadium and then announced that so far as he was concerned, ladies with .38s were a little freaky, anyway.

To Be Continued

July 27, 1974

Leon wrote this column when he left Competition Press and AutoWeek *in 1974. This was the second time he left—the first time he went to* Car and Driver *for three years in the late '60s. This article includes a little pocket history of the publication. This was only a few months after the publication of* Speed with Style, *which he co-wrote with racing driver Peter Revson, who'd died in an accident in South Africa just as the book was going to print. The book was well received, and Leon was pursuing other book ventures, which eventually included a biography of casino impresario and car collector William F. Harrah;* American Cars, *a history copiously illustrated with photos of Harrah's collection; a mystery novel,* Murder So Real, *under the pen name Al Bird; and* Driven: The American Four-Wheeled Love Affair, *an analysis of both the benefits and the problems facing the car industry in the late 1970s. Before Leon returned to* AutoWeek *in 1983, he would toil three years as editor of* Motor Trend *and then write what turned out to be his last book,* Fast Lane Summer, *a first-hand account of a racing season with driver Danny Sullivan and Garvin Brown Racing in the second iteration of the SCCA Can-Am Series.*

IT IS ODDLY DIFFICULT TO REMEMBER THE MOMENT, 11 years ago, that I wandered innocent into the San Francisco offices of *Competition Press* asking for a job.

The moment of my arrival at *Comp Press* is gone, lost in the swirling mists of a middle-aged memory. Of course I remember the cast of characters: Bill Finefrock, now departed, a graduate of the *Cleveland Plain Dealer*, fussy, meticulous, a hard-nosed newsman; Don Bice, the prototypical art director type. He's gone now too.

Russ Goebel is not gone. It's hard to imagine that he ever will be. If you can anthropomorphize the generators at the Grand Coulee Dam and combine their energy with the fierce and intimidating presence of the mushroom cloud, you begin to see Russ Goebel.

There they were, on Boardman Place, right across from the San Francisco jail. And although the days were full and the offices small, I recall only a kind of tranquility, a peacefulness amidst the turmoil of growth.

Cover of *American Cars*, published by Random House on July 4, 1984. The illustrated book featured Cindy Lewis and Baron Wolman photos of cars in the Harrah collection.

Growth there was, and at an astonishing rate. Finefrock, Bice and Goebel had bought the fortnightly *Competition Press* from *Road & Track*. It had been a disastrous adventure by *R&T* even though the magazine had hired the remarkable Jim Crow to be editor. Circulation was about 8,000, nobody advertised, nobody took the 12-page newsprint competition supplement very seriously.

But when the energies of Finefrock and Russ Goebel and Don Bice were applied, astonishing things began to happen. Circulation began a crazy climb; the book went weekly, people began to pay attention and almost before anyone noticed, *AutoWeek*, as it was newly named, had become a genuine force among car books and clearly the head-and-shoulders leader among motor racing publications.

By then, offices had moved to the San Francisco suburb of Lafayette. I had mixed feelings about that since the charm of the bail bond district of the city had showed itself in the occasional quixotic fashion.

Well, *AutoWeek* had moved to Lafayette in its inexorable climb upward and I suppose that made sense. My editorial associate then was Charles Fox, certainly the most talented motoring writer I'd ever encountered. I still think that's true and I measure him against other alumni of *Competition Press* who are no slouches themselves.

For example, Denise McCluggage, a fine writer, a courageous driver, a lady whose mind is sharp as diamonds, whose wit is sharper than an Ehrlichmann's tooth. For further example, Brock Yates, an early contributor of words and, believe it or not, cartoons. His drawing was execrable; his words were as filled with vitality then as they are now. Steve Smith, ex-editor of *Car and Driver*, and Mike Knepper, now feature editor of *Road & Track*, David Abrahamson, managing editor of *Car and Driver*. And, of course, Jim Crow.

All of this is to say that I lived in some very imposing shadows.

I thought about those people last week as I walked down the long, long hall in our immense new building in Reno toward the press room. We'd never had a press room before we came here. Somebody else had done our printing, somebody else our color separations, somebody else our mailing, somebody else our subscription fulfillment.

Now it was all here in a huge, automated plant in the high desert. With it were our new sister publications: *American Boating*, *American Collector*, *Our Town* and one about to be born about general aviation. From perhaps five employees, the company had grown to 80 or more.

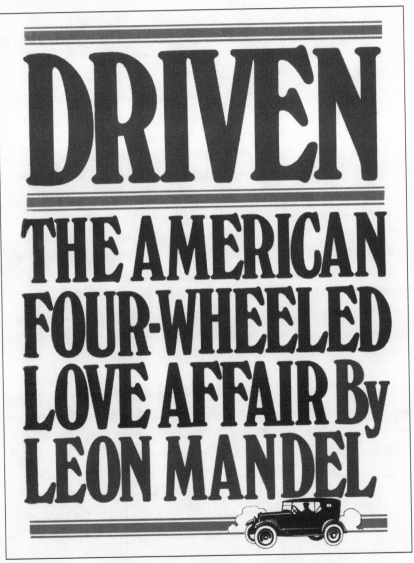

Cover of *Driven*, published by Stein and Day, Jan. 1, 1977.

I reflected that *AutoWeek*, with slightly more than 100,000 weekly circulation, had come further than anyone had dreamed; mostly due, I suspected, to the extraordinary talents of Russ Goebel, who had emerged in my perception as a unique combination of turn-of-the-century entrepreneur in the mold of James J. Hill and Jay Gould and the modern American manager, celebrated by *Business Week* as today's folk hero.

Well, there we were, I thought. A presence. But more than that, a publishing institution. And at that moment, I was probably sadder than I'd been since 1963 when I walked in off the street with small hope and a smaller savings account.

A publishing institution does not need, cannot afford, to have a wild-eyed journalist as stationmaster. To do justice to what Russ Goebel had built required a modern American manager much in his mold. I was not one, I realized, nor did I want to be.

That Sunday I resigned. I am left with genuine affection for his company and for the readership of *AutoWeek*. Both have offered infinite stimulation, endless challenge, moments of rage and moments of intense pleasure. I shall remain as a senior editor and for that I am grateful.

But not, I hasten to add, any less abrasive.

The Opel in
the Junkyard

A LESSON IN
BUFF BOOK FOLKLORE
Dec. 10, 1990

IT IS 22 YEARS SINCE I WALKED UNCERTAINLY onto the bridge at *Car and Driver* and took the helm. You will not be surprised to hear that things have changed. Looking back can get downright scary. Return with me now to the days of yesteryear, and see if you don't agree.

Introducing the '68 models to America, *Automotive News* posted a market-share box score for the United States. GM had just south of half of all the business in the country (48.3 percent). Ford had a quarter, Chrysler 14.9 percent, AMC 2.5 percent and everybody else (mostly imports) 8.9 percent. The top five selling cars? Impala, Galaxie 500, Mustang (sic), Chevelle and Tempest.

A September issue of *AutoWeek* (then called *Competition Press and AutoWeek*) said in its "Late News" that Mario Andretti would test two Ford Can-Am cars to decide between the Calliope and the Honker and that Firestone was conducting secret tests at Daytona. Elsewhere in the book, American Motors vp Bill Pickett announced that with the new-for-'68 Javelin, "AMC was here to stay."

Sounds odd to the '90s ear, but not nearly as odd as the cars and prices in the classifieds. For example, there were two ordinary, everyday American beaters some people were obviously desperate to sell: a '36 Chrysler Airflow for $600 and a '48 Continental you could buy for $1,500. Something a little more pretentious? How about a '62 Ferrari 250GT Pininfarina convertible for $5,400, or maybe these two: a '59 Mercedes 300SL roadster for $4,550 (or best offer) or a '66 Cobra 427, 5000 miles, best offer over $5,500?

A different world, no? Different too in the new cars that were being offered for sale. Renault was running full-page ads for the Renault 10 that bragged its price was "under $2,000, way under $2,000." For that two grand, buyers got a car that would deliver 35 mpg, had its engine over the drive wheels, rack-and-pinion steering, four-wheel independent suspension, four-wheel disc brakes and a four-speed synchro transmission, all true. Except that the Renault 10 was a lousy car.

You'd go a distance in model year 1991 to find a car as nasty as a Renault 10. These days almost everything in the market is at least acceptable; most are pretty good. Trabant is a running joke in the buff books precisely because it is alone on the end of the spectrum reserved for the truly dreadful. (Plus the fact it's been a while since American car magazines ran very much Trabant advertising.) Because cars have gotten much, much better and because these days auto magazines are mega business, you are as unlikely to find a zinger of a road test in a mainstream car book as you are to find honor in the savings and loan industry. But this is 1990 and we were talking about 1968.

What follows is the story of a moment in the history of one mainstream car book when its editors said what they really thought about a car. The piece, the moment, indeed the milestone, have come to be known collectively as the Opel in the Junkyard.

In September of '67 (when the piece was written) the name on everyone's lips was Ralph Nader, then not much more than a missionary lawyer who had made his name as a legislative consultant to Senator Abraham Ribicoff during that senator's subcommittee hearings into auto safety. Not so coincidentally, a heretofore unknown publisher named Grossman came out with a book by Nader called *Unsafe at Any Speed*, an indictment of the Chevy Corvair, and Nader became notorious. So far as the car magazines were concerned, the Corvair was a back-engined marvel—the little car Detroit should long since have built—and Nader was an ogre. "Naderian" became a cherished buff book expletive and the proper noun a code word for "enemy."

Car and Driver magazine was almost uniquely positioned to respond to the attack on the Corvair. It was the headquarters of iconoclasm and had been ever since David E. Davis Jr. accepted its owner's charge to resurrect it, and stunned the traditionalists with a comparison of two GTOs: Pontiac and Ferrari—invidiously to the, gasp, latter.

Opel chose the moment to introduce a thoroughly innocent, utterly undistinguished, absolutely ordinary—albeit shabbily built— new Kadett to America. Now it happened that one of the periodic changes in the palace guard was taking place at *Car and Driver*. Editor Steve Smith and tech editor Peter L.V. Hutchinson were leaving for paying jobs and persuaded the current publisher of *AutoWeek* and a not-yet-famous tech genius called Patrick Bedard to replace them. On their way out the door, they left a few messages for the newcomers, one of which was they had just tested the new Opel Kadett and found it Naderian.

Thus did the Kadett became the first full test for the new administration, which was filled with all sorts of silly notions about the Higher Purpose of the Car Magazine. A repeat test of the Opel by the newcomers confirmed the judgment of their predecessors. The Opel was genuinely awful. Well, then, where to photograph it? Happily for an apprentice editor, *Car and Driver's* art director, the legendary Gene Butera, was an old hand at finding locations. And his notion for this one seemed inspired.

The February 1968 issue, the first under its new editor, carried these words on the cover: GM STRIKES A BLOW FOR MEDIOCRITY AND CREATES THE ULTIMATE NON-CAR.

That was just the beginning. Inside were not one but two photos of a shiny new Opel posed in a junkyard. And the piece itself was without mercy: "[The Opel] is an electric car without batteries, a paragon of Naderian virtue, a eunuch on four skinny tires . . . it's your definitive non-car, a limp, unending mass of tapioca, an embodiment of zeppelin-sized boredom on an economy scale."

Within a nanosecond of publication, every General Motors entity with an advertising budget canceled everything in *Car and Driver*. It was the biggest dollar disaster in the magazine's history.

It is not likely anyone outside the car magazine business remembers the Opel in the Junkyard, 22 years later. But inside the buff books it became instant folklore—and as the competitors counted the diminished ad pages in the following month's *C/D*, a lesson learned by all.

On second thought, a lesson yes, but maybe not learned by all.

The AAA Magazine That Wasn't

THE TESTS OF TIME TAKE TOLL ON SOME CAR MAGAZINE 'FIRSTS'

AutoTest

April 15, 1991

One more thing that happened in the 1970s while Leon was away from AutoWeek: *a flirtation with the AAA, recounted here.*

"DEAR LEON," READ THE LETTER, "just a note to introduce a new publication from the American Automobile Association—AAA *AutoTest*.

"*AutoTest* is AAA's first comprehensive new car buying guide available to the general public.... If you have any questions ..."

The letter was signed, "Geoff Sundstrom, manager, public information."

Now Geoff is an alumnus of our sister publication, *Automotive News*, so if for no other reason than simple courtesy, of course we'll give *AutoTest* a mention. And while we're at it, discuss its merits which are many, including mainly that the car evaluations—while by no means aimed at the enthusiast—are to the point and as objective as these things get.

Well, almost. Once upon a time the AAA did evaluations itself. They were called "Autographs," two-page summaries of cars driven by the national staff who owed no favors to anyone and who—in the way of consumer professionals serving no single master but instead large, impersonal, insensitive nonprofit bureaucracies—were very outspoken. Trouble was that a staff collected to serve the automotive engineering needs of a club as large and diverse as the AAA had only so much time to do car tests. Enough time, it turned out, to do just a handful a year—so that however crisp and interesting and worthy they

A mock cover, with Leon lying on the pavement, created by the team that worked on a proposed—but never published—car testing magazine for the AAA. *Mandel Family Archive*

might have been, they just couldn't keep up with all that production overcapacity that was churning out makes and models, which in turn reproduced like particularly fecund rodents.

Still—given the 32 million members of the AAA's 157 clubs and divisions in the United States and Canada, and given further the club's strong and hard-earned reputation for fair treatment—it was clear there was a place for a collection of evaluations bearing the AAA imprimatur.

Enter the nice people from *Consumer Guide,* who were prepared to do a deal to produce the reviews in *AutoTest*—with a caveat. That being—to nobody's surprise—that when the *CG* people were done testing, the words and music went over to the AAA's automotive engineering department, where they were reworked and rescored and (the impression remains) all but recreated. In other words, maybe the AAA couldn't justify generating a whole department for the single purpose of providing its huge membership with car tests, but it could find a pretty fair subcontractor and then run a quality control program over the subcontracted pieces that would ensure that fit and finish were to standards.

Now then, thus far everything is as represented, right? Only more or less. Because while the AAA is absolutely accurate in saying *AutoTest* is the club's "first comprehensive new car buying guide available to the general public," it is not the first new car buying guide the club has ever tried to do.

Return with me now to the glorious disco days of the weary '70s, to a modernesque building in lovely Falls Church, Va., to the office of a furiously ambitious, clever fellow whose engineering career was somehow sidetracked from the Ford Motor Company to a sleepy, balkanized service club called the American Automobile Association.

Jim McDowell, chief of automotive engineering and road services, was operating under false pretenses. Ostensibly, he was there to streamline all the various services offered by an old-fashioned organization so that members, then 18 million of them, could feel attended to efficiently. And perhaps more important, so that members of the board of directors of the club could feel useful. And productive. And virtuous. But at the same time not too useful and productive and virtuous. Because the secret of all non-profit organizations, and particularly those brought to full bureaucratic flower in and around the District of Columbia—home of the mother of all such organizations—was that it should seem to be central to the lives of those it served, while at the same time making almost no demand on the effort or commitment or talent of those who ran it.

Most of all, it should never under any circumstance put anyone or anything involved with that organization at risk of losing either his job or so much as a moment of his afternoon nap.

Into this paradise of inactivity came Jim McDowell, a whirling, churning vortex of aspirations. One of which—seeing as the AAA had a potential 18 million subscribers—was an auto magazine.

In little or no time, McDowell organized a magazine SWAT team—a pair of ruthless consultants, one editorial, one circulation. An in-house accounting whiz; a careful, meticulous, highly qualified test engineer, an overseer in charge of adherence to procedure and—where he got him nobody knows to this day—the resident wit-cum-skeptic-cum-jack of all deals.

What emerged was a down-to-the-last-detail plan for one of the most ambitious, clever and useful consumer magazines ever to set word to page—drawing on amazing resources the AAA didn't even know it had. Imagine a car book that harnessed a data base gathered from 25 million-plus road-service calls a year. Think for a moment about a magazine concerned with things like longevity, serviceability and durability of cars that were routinely serviced in a club-overseen repair program in 26 states. Contemplate the resources of a huge national club focused on a test facility with no other purpose than to examine how well cars were designed and made. And imagine all this in a magazine that took no advertising and was responsible to no one other than its members.

Sound too good to be true? It was of course. Cost was too high, effort too great, and worst of all, the risk inherent in publishing a magazine that took a stand and actually helped its members make decisions was far, far too high for its timid board of directors.

McDowell, as clever as he was ambitious, rode out the storm and today is the No. 2 man in the AAA, responsible for much of its recent competitiveness, not to mention its sudden appearance in the 20th century.

The test engineer went wiser into the night. The editorial consultant survived and his name appears on the masthead of this very magazine.[5] As for the resident wit-cum-skeptic-cum-jack of all deals, the experience was too much for him. He had seen the outside world and would never be the same. His name is Bill Lovell;[6] IMSA and *AutoWeek* are far the better for his miraculous enlightenment.

---

5. *And in the byline of this column.*
6. *Senior editor at the time, covering sports-car racing.*

Chapter Two

The Open Road

"A summer's voyage should begin with the discontent of a city spring, the lure of an unexplored horizon. A delicious May evening descends, filled with the scent of the unknown, and there, at the curb, is your car. It is ready—it is always ready—because you keep it that way for exactly this moment. You have no idea where you are going, nor why, but you can no more stay where you are than you can stop breathing. It is the migratory urge.**"

In popular perception, the working life of a motoring writer is all glamorous travel over the world's best roads in the world's best cars. Never mind the mundane realities, the fact is that exotic cars and great drives are the high spots and plentiful enough for anyone. Leon Mandel had managed some pretty exotic automotive experiences even before he became an automotive journalist, and as this chapter demonstrates, his career included some spectacular drives—and rides.

Rumbling Toward Bethlehem

A NEW WIFE, AN AIREDALE, A PORSCHE
AMERICA AND 3,000 MILES TO GO . . .
LIFE HAS NEVER BEEN THE SAME SINCE
May 12, 1973

I THINK I BEGAN TO NOTICE THE PORSCHE population explosion about a year ago when the girl-next-door stewardess on National to Tampa told me that all she wanted in this world was a Targa.

There had seemed to be more and more of them, more 911s especially, on California freeways and New York throughways and Pennsylvania turnpikes than even Datsuns, but I wrote that off to their visibility; oranges and silvers and deep metallic browns as well as the fact that somehow you look for Porsches and you rarely notice a Datsun when it whooshes by.

But when the squeaky clean girl on the DC10 told me about her dream, I began to check seriously and I noticed that the Porsche column in the classifieds was getting bigger and bigger. There is not yet a Porsche plague; thank heavens, 911Ts are not behind curtains on *Let's Make a Deal*. But Porsches have clearly become the patched pocket of the bachelor, the Garrard of the single girl. And while I understand it as a social phenomenon, I do not understand it economically, and my inherent snobbery tells me that it is regretful. The last time I asked the price of a 911S with Sportmatic it was something over $10,000. Since then there have been clean and dirty floats and devaluations and revaluations, and now, I expect the cost is somewhere near $12,000 or $13,000. If ground round is up to $1.36 a pound, I suppose that makes sense. But where do the young get $11,998.64 more than that to spend on a car? I simply don't know.

Envy is part of it, I suppose, and bafflement too. But more important, it means that Porsche has emerged from that secret, select circle of magic objects for magic people and become a common artifact of our culture.

It was not always so. Very much the opposite in fact. The one and only Porsche I ever owned was a 1952 America coupe bought new from Max Hoffman himself through a Buick dealer in a New York college town because I had been struck by a ray of the moon. I did not then know what 1 had; I would be embarrassed to admit today that I still do not know much about the car. It has come to me since that it was the first of the "Normals." No split windshield, no crashbox, no roller bearing crankshaft. But those were enormously recondite matters, far beyond any understanding of mine when I bought the America coupe, so I conclude now that however unconscious I was then of the reasons, there must have been powerful cause for me to wheedle and cajole the $3,495 from a local banker who had never heard the word Porsche in his life before.

I suspect it had something to do with a desperate need to be one of the chosen. Certainly there was no foresight, no avant garde understanding of what sports cars really meant, no inkling that with the Porsche I was getting a piece of the future.

It was still a primitive world that surrounded the sports car owner and racer in 1952. The headquarters of the SCCA was in a great gray stone house in Cazenovia, N.Y., and John Bishop had yet to make his decision to become a member of the club's Central New York Region. There was a race at Watkins Glen and one at Sebring. *Road & Track* existed, but its circulation could not have been large enough to keep even the printer alive. Its attraction was not merely that it discussed the unknown, but that it was on the West Coast, a kind of Sports Car Paradise where Strange and Marvelous things were happening. Those of us in the East knew that the Western littoral was vibrating with vitality (*Road & Track* was telling us that), but we had not seen it; we could only imagine. Almost everyone I knew was headed west as a result of the inexorable lure of what we were convinced was sports car Nirvana, and it didn't change our minds much when we opened an issue of *Life* to see a photo spread of TCs driving underneath lumber haulers. If they were doing that out there, what other marvelous, delectable affairs were offered to sports car owners? A Porsche or an

MG or a Jaguar on the West Coast was obviously a passport to a life so filled with delight and excitement that it was almost unimaginable.

So although I bought my Porsche in New York, it was really the West Coast that provided the dream, and therefore the urgent need to own it. I couldn't drive it properly, and looking back, it is very likely there was not much there to be driven. The early Americas were ill-handling, sluggish, uncomfortable animals fitted out in corduroy. My guess is (although I do not know) that a Super Beetle of current vintage would probably have outperformed it. I do know that the car swapped ends at will. In corners, on straights, in parking lots, sitting in the garage. I had owned (and still did) an MG, which in no way prepared me for the Porsche. Its failing in that respect was surely not a deficiency in its own character. Nothing prepared the neophyte for Porsches in 1952.

It was not that they behaved so oddly when they were set in motion; it was more what they represented as social appurtenances that dramatically altered the early Porsche owner's life.

It is hard to imagine a world without the VW, but that was upstate New York in the early '50s. And if the sight of a VW was enough to startle, the vision of a Porsche was purely paralyzing. Those were the days of waving on the highway between sports car owners. The Porsche was such a shock that even the sports car owners did not have the presence of mind to wave. They simply stared.

The simple, distilled effect of owning a Porsche America in 1952 was enough to define my life forever after. Had it not been for that car I might have found myself enmeshed from then on in the corporate structure. If I saw the car as a reflection of my need to own a rebellious and distinctive object, it made clear to me that I could never be a satisfied dweller within the fabric of conventional America. I do not regret it. My debt to Ferdinand Porsche is probably enormous; I repaid him by spending the next 10 years as a BMC salesman and dealer and racing MGs not to win, but only to beat Porsches.

Of course the lure of the West could no more be resisted by me than anyone else who was addicted to sports cars and *Road & Track*. Each day's vision of the Porsche, each month's *R&T* fix heightened the addiction, made more vivid the vision, more ineluctable the decision to migrate. And when the day came, although it seemed to come on impulse, it was the result of a long-built restructuring of my soul.

The trip itself was madness. From upstate New York in the snow, with a new wife, collected belongings discarded almost immediately on arrival, a roof rack filled with the absurd detritus of a Victorian wedding and a great slavering Airedale in the back. The roof rack went in Texas, the wedding presents in New Mexico and the gearbox in the California desert.

If the lunacy of Porsche ownership at the dawn of sports car civilization in this country has not yet penetrated, understand that we were not going for any defined purpose, nor to waiting friends, relatives or jobs. We were going to the inside of Turn 6 at Pebble Beach. That was the beginning and the end of it. The whole and only reason for the air-cooled Conestoga caravan across 3,000 miles. Pebble Beach was somewhere at the end of the road. Pebble Beach was driving the Porsche, not I. We watched the race, only dimly understanding what we saw and remembering nothing, and the Airedale would never come near a car again. Especially a loud car.

So far as conscious direction was concerned, it was the merest coincidence that Pebble Beach was in Northern California and that San Francisco was closer than Los Angeles, and after the race it was there we settled. So Ferdinand Porsche had bestowed another gift upon us, the decision to live in what must be one of the loveliest parts of the world.

There was no money left, the trip and the new gearbox had seen to that, and so the Porsche could not be kept. It was traded for a Rover 75, another *Road & Track* legend, the poor man's Rolls-Royce. But you cannot go from foie gras to okra, and since the hues of each day had come to be colored by the car in the garage, life was soon unendurable. That meant some kind of job having to do with cars because only that way could the vivid car that had become so integral a part of our life style be afforded. Still, not even then did I understand what the Porsche America had etched as my destiny.

Olivia and Leon shortly after settling in California with their cross-country companion Airedale, Siddley. *Mandel Family Archive*

Leon in his days as a car salesman, with his MGA at Kjell Qvale's store in Burlingame, Calif. Leon not only sold MGAs, he raced them, not very successfully but sufficiently to prove they could be used both as daily drivers and as competition cars. *AutoWeek Archives*

Curiously, the car ended up belonging to one of the first friends I made in the West, although I did not know it until six months after we met. He remains a friend and it is now 20 years.

Last night contemplating this writing, I felt about the Porsche as I feel about Scott Fitzgerald. There was a period in my life, when I was in high school and Fitzgerald had sunk from prominence to a point where his name was all but unknown, that I discovered *Gatsby* and *Tender Is the Night*. Something of my very own. A treasured possession that only I had taste and perception enough to seek out and relish. Since, of course, Scott Fitzgerald has become kind of printed Norman Rockwell, Mia Farrow as Daisy Buchanan for God's sake. But the clubby, trendy, insy people who talk about *Gatsby* as though they had written it themselves remain ignorant of *Diamond as Big as the Ritz* and Fitzgerald's only play, *The Vegetable*, or *From President to Postman*. Those, at least, are still mine.

And so, however dim, the memories of how delicious it was to own a Porsche in 1952 remain. How special it was, how marvelously bewildering.

I see the 911s and the 914s parked by the singles apartments and listed three columns full in the *Chronicle* classifieds and I wonder now, can it be the same for them?

Heroes, Artisans and Rogues

THE HEART OF THE GREAT AMERICAN CAR REVIVAL
June 12, 1995

IT IS A CAREFULLY POSED PHOTO, shot in the bright Arizona morning against the stunning stagedrop of the oldest and perhaps the most imposing mission in America.

There are 82 cars in the photo. There are too many Ferraris to count. There is a Miller Indy car, enough GT350s and Cobras to bring tears to Carroll Shelby's eyes, the one and only Excalibur prototype, a 4.5-liter Bentley Tourer, a Porsche RS61, Morgans and Corvettes to spare, an international delegation of Jaguars from SS100 to D-Type, a late '01 Yaller and enough 356s to have set the Family up for life. They are arranged squadron-like on the apron of the Mission San Xavier, dotting its parking area with famous national racing colors, coy pastels, signature yellows and blues, all the shades and hues peculiar to the tastes of their owners.

Ah, their owners: a collection as diverse, rich, oddly shaped and individual as the cars. Even more so, they are authentic heroes, poseurs, artisans, famous corporate managers, retired raiders, dilettantes, demure billionaires, great collectors, money predators, international art dealers, shills, attendants, sheetmetal handmaidens, courtesans and camp followers.

This is the Copperstate 1000. Like the Colorado Grand, the California Mille and New Mexico's Las Milas Encantadas, it is one of the new enactments of car enthusiasm in America. It is an orgy of automobility, an evocation of great tours and rallies of the early part of the century: Chicago to Milwaukee, the Glidden Tour, New York to San Francisco. The Copperstate and its brethren are testimony to a wonderful fact of the ultimate decade of the millennium: After all these years, America has finally discovered the automobile *qua* automobile. A device to relish. Not a vacation module. Not a pretext for adolescent revolt; much less a street racer's marital aid.

And on this brilliant April weekend in the American outback, 200 people (give or take) with 82 cars are gathered to participate in four days, 1,000 kilometers, of unrestricted, unreined, untrammeled enjoyment of the car as pleasure object.

. . .

When Phil Hill took off his helmet, climbed back into the C-Type Jaguar he had just raced at Watkins Glen, and headed out across America for home in Santa Monica in 1951, he was setting a course across a car country profoundly different from the one that would become so hospitable 44 years later to the likes of the Copperstate.

It would be five years before Congress would pass the Interstate Highway Act. There were no McDonald's. Kemmons Wilson had yet to open his first motel, called Holiday Inn after the 1942 movie.

And these are mere superficial examples of how far the country was from embracing the automobile—how much closer it was, emotionally, to the Conestoga epoch.

In these car-sophisticated days, it's hard to imagine a landscape dominated, Jurassic Park-like, by '49 Buicks and their ilk. But the two- and three-lane roads taken by Phil Hill as he roared across middle America were littered with absolutely dreadful cars. It's a measure of our malleable memory that these days we think of '50 Studebaker Champions as delightfully quaint and that we collect Edsels and make movies about Tuckers. In fact, almost without exception, the cars of the early '50s were abominable.

The rolling roadblocks along Hill's charge toward California were awful because they didn't need to be any better. At that time— and for three decades forward—Detroit designed cars to satisfy its accountants, not its customers. There was no competition. Volkswagen had barely arrived in America. Toyota, which had just started building cars in Japan four years earlier, and didn't begin importing them to the States until 1958, was hardly a threat.

The postwar economy enabled people to afford things they never before could even aspire to—mainly cars. It would be four more years before the insatiable demand for cars and other civilian products could be satisfied by industries that were still converting from wartime production. In the meantime, people would buy anything that moved, up to and including prewar Hudsons at postwar prices. In 1951, it was still the practice at dealerships across the country to move a long-suffering customer up a waiting list only if he responded to the open solicitation of an under-the-table cash payment to the sales manager or the owner. When the customer's car finally was delivered, it included every add-on and furbelow imaginable to jack up the price, including windshield visors and port-a-walls. But such things made little difference to people who hadn't owned a new car since well before the war, if ever.

Nor did it matter that we didn't know how to drive. It was a vicious loop: We had no need for engineering excellence in our cars because we couldn't drive, and we couldn't drive because our cars required simply that we know how to start them, point them and stop them.

The right-hand-drive Jaguar that Phil Hill pointed from the Finger Lakes toward the Pacific had an aluminum body, space frame, overhead-cam engine and Alfin brake drums. It was so much more sophisticated than a contemporary American passenger car that it might as well have been a UFO to people who saw it on the highway—they knew neither what it was nor its reason for being. And if they had been told that it was being piloted by a future Formula One world champion, they would have been bewildered; the notion of "world champion" was as immediate as "moon walk." In 1951, we were a nation of car ignoramuses.

But the revolution was upon us.

For all the remarkable facts of Hill's pioneering journey across America in the C-Type, it was the man far more than the car who represented that real car revolution. Forty-four years later, driving his 1930 Pierce Arrow Cabriolet in the Copperstate, a 68-year-old Hill would anchor the event in history.

The object of an enterprise like the Copperstate is to celebrate the automobile and the legends that surround it. Not only does Hill accept it as his responsibility to guard those legends, but everyone who knows him agrees that it is Hill who provides their authentication. In the tradition of the greatest world champions, Hill honors his past. The Pierce Arrow he brought to the Copperstate has been in his family since it was new, and it had carried him twice daily on his college commute to the University of Southern California. Hill dressed every evening during the four-day Copperstate trek in blazer and tie, and verbally brought his and Ferrari's world championship days to life in detail so vivid and imaginative that the experience of listening was almost theater. He has spent his life researching the car culture, as if he were a curator in its worldwide museum. Would you like perspective on Alfred P. Sloan and his contribution to the notion of Planned Obsolescence?

Hill will as readily talk about the value of authenticity in restoration as he will about current drivers and their techniques—and he is very explicit on that subject. Of all the people in the car universe, he is as worthwhile listening to as anyone imaginable. He punctuates almost every point he makes with "What do you think?" or "Don't you agree?" During the Copperstate he mingled with strangers and friends equally, and accepted dinner companions whether they came boldly or with diffidence to his table to ask if they might sit with him. He is an intensely animated man whose presence fills the air with electricity, and whose immense energy suffuses his still-young face. In the old days he was merely California handsome; now his regular, pleasing features are traced by character lines acquired in a life of risk, insight, disappointment and success on a world stage. If the Copperstate is a cross-country revival, he is its high priest. It is one of the great joys—indeed one of the principal purposes—of an event like the Copperstate that there are evenings filled with the dynamism of the thoughts and words of a man like Phil Hill.

The second day out, Harley Cluxton's absolutely perfect lightweight 427 Cobra broke, providing gentle fodder for everyone who knew him—which is to say everybody in the entire car world, Arizona and otherwise—to needle him. While it is true that the world knows Cluxton, and he is everyone's favorite target (a role he accepts with *elan* and grace), almost nobody knows exactly who he is, despite the fact that he has been mostly everything and mostly everywhere. He passes himself off as conventional by dressing as if he were modeling for a Brooks Brothers store on the Italian Riviera. Think of a lean Jack Nicholson in his best years. Think of a leprechaun attached to the CIA. The son of an immensely successful physician, young Harley grew up in suburban Chicago with three commandments. Don't play football. Don't ride a motorcycle or drive a race car. Don't have any truck with lawyers. The outcome was absolutely predictable; at Culver Military Academy he was a football star, he graduated from Tulane law school, and in between he was a marvelously successful racer, including a stint in Formula Two with backing from the legendary American Ferrari impresario Luigi Chinetti. Cluxton's significance to the Copperstate— indeed, to the entire car revival movement in America—comes not from the fact that his international credentials include ownership of the Mirage team, a winner of the World Manufacturer's Championship. Nor that he also once acted as entrant for the Renault Formula One team, back when Renault needed a prominent front man—a beard— because it was unwilling to admit its involvement until it was sure its engines were competitive: *"Plausible deniability"* (as it was called during Vietnam) was what Cluxton provided for Renault. Nor even that during that war he was a Special Forces officer very active in Southeast Asia, and afterward is said to have continued his relationship with its overlords. And to this day.

Cluxton's highest importance to the Copperstate does not even come from his relationship with Ferrari and Arizona. After he had decided that lawyering was a pain in the neck, and was looking for something to do that was more central to his life, his friend Luigi Chinetti—offering his blessing, encouragement and perhaps even backing—asked him to point to any place on the map where he might want a Ferrari distributorship. Harley chose Phoenix.

No. Cluxton's significance comes from his remarkable evocation of a pair of extraordinary figures who were giants in the international art world during the early part of the century. Joseph Duveen was a

London art dealer who filled the mansions of the new American rich with *objets d'art* and furnished much of the grand collections of the great museums of the world. He was a scoundrel but also a very great man, and his guru was a former art student turned Delphic oracle named Bernard Berenson. Whatever Duveen proposed to his clients the immaculate Berenson blessed. With their trendsetting imprimatur, both state collection and nouveau riche were assured that they were buying only the authentic, and the best.

In the car world, Harley Cluxton these days is a wonderful combination Duveen and Berenson. With the exception of the narrowest of specialists—automotive analogs to collectors of the Clouded Yellow Butterfly—nobody knows car history, car worth, values and prices better than Cluxton. More important still, like Duveen, indeed *all* the legendary international art dealers, Cluxton's genius lies not so much in selling *objets d'art* as in knowing where they are to be found. Equally important, he knows his buyers. "If a second, expressed in terms of money, is ten dollars," Harley asked on one exquisite outdoor dining night at the Copperstate, "how much time do you suppose a billion would be?"

Thirty-seven months, he said, and looking around the assemblage, he ventured that there was enough time at the tables to take us well into the next century. "Before the Mirage deal," said Cluxton's banker, "he had a very big line of credit and he used it." Now, the banker says with some wonder in his voice, while the credit line is still there, Cluxton hasn't touched it in a long, long time.

If Cluxton is the Copperstate's figurative ambassador to the art world, he is also its cruise director. (Mind you, he doesn't make it run. That is Mike Mullen's job, and he does it with the efficiency of an old-fashioned stationmaster.) Cluxton is everywhere with everyone, bringing along his wonderfully self-deprecating sense of humor to put people at ease. Chatauquas and other travelling communities have always needed a maker of jokes and a mender of resentments. Cluxton is both those things, and his touch is very light indeed. "Everybody likes him," said Phil Hill, and when it was mentioned that Cluxton nonetheless had his critics, he replied, "Good. That makes him even more mysterious."

When the Copperstate ended in Phoenix, most memories were certainly of an almost magical trek through southern Arizona, a diversity of cars, a mosaic of people. Six months later, when Cluxton's name comes up, everyone who was on the event will recognize it. What they won't quite recall is exactly what he did. Much less who he really was.

. . .

The presence of a world champion/historian and a latter-day Keeper of Provenance on the Copperstate is not to say that its population was elitist, except, naturally, for its considerable automotive elitism. The representation of Jaguars, as if stirred and spawned by Hill's original swath over the country in his C-Type, reflected this healthy appreciation of Automobility. Cardiologist Philippe Reyns— classmate of Jacky Ickx, former neighbor of Paul Frere—and wife Francoise entered their exquisitely restored SS100, the crown jewel of a group that included a wonderful XK140M driven by an exchange team from Switzerland, a 150S, a D-Type and a C-Type. The Coventry cars on the Copperstate were shepherded by a singular figure both in the event and in Jaguardom. His name is Terry Larson and his own collection is extraordinary, but he is best known as the registrar worldwide for Ds and Cs. Beyond that, and more to the point on the Copperstate, he represented a critical element in the Great Car Revival: the artisan. It is the artisan whose role it is to preserve the era.

On appearance alone, Larson could be either a telephone lineman or a Silicon Wizard. He is compact, neat and so absolutely unassuming that it is crystal clear there is much more to him than there seems. However, his wife Darlene couldn't be anything other than what she is: the enabler/office manager for a partnership of neurologists. She is attractive and comforting, she is warm and reassuring; it must be very hard for a patient in the office to leave her side for the forbidding reality of treatment. Both are younger than might be expected, given their interest, but older than they look.

You would probably have very much wanted your Datsun touched by Larson when he was a mechanic at the local dealership; even then he was meticulous, and possessed of a mechanical intuition that provides certain and quick understanding. Darlene financed his first restoration job, on an XK120 roadster, and it turned out to be a labor of discovery. Of a vocation. He sold the car, and she financed his second restoration.

Today they live outside Phoenix, in a house he designed. It abuts his restoration works, a shop whose ambience is what you might expect of a sculptor's studio. It is open and airy under a beamed ceiling and sunken below a seemingly random collection of Ocotillo, Saguaro, Creosote and Lantana, which ring the building's stucco walls and Spanish tile roof. It is exquisitely orderly.

There, in one of the three separate spaces that make up the shop, is Larson's collection. A '54 XK120M; a '61 E-Type Competition roadster that used to belong to Sir Gawaine Bailey; another '61 E-Type, the 50th roadster built; a '38 SS100; a '33 SS 1 Landau Coupe (up for sale); a Lotus 51; a Crusader Sports/Racer he shares with Philippe Reyns at vintage events; and in the corner the motorcycles: a '53 Ariel Square Four, a '38 Indian Sports Scout and an '81 Harley Sturgis. "I've got all the cars I can keep the batteries charged in," Larson says. "Anything beyond that would be ego."

All these, of course, are in addition to the ex-Le Mans D-Type and the C-Type outside the shop entrance, breathing heavily, flanks heaving, having just come from a 1,000-kilometer charge through southern Arizona in the Copperstate. "The point to any car is to use it," Darlene says. Use it indeed. Larson has driven the D not only on the track but on the Copperstate and the Colorado Grand. He has raced the C more often in its vintage career than it was ever raced in its salad days.

It is this commitment to the use of such precious artifacts (the C is worth somewhere in the neighborhood of $400,000, the D half again more) combined with Larson's worldwide reputation as a Jaguar restoration expert (a great deal of his work comes from overseas, principally Switzerland and England) that makes him a legitimate guardian of the Jaguar legend.

Not that he is universally appreciated. Some of his competitors on the track think he goes too fast, while the local Jaguar club thinks he is insufficiently appreciative of the social aspects of Jaguar ownership. To the first charge, he answers that nothing appears on his cars that was not on them during their international racing days. To the second, he sometimes replies with an illustrated fax of a naked man bent over with his head disappearing into his backside and the legend: "Your Problem Is Obvious."

. . .

It is evening on the next-to-last night of the Copperstate 1000. There will be a traditional awards banquet tomorrow, and the expected will be said; but really it is tonight that speaks of the sweet spirit of the event. It may have been true that few of the participants knew one another before the beginning three days previous, but only literally. They shared a bond of car appreciation, a vision of the world through the prism of the car, and a belief that no time could be better spent than in an interesting car on a mean road in the company of like-minded people.

The spirit of rediscovery of the pure pleasure of the car is the hallmark of the Great Car Revival, whether it is found at one of the many concours d'elegance across the nation or rising like a heat wave from the racetracks at the growing number of vintage events. And the flavor and character of the new/old road trips and tours around the states are what hark back to the earliest age of the car in America. To the wonder and delight at its performance; to the grand adventure of driving. And to the astonishing affection that wells in the soul at the sight of a great car.

The C-Type sits in the cool Arizona evening, the last glints of sunlight gleaming off its black bonnet and the bark of its unmuffled exhaust still somehow lingering in the mountain air.

It's so beautiful it could break your heart.

Strafing the Alps

April 24, 1989

ON THE OCCASION OF THE APPEARANCE of a super Corvette *[1990 ZR-1]*, some memories. Nineteen and fifty-three is a century ago; but several of us still breathing inhabited the earth then, too. Those were the heady, champagne days of car discovery, *foreign* cars, as they were know. MG was in the flower of its reputation with the TD. Jaguar was still building the most exciting car it ever made: the XK120. Out on the three-lane, Roadmasters wallowed. Dodge Travellers made their quirky way. When looking at those, which of us could be self-critical of the love affair with the sultry foreigners?

Whereupon came the announcement of the Blue Flame Corvette—a car made of *plastic,* for heaven's sake. Worse still, a six-cylinder, automatic-transmissioned plastic car. No fanatic is so intolerant as a newly minted fanatic, and we were all that. So did I foresee a dynasty when I laid eyes on the first production sports car in what was to be a landmark series? Of course not.

I thought these thoughts as I drove a ZR-1 through Geneva with the chief engineer of Chevrolet, Fred Schaafsma, riding shotgun. That thought and the memory that the last time I drove a big-American-engined car in Switzerland was two decades earlier. It was something called a Monteverdi. It was Swiss and it was filled with excess, but it was foreign. Foreign was still good. Scratch that. Foreign then was still better. If memory does not fail (something it spends most of its time doing these days), my then-colleague Patrick Bedard tried to tell me the Monteverdi wasn't much. What did he know?

He was a recently reformed drag racer; worse, a just-saved Chrysler engineer. In fact, the Monteverdi was more than moderately terrible—and last month all the evils of that car, at the time hidden by the mist of foreign car intoxication, came finally into focus even as the virtues of the ZR-1 were making themselves winningly evident. Geneva is a lot like most cities on the Continent. It's old and it's crowded. Both conspire to make driving a big car an absolutely dreadful experience. The Corvette was not at home in Geneva, but it slipped on its citizen-of-the-world personality and behaved as though it belonged.

The route from Geneva took us along the shoulder of the French Alps and through Grenoble on its way to the Mediterranean coast west of Marseilles. It was a part of France I'd never visited and it was glorious.

We steamed along in formation, 15 big American warships on a reconnaissance in force. Some of the time we blasted down the autoroute, more often we were on superb French blacktop. As the Alps surrendered topographical suzerainty, the road turned tight, twisty and two-laned, carved trails through ancient foothills. The route was goatpath narrow and viciously treacherous as it paid out down the granite walls of deep gorges. Way, way down below—visible from the car only because there were no guardrails—were ancient villages, like tiny Monopoly buildings, huddled on the valley floor.

As the ZR-1 boomed through high meadow sweepers, and gathered its haunches to leap out of the mountainside hairpins, I remembered a summer not long after the end of the Second World

A chat with officialdom during the drive of the original Corvette ZR-1.
AutoWeek Archives

War when I drove a Belgian-assembled American Ford over the Italian Alps not far from that very spot. It was a trip of agony, not because the drive was so demanding (it was), but because in those early days I was a product chauvinist. An America-firster. And for the likes of me, sitting high in the cabin of the Ford, watching the Topolinos stream by, there came a confrontation with reality that forced a wrenching recalibration of attitudes. What would it have meant to me to know that someday there would be an American car that could traverse those brutal roads with the best the Euros had to offer? Lordy!

The route carved its way along until it brought us to the Med, to the sunny coast west of Marseilles. There, on a bluff overlooking the sea, sat the newest of the Goodyear test facilities, Mireval, which began life as a Formula Two circuit. On a brilliant blue day, they let us out to play. The place is eerily reminiscent of Bridgehampton, neighboring ocean and all. Its plummeting right-hand first turn off a high front chute sucks the hubris right out of foolhardy Americans. Although there is not even the remotest chance that a real race will ever be held there again, the fine, challenging switchbacks and sweepers are bracketed by gravel runoff areas to the exacting specifications of the Formula One constructors.

Do I remember 1957 as the first year in which Corvettes demanded we pay attention to them on American racetracks? Names popped into my head: Dick Thompson, Jim Jeffords, Bob Bondurant; those were big guns, did they appear so early in our sports car history? My Corvette-racing neighbors in Northern California then were Sandy Greenblatt, Bob Bent and the late Red Faris. On a day as bright as this, the spring breeze as gentle, the sun as warm and friendly, the first Corvette I ever saw raced made life miserable for Bob Winkelmann in a 300SL Mercedes and a flock of Jaguars led by Cloyd Gray at a place called Buchanan Field. That the still-scorned (at least by me) plastic pachyderm could be so formidable in such company came as a nasty surprise. Attitude recalibration time again.

We were loosed half a minute or so apart to try Mireval in the ZR-1; no wheel-to-wheel, just a joust with the clock and with memories. I expected the Vette to be fast, but to my absolute astonishment the car was as refined as anything I have ever driven on a racetrack.

Superbly balanced. Marvelously capable. Supremely able to make up for the mistakes of its driver.

Even mine. Even a wild, uncontrolled loop from one side of the track to the other, out into the verge and back again with gravel spewing up from the big rear tires, while the car lurched and wove and bucked along very much against its will or nature.

Ah, well—even that didn't dim a glorious trip. A journey on the secret passageways of native Euro Builders: Porsche, Alfa, BMW and Mercedes. A raid in force along bristling borders, which, until now, have kept our homegrown performance cars cowering in their backyards. Never again. And so now I have this to add to my Corvette memories: When the Super Vette paraded the flag on Ferrari's front lawn, it took me along for the ride.

Maximum Driver, Maximum Car

SPORTS CAR ACE AL HOLBERT COMES TO GRIPS WITH THE ULTIMATE STREET PORSCHE
Feb. 1, 1988

THESE CIVILIZED HILLS HAVE SEEN many December mornings as crisp and sunny as this one, but few dawns that have in store such a dramatic surprise. It is an early winter Monday at Weissach, a place where the shamans of Porsche concoct their magic safe from searching eyes. The ground here is bare, brown and hard, covered only with the sturdy tufts of seasonal growth that shrug off morning frosts and nighttime freezes. The ice of darkness is just now beginning to relinquish its hold over a winding, two-lane road from Tiefenbronn. It is just a country lane, really, filled with twists and surprises, lined here and there with stone fences.

Test track gate guards are the same all over the world. They are the commandos of the Rent-a-Cop corps.

"Remember," I have been cautioned, "you do not see what your eyes show you here." I know the drill.

So, as I stand by the break in the Armco barriers and look across the start/finish strip of test track at Weissach, I neither see the prototype 964 at my elbow nor do I hear the unmuffled hoarse shriek of the vehicle tiny in the distance that shatters the postdawn peace of this swale. It makes its metronomic, rackety way up one side of the opposite bank, turns abruptly on its tracks like a toy in the F.A.O. Schwarz window, marches alongside the fence for 100 feet, and pitches mindlessly downward again to the same beat and sound all morning long.

This maniacal puppet is so hypnotic I fail to notice the car.

Fail to notice the car! How is it possible to overlook a device its creator said is endowed with "the closest approximation to racing car performance ever seen in a series production car"? To overlook likely the most coveted performance piece in the world? To be so distracted that the meanest, nastiest, sleekest, toughest, angriest, fastest, costliest, rarest automobile in the world sits whitely and serenely in the Swabian sunshine, unseen?

The answer is: I am not a believer.

The orthodoxy of the followers of Weissach demands the most exacting understanding, requiring an absolute dedication. Theirs is an ornate worship. The text of everyday gospel is intricate enough and has always been difficult to follow. Before me now is the centerpiece of that gospel as it is revealed to today's congregation. The litany of the 959 is elaborate. This is how it reads.

The car designated 959 is the sheetmetal realization of the intentions of Professor Helmuth Bott, Porsche head of research and development, and Peter Schutz, former chairman, to use the 911 as the basis for a limited production precursor to the product future of the company.

But it is not a 911. Almost none of the stampings, pressings, forgings. castings, parts and pieces, tools or dies of the 911 are anywhere involved in its building. Almost unbelievably, it shares only engine placement and number of cylinders with the 911.

The 959 is, however, clearly that car's spiritual heir. The 959 is the car that keeps the 911 alive in the hearts and minds of Porschephiles and holds the front-engined car heretics at bay in their quest to breach Porsche's philosophical gates. Not only does it have four-wheel drive, unlike the 911, "the 959 features new axles, new damping and ride-height control systems, a new antilock brake system, a new six-speed gearbox, water-cooled four-valve cylinder heads, a load-dependent limited slip differential on the back axle, electronically controlled front/rear axle torque split" and more and more, in the rhapsodic words of Professor Bott.

Oh, yes indeed. This wholly new car surely does bristle with hardware and software enough to preoccupy a war lover for a century of gaming, or more important, to induce a sports car fanatic to part with about $302,700 F.O.B. Warrington, Pa., if he could buy one of the 26 coming to the United States, which he cannot. It looks disdainfully upon its inferiors from a perch of technological marvels made up of a 2.85-liter, four-valve, quadruple overhead-cam engine, with water-cooled, three-chambered heads that, with the assistance of twin-intercooled, sequential turbos, makes 450 hp at 6,500 rpm. This, in short, is the maximum car.

. . .

And now, on this ice-bright morning in December at the wizards' lair in Weissach, a white 959 crouches by my side, awaiting only a worthy driver. That is not to be me. An old friend is on his way from the Stuttgart airport. A.J. Holbert is coming to play. Maximum driver, maximum car. What hath Bott wrought? We are about to find out.

As part of his baggage, Holbert willy-nilly carries the reputation for being a highly competent driver of wide experience whose great strength lies in his technical proficiency. This was a judgment I shared for many years—the times of Holbert's seasoning during which he drove in the Trans-Am, IMSA and NASCAR. In 1980, when I spent a year with the Can-Am, and in 1981, when I returned for most of the summer, I discovered once again how witless it is to accept stereotypes. Particularly at Riverside in that second year, I saw a raw, determined, tough side of Holbert he almost never gets credit for.

Suddenly, a blue Rent-an-Opel wheels up and out steps our driver, gloriously outfitted in a red, white and black Porsche Motorsport jacket. He wears no hat, his shoes are not Gucci/Simpson/Air Jordan winkle pickers, but the same kind of loafers he might put on to work in the office over a weekend. There's a big grin on his face, which stretches the already taut skin tight. The Holbert presence has grown so much lately, and his reputation as a taskmaster remains so close to the surface, that any encounter is filled with the same kind and quality of misapprehension as exists about his driving: that he is cool, aloof, not far from being barely civil. So it is forever a surprise at each meeting to rediscover that his manner is utterly relaxed and his voice easy. What's more (I'm not sure how often or how publicly he shows this), Holbert is a man who sees the world's drolleries. Thus his humor, which he uses as a liberal conversational condiment, is wry.

We ease into the car and settle in. Holbert suggests it might be a good idea to fasten my shoulder and lap straps. Out we go, out onto a circuit that's legendary as the test track for Mark Donohue's development there of the brutish 917/30 and on which Niki Lauda set the record in his McLaren-TAG Formula One car of 1:04.6. By the time we get to the first turnoff start/finish, a rising then swooping left-hander, Holbert has the 959 going quick enough that I feel the g's. There is an enormous smile on his face. "You're smiling already," I say, surprised to hear myself speaking so quietly. Holbert nods silently, the smile fixed on his face. He is at work, concentrating, feeling, seeing, absorbing the car's reactions to his movements of the steering wheel, his foot's pressure on the throttle, each shift, each squeeze of the brake.

The first lap is surprisingly fast, the second faster. From then on the speeds rise in astonishing increments. At least it feels that way until the fifth lap or so when we are going as fast as I have ever been on a racetrack. I am outside myself observing me observing Holbert. Holbert is reading out the car's behavior, which has by now become an extension of his own. He has not driven the 959 very much, he says, only to follow Professor Bott home one day, a drive Holbert will remember as one that gave him a whole new dimension of respect for the gentle, scholarly, late-50ish genius whose personality the car so vividly expresses. "He scared me trying to keep up," says Holbert later, with surprise still in his voice.

Now, he's talking to me and to the car and to himself and he's using the same word. "Normally, I'm scared to death here," he says, his body parts working as though the car were connected to them. "Those poles?" He nods his head to indicate striped sticks that line this tight, twisting, defiantly cambered blacktop, set down inside banking that drops away on the driver's side at just the moment he is busiest, revealing dramatic views of the nearby valley. "I used to think they were steel. Then I found out they were just plastic. I found that out the hard way."

We are going blindingly fast. Holbert is into his rhythm, and it comes to me I am watching no mechanistic, emotionless driver. A technician, certainly, the surgical correctness of his movements is there to detect, but detect is the operative word because it is covered over by a kind of joyfulness. Holbert's driving this morning in this legendary place in this extraordinary car is, well, it's almost lusty. He is a confident master of his craft, disdaining even a pretense of being unaffected by its pleasures.

In my day, I have ridden with some accomplished drivers. Dan Gurney I remember as playful. When I think of Mark Donohue, the word "mischievous" leaps to mind. He was full of surprises, most of them on the edge of lunacy. Peter Revson was, as you'd expect, almost sedate. I never remember driving even a lap at close to race speeds with him during which he was anything but serious. I come close to being tempted by "irrepressible" when I think of Danny Sullivan, whose sense of what most of us would think of as responsibility seems to be placed on hold when he gets in a car. As a result of his Speedway spin, he is a man more credited with luck than with the uncanny talent for car control, which is his true strength.

This morning, I am seeing in Holbert not just the immense technical mastery I expected, but something well beyond. A great pianist has a genius for fully exploiting his instrument, but he has more. His empathy with the music it produces invokes the emotion in that music and so evokes its feelings in us as we listen to him play. Holbert clearly understands the rigorous technical demands of this instrument. Because he is so much the master of what he does, his driving can go beyond the boundaries within which the rest of us live and into what is almost art. Holbert's driving is a sequence of movements filled with shadings and subtleties and nuances—an act that can only be thought of as Performance: The Dance at the Edge.

. . .

Ah, the instrument. The 959. The car. It is quietly, efficiently, remorselessly inhaling the road surface. "Feel the sequential turbos?" Holbert asks, as we accelerate off a corner so purposefully we seem to be shoving the entire world behind us. "Let's see what the brakes do." Down we come straight but brutally from 250 kph. "It tracks so well," says Holbert, marvelling. "It is just so consistent around a corner, it just hunkers down."

We have turned so many laps I can't count them anymore. Holbert has become a little pensive; he is quiet for two or three circuits, then says softly, "In this car I can appreciate a whole new threshold."

I ask him what the lap record is. He doesn't know but race driver's mischief, perhaps contracted from his late friend Mark Donohue, steals into his voice. "Let's find out how close we can get to whatever it is."

If I had thought Holbert was hustling, I see another side to him now: the intent Holbert, the professional at work, the competitor with just a hint of the glow of the fire in his belly. One forty-four flat. Maybe not Formula One time, but Holbert, deeply though quietly impressed, says it is the fastest he has ever been in a production car and that the time is not outrageously off Mark Donohue's time in the 917/30.

. . .

I am elated. Why? When I climbed into the padded seats of this car, I may have been unconsciously disappointed by its almost sybaritic interior. More room in the footbox, I said to myself, thinking this brand of 911 had solved at least one problem I had with its forebear. Good heavens, another elaborate radio, I recall thinking, looking into the middle of the dash. Nothing remarkable here, it seemed to me, but then what was I expecting? In fact not much.

My first surprise has come from Holbert's bravura performance. My second from the brilliance of the car, which has been almost as subtle. Now we have turned an absolutely stunning lap time in what is no more, no less than a passenger car. As we slow to exit the track, Holbert turns with a giant grin on his face. "Let's take this thing out on the autobahn," he says in defiance of what he has been told. Hell, everything he's done up to now has defied his orders. No racing speeds, he has been instructed. Drive well within the car's limits was his mandate. You don't tell a racer that, particularly one who loves his work as much as Holbert does. Now his blood is up. He wants to take the car out on the still-slippery two-lane and then the autobahn and do something he'll never be able to on the roads at home. Drive it on the public highway.

Holbert nods pleasantly but with appropriate condescension to the gate guard and launches on the road to Tiefenbronn. The car, which should be breathing hard, is not showing any sign of heaving flanks. No whiff, however faint, of hot brakes. The idle is smooth, all instrument readings normal. We snake down the two-lane as gently as if we were delivering loose eggs in a paper sack. It's a little hard to bring myself to realize the magnitude of what this car has managed to accomplish within the last five minutes. It's gone faster than a greased weasel on a viciously demanding track, stopped from 150 mph in race car distance, and is now pottering along as though it were trying to coddle the sensibilities of an octogenarian suffering from congenital car sickness.

We amble through the center of town, a typically crooked, crowded, cobbled market street, lined with carts and bicycles and shawled women. In and around them stand workmen leaning on their shovels or cradling lunch, some even tending to barrows or mounds of earth. The 959 is as happy here as on the Can-Am track at Weissach. It neither bucks nor barks.

"Let's see something," says Holbert as the road out of town opens. Putting the car in sixth, he points to the tach which is reading 1,000 rpm. Then he puts his foot in it. As smoothly as though it were powered by steam, the 959 gathers momentum, never hesitating on its way up, up, up . . . until the entrance to the Stuttgart-Karlsruhe autobahn looms and we are on it.

This is not one of the new roads. It is just two lanes in each direction. Traffic is on the heavy side today, the inevitable trucks lumbering along on the right. In this countryside their wallow and pitch seem to mirror the topographical elevations of the landscape. They are like ships in a long and heavy sea.

From the moment we entered the autobahn, Holbert has had the car on full throttle. If he had not put me so in regard of his ability

73

on the track, I might just be uncomfortable in traffic at these speeds. Uncomfortable, hell, petrified. "Look," he says, nodding downward at the speedometer, "300 Ks." Just as I realize that's almost 190 mph, a tiny little box of a car, 2CV-sized, bounces out from behind a truck rushing backwards towards us, blocking our lane completely. "Ohshitohdear," I hear someone say. It is me. But my voice sounds like no voice I've heard from my mouth before. Holbert is absolutely expressionless as the brakes haul the car down without even a hint of abruptness. No loss of balance. No pitching forward in the seat. Just the insistent, firm hand of deceleration and suddenly we are three lengths behind the little box, ambling along at 100 kph, just another car moving at an idiotically slow pace in the fast lane.

Minnow-quick, the box dives in ahead of the truck. It has taken it exactly the same time to dart out, pass and dive back as it has taken us to catch it up and scrub off 200 kph. We pass and I look over casually to see a young woman who is staring at the road ahead, frozen in terror. She has seen us in her rearview mirror. I wonder idly how, when she arrives at her destination, she is ever going to manage to unfix her hands from the steering wheel.

An immense, catastrophic wreck on the other side of the road, the side on which we will have to return, has traffic backed up beyond the rise of the far hill, so we dive off at a handy exit. Holbert knows these roads well. "I'm lost," he says within five minutes. It makes absolutely no difference. We have discovered a few back roads with mixed surfaces, some have patches of ice on them, some have hollows filled with water. Holbert, delighted, begins to use the lever that shifts programs for distributing power between the axles. Whatever he is doing, only he can appreciate. When we see ice ahead, he switches the program but I don't notice a thing when the car gets there. No slipping, no sliding, in fact, no drama whatsoever. Another immense accomplishment that superb engineering has reduced from the astonishing to the mundane.

Sooner than I would want it is over. It could have taken all day and it would have been sooner than I would have wanted. Holbert feels the same way. We enter the gates of Weissach, and putter down to the racing department called "Falkland" for Peter Falk, Porsche's racing chief.

I climb out of the car absolutely elated. I feel very slightly intoxicated but at the same time I feel as though every sense were sharpened. The air is cleaner and purer, the spring to my step livelier, the sounds of far-off engines on the track seem almost melodic.

If I were willing, I would admit to myself I have been touched by a kind of automotive spirituality I did not think myself capable of feeling any longer. It has been years since such primal chords have been struck inside me—the mind bypassed but left to observe, while feelings have been so exquisitely played and the soul so stirred.

The thought arrives whole in my mind that I have been to visit a place where there is great power to affect human responses, an almost mystical place. I have been taken there by an extraordinarily accomplished practitioner in its arts. The intensity of the feelings at the tips of my senses will fade, although not quickly, not even soon, but they will leave an imprint.

So it requires reminding at this transcendent moment that I will not be a convert, I will not. I've spent my life resisting, and besides, I can't afford it.

Not a convert, then, but no longer an unbeliever.

Miami Advice

YOU DON'T HAVE TO BE DANNY SULLIVAN TO DRIVE THIS CAR WELL—BUT IT HELPS
Jan. 13, 1986

ANY MAN WHO CAN DO A 195-MPH PIROUETTE practically in front of Mary Hulman George's Turn Two Indianapolis Motor Speedway suite and not so much as *ripple* a guest's mint julep ought to be able to terrify your basic overage, cowardly passenger in a 911 Turbo on the streets of Miami, no?

Not a chance.

Danny Sullivan didn't become the driver/spokesman for Miller Beer, contract representative for Marlboro and all-around role model for Alberto Culver users by indulging in unsanctioned displays of vulgarity.

Nor did he come to be the public presence for all these Great Companies by revisiting the incorrigible public behavior that marked his growing up years in Louisville. We are dealing here with a civilized, polished gentleman driver who would be aghast at the thought of twirling a test car like a baton.

Unless, of course, it were at night.

Somewhere no one could see him.

Away from the cops.

In a place with nice tight switchbacks and big ol' sweepers.

Which is where Danny has by now already been, and without me, so that my hair has been spared being shaped into a Jim McMahon spike.

Hair acts like iron filings and magnets in the presence of fear. I know this because I have served my terror and resultant cone-head time with Sullivan in the salad days of the Can-Am. We did a rental car trip through the infield at Brainerd I shall never forget nor my linen supplier either. I rode shotgun with him once on Mulholland Drive in a Scirocco he had just had fitted with a dry sump Super Vee motor. I'm not about to claim he shamed the canyon running regulars,

Leon with Danny Sullivan (middle) in 1991, the year in which Sullivan drove the Patrick Racing CART car. *AutoWeek Archives*

but police reported very little, urm, lively activity on Mulholland for two weeks thereafter.

An almost apocryphal story, that one, but this is not: Allow me to report the astonishing fact of sitting in the right seat with Danny Sullivan in a Porsche 911 Turbo through Coconut Grove, the appendix of Miami, and never exceeding 50 mph.

All right—80.

There are some very sound reasons for this. First of all it is Sullivan I am sitting next to because he does this sort of thing for *AutoWeek* from time to time. He is a first-rate tester and Olympic-level racing driver, and he can discern the characteristics of a car without all the thrashing and heaving you and I have to go through just to get a sense of how things begin to feel. But specifically, he is driving slowly because he has the craze to put the landscape rapidly behind him temporarily out of his system. Sullivan has spent the previous day outrunning one Rahal, a pair of Unsers and various other persons of high-speed inclination and collected almost $60,000 for his trouble. Call it speed catharsis. For the time—this can last as long as 48 hours—Sullivan's bloodstream is cleansed of nature's amphetamine, the special drug that seems to be generated in the systems of world-class drivers.

There is a more important reason, though. The car. Reintroduced to this land after a six-year, emissions-motivated sabbatical, it is still one of the most ferocious vehicles this side of Al Holbert's Porsche 962 race car—and possibly more difficult to drive quickly. Danny is here to tell us how to approach this wunderwagen in order to enjoy it fully, which does not include wrapping $48,000 worth of whaletail Porsche around the nearest stone crab stand. Hence, the (relatively) sedate pace. Sullivan says it succinctly: "This thing can eat you."

Let us pay attention.

We are cruising underneath palm trees and through the balmiest day a weather-obsessive could want. It is so bright and sunny it could break the hearts of Rust Belt dwellers; for the PPG Indy-car season ender is in November, and, up north, the frost is on the earlobes. Foot traffic is heavy. Sidewalks and streets, too, are populated by those languid walkers who seem to dwell in the tropics in perfect safety despite their disregard for the difference between highway and footpath. Don Johnson is right: The world around us is pastel.

Not the Porsche. It is a nasty shade of black-and-blue, like a bar-fighter's eye the day after. The car profiles nicely through this equatorial scene, and that is Sullivan's point at the moment. "It can deceive you into thinking it's inoffensive, particularly around town, and that is dangerous.

"Why? Because if you live in town and drive the car around town mostly, you can come to have contempt for it, which may be one of the most dangerous things you can do with this car."

Look, says Sullivan, who knows the upcoming topic better than most racers—people buy a high-performance car like this one because it's fashionable. Or because it's the hottest car on the road. Or because, in their minds, it's the ultimate sports car. But like anything else, he says, a new offshore powerboat, or high-speed bass boat, or fishing rod, or any instrument that is made by one craftsman for another, you have to learn how to use it.

It begins by starting to understand the Porsche's eccentricities, of which, according to Sullivan, there are several, starting with where you sit. The seating position is offset, which can be disconcerting to the unprepared. Sullivan has spent the last 15 years or so driving sports and formula cars, most of them with offset seating; he barely notices his slightly sideways position. The trouble, and the only trouble, with offset, he says, is that if you're unaccustomed to it, you're unconsciously insecure in your feeling of control. "So, as with any car, get secure," says he.

We are hearing, incidentally, the professorial Sullivan. It comes naturally to him. There was a time just after his return to the USA when he was out of a drive. Flat. Nothing in prospect. But instead of flopping around on the beach and feeling sorry for himself, he took a job as an instructor at a drivers' school.

At the school, Sullivan learned to teach and teach patiently. So he is harking back to those days when he talks about feeling securely placed in a car before trying to drive it near its limits. Initial insecurity for the first-timer in the Porsche, Sully suggests, is exacerbated by the steering wheel, which he plain hates. The wheel has a wide cross plate in the middle with a top and bottom bar an inch or so above and beneath it. Porsche, in effect, is telling its owners where they can put their hands. Very Teutonic. Trouble is that's not where many people are accustomed to having their hands, nor is it the position some high-speed driving schools teach as proper for grasping the wheel. Mainly, though, Sullivan hates the wheel because it looks like a Blue Light special. Cheap and ugly. "It does not befit a top-of-the-line Porsche," he sniffs.

If Sullivan does not like the steering wheel, he is even less complimentary about the fact the single turbo does not come in strongly until the aluminum-block engine has been twisted to about 3,500 rpm (maximum torque and horsepower come on well up the chart, at 4,000 and 5,500 rpm respectively). For all its high-rev huffing, the 911 Turbo remains a bafflingly weak performer off the line. Even with the extra 29 hp Porsche engineers have found in the intervening six years. "The acceleration is not progressive. And, at least for me, it's simply not strong enough until you get into relatively high revs."

All those are merely peculiarities compared to Sullivan's real complaint: the lack of a fifth gear. Porsche says the car doesn't need a fifth because it is so strong you don't need to compensate for lack of power with gearing. In fact, Porsche is absolutely right about the power: There is almost nothing else available to the common man that will set you back in the chair like the 3.3-liter, 282-hp turbo-motor in this car. And top speed is a more than adequate 155 mph.

This does not occur to Sullivan, however, whose office is powered by a 750-hp turbo-motor of its own, good for 225 mph. Compared to the Cosworth, the Porsche probably does feel a little limp. Compared to what you and I are used to—and after the turbo has spooled up enough to take up the initial slack—it feels like a boot in the butt from an angry rhino.

"Make this car a five-speed or change the gearing, particularly since the splits in the gear ratios are just not that good."

Okay, so maybe you've heard a lot of this before. The 911 Turbo has been around for better than a decade now. It's been said and said often that it's faster than almost anything you can imagine. It's been said that it suffers from grievous turbo lag. It's been said that it could use a five-speed. You knew all this. It doesn't take Danny Sullivan to tell you it again.

But you also know the 911 Turbo's darkened reputation for handling. The car is tail-happy, they say. Get it right and it's as fast and satisfying as anything on four wheels. Get it wrong, they say, and you'll be hurtling off into space. Backwards.

A surprise, then, courtesy of an expert: "If you get it and take it up to speeds you have never experienced before, the car will do something you don't expect . . . it'll fly."

As in pick up its nose and take off.

An explanation. "All the weight in the 911 Turbo is in the back end. Now accelerate. You get additional rearward weight transfer, and the car will fly its light front end," says the Indy winner.

Sullivan seems truly perplexed by the notion that the 911 Turbo oversteers in an excessive manner. Part of this is due, no doubt, to the fact that Porsche has changed the Turbo's cornering nature recently, in part by installing even wider rear rubber.

And part of it is Sullivan. A later conversation with the man responsible for setting up the handling of his 1984 Indy racer, Shierson Racing's Ian Reed, puts Sullivan's seeming innocence of the notion that Porsches oversteer into clearer perspective. "Danny wanted the front end of his car [the Domino's Lola] pinned," said Reed, by which he means Sullivan wanted his car to rotate around a front end nailed to the road. "Al [Unser Jr., Shierson Racing's current pilot] likes the rear end pinned. So, in effect, Danny wanted his car in an over-steer mode, Al wanted understeering."

Sullivan, however, is far from being as unaware as he seems. "From understeer comes oversteer," he says in a wonderfully quotable comment on what happens when the front end either resists going around a corner or toys with the pavement without coming to grips with it ("flying"). Sullivan is saying that when the wheels that steer the car ultimately do get their bite, hell can break loose. "When the front end finally bites, and it will, the car snaps around."

This is something the new sports car owner, particularly the 911 Turbo owner, must learn to control. But how?

The quick way, of course, is to get going too fast in a corner and lift out abruptly. Instant vertigo. Think of yourself in a centrifuge. Hell, think of yourself sitting right smack over the point around which a spinning Porsche is revolving.

The safer way is to learn the car in an environment in which mistakes aren't likely to be final. Find some country roads, he suggests, and be sure they're empty. (Danny's brother Tommy reports a hair-raising number of incidents in which his older sibling went exploring the berms of exurban Louisville and had to be towed out, to their father's exasperation. So when Sullivan says "country roads" be wary.)

Sullivan also recommends empty parking lots. You can replicate high-speed dry road behavior on icy concrete at very low velocities, he says. Or, if you can afford a 911 Turbo, get really smart and rent a day at a local racetrack, complete with attendant ambulance. (Some tracks, Lime Rock is an example, have test days that allow you to share costs with several others. Several performance drivers' schools allow you to use your own car.)

At any rate, the Sullivan advice is indispensable: "Experiment. Sneak up on the car's performance. Don't go out and expect to find the car's limits for some stupid reason like impressing a girlfriend.

"Another thing, this car has really great brakes. But just because it does, maybe especially because it does, you should remember that unlike a muscle car with a normally aspirated engine, a turbo motor doesn't work for you on deceleration."

Once you've learned a car like the 911 Turbo, Sullivan suggests you go back to your Porsche dealer and tell him how you want the car to behave to suit your own inclinations. Don't be bashful about wanting it set up to your needs. Perhaps you want the boost to come at a lower range. He would, and he would ask for it. Maybe you are adamant about more or less roll stiffness. The point is that cars are adjustable.

The further point is that you must begin by adjusting yourself to the car, but when you have, the car can be tuned to suit you.

It is dusk. A pastel dusk. Pink and blue, just exactly as it's supposed to be. We are in the tiled and covered entrance of Sullivan's hotel, a great rococco monster that is merely one component of a great shopping center dripping with Gucci and Giorgio Armani and adorable little shops selling tiny cups of avocado yogurt for roughly the same price as the Porsche. The valet parking attendant is hovering nearby. Earlier, when he went to fetch the Turbo from the downstairs garage, he came back empty-handed. The steering wheel was locked, as wheels are required to be able to do in cars sold in this country, and he wasn't inclined to wrestle it back and forth. Had this been any other car, had Sullivan been anyone other than the Indy and Miami winner, the kid would likely not only have shaken the wheel like a rat but pulled the damn thing off rather than return sheepish and on foot. It is an incidental discovery of what you have to do to be able to intimidate valet parkers.

Before the Miami race, Sullivan's car owner, Roger Penske, said almost offhandedly that if Sully won the finale he could take his, Roger's, 77-foot Hatteras sports fisherman and cruise down the Keys for a week. Penske is famous for being as good as his word, Sullivan famous for relishing such hedonistic moments as lie ahead.

Time for Sully to say goodbye to the Porsche, which he does with true reluctance. He has become fond of the Turbo, steering wheel and all.

Goodbye then, and an oblique word of warning to me as I embark on the long trip from Miami to Detroit. "I think it was Vic Elford who said maybe people who own cars like this should have to have a different kind of license." If it was Elford, he wasn't the only one. The Porsche points its nose northward to an office where sits an *AutoWeek* editor who, not a month before, wrote the very same thing.

It will turn out to be a lovely trip home. The Porsche performs flawlessly, if somewhat thirstily. It gobbles up whole states at a time without effort, without a gasp, without so much as a shrug.

It also is a trip that serves as a reminder of the vast respect required by automotive predators like the 911 Turbo.

Lure of the Open Road

June 26, 2000

COME JULY MY DAUGHTER is packing her daughter and her son into a far larger than necessary Buick and wandering from Tucson to Portland; about time, too. It is a grand tradition in her family. She is a late-blooming Bedouin; her mother and I took to the road well before she was a gleam.

There are such things as carefully planned trips, but they were not for us. A summer's voyage should begin with the discontent of a city spring, the lure of an unexplored horizon. A delicious May evening descends, filled with the scent of the unknown, and there, at the curb, is your car. It is ready—it is always ready—because you keep it that way for exactly this moment. You have no idea where you are going, nor why, but you can no more stay where you are than you can stop breathing. It is the migratory urge.

It began for me one year—began and continued without reason or particular awareness—when I pushed out on the West Side Drive of Manhattan every night farther and farther to wherever, coming home for no particular reason in the early dawn, until one day I just kept going to discover thereby there was no reason why not.

It seemed only natural that this should spill over into college where my then-fiancée and I would wander over upstate New York and Pennsylvania. Do you remember the allure of places never seen, names long known but not discovered? Wall Drug Store ("Offering Famous Free Ice Water to Thirsty Travellers for Over 50 Years") or Little America ("The Only Truck Stop in the Nation with a Concierge").

Your neighbor came home with slides of the Grand Canyon, you came home, if at all, with grainy black-and-whites of the Sacramento Mile, Pikes Peak or race shops with signs that said "All American Racers" or "Vel's Parnelli." Thus did car people migrate—in this way were whole new careers created out of nothing but movement. Car people went to California, of course, and Nevada and from there up and down the West Coast. The names of the frontier camps would have been familiar to Mark Twain or Parnelli Jones: Virginia City, Altamont, Carson City, Monterey. Wherever car people gathered to show or race, there we were. Did you say Aston Martin? My wife was offered a ride in one in Denver. How about OSCA? A fine fellow called Jim Simpson thought it would be nice to see me drive one of his at Janesville, Wis.—the very idea terrified me and I never did. I crewed at Riverside; my wife worked communications at Pebble Beach for Mary Jane Rothermel.

So now my daughter is wandering up the West Coast with her kids. She is settled in Portland and immune, I suspect, to the migratory urge, but her children aren't. To this day I feel the freshness of the first moments of travel, the adventure, the breathlessness at the prospect of what lies ahead. It will be there for my grandchildren if only they are open to it, and if they are, it will live in them forever.

Chapter Three

Off to
the Races

I was standing in the pits at the Speedway during practice one afternoon when Peter Revson blasted a truly evil-handling car up to Tyler, ripped off his helmet and demanded, 'What in the hell are you going to do to keep this s - - - box from killing me?'

"'Don't ever ask a question you don't want to hear the answer to,' said Tyler.

When Leon joined Competition Press *in 1963, it was barely five years old and devoted almost entirely to racing. He'd been immersed in the Northern California sports-car scene for more than a decade, working as a salesman for Kjell Qvale's import-car operations and participating in SCCA racing as an occasional driver, more often as a volunteer worker, flagman, track announcer and race steward. Race reports by their nature don't have a long shelf life, but we've chosen a few representative samples of his early work. About these: In the '60s and '70s, television was not a factor in auto-racing coverage, so the reports tended to be very thorough, detailed and long. I've taken the liberty of editing them down. Long after he stopped writing actual race reports, however, Leon's interest and expertise in motorsports continued, and that's reflected in the other selections in this chapter—note especially his continuing campaign on behalf of safety in racing, rarely strident but always insistent.*

Andretti Wins Daytona 500

Daytona, Fla.
March 18, 1967

IT WAS ONE THING FOR PARNELLI JONES to win NASCAR's annual road racing exercise last month in California.

But when USAC national champion Mario Andretti won the big one at Daytona today, it had the good old boys talking to themselves.

Andretti took the measure of the "Big D" in NASCAR's biggest race, winning convincingly from a fine field that disintegrated trying to stay with him.

Nine caution flags held his race average to 146.926 mph, but when he was on the green he purely flew, turning 179-mph laps with regularity, several at 160, an official 181.818 mph and two unofficial tours at over 182. Time for the 200-lap, 500-mile event was 3:24.11 and over 94,000 fans braved near freezing weather and knife-cold winds to watch.

Andretti's virtuosity gained him $43,500 to second-place man Freddy Lorenzen's $14,000.

The 1966 NASCAR rookie of the year, James Hylton, was third in a '65 Dodge, Tiny Lund was fourth in the second Petty team Plymouth, and Jerry Grant took a fifth in Tommy Friedkin's independent Plymouth.

NINE LEADERS

Nine drivers led the event, but it was clearly dominated by Andretti in a Ralph Moody-supervised and built Holman-Moody Ford Fairlane 427 CID.

Curtis Turner led from the pole in a '66 Chevelle that had Chevrolet's chief resident engineer, Ralph Johnson, in attendance. (Said Johnson, "I am not here on anything official, actually I am on vacation.")

But the early laps looked like a Dodge showroom with Lee Roy Yarbrough in second with a purple Charger accompanied by David Pearson and Buddy Baker, also Charger-mounted.

Still, it took them a while to get there and drama was in store early. Frank Warren's '66 Chevy spun on the west turn and out came the yellow for the first time on lap 6. Paul Lewis' blue Charger came weaving into pit lane nearly flat out and obviously without brakes. He had a small fire on the underside but no one could get to it because he couldn't stop the car. Lewis went on down the short straight on the inside verge and finally managed to bring the blue car to a halt with the fire already out.

Two of the great names in NASCAR stock car racing, CooCoo Marlin and Friday Hassler, had already retired along with George England and Warren. Lewis' demise was the fifth in a race that saw only 20 of 50 cars last the distance....

ALL-IMPORTANT DRAFT

Passing at Daytona is done on the back chute, taking advantage of the draft. Andretti went it one better. Each time he set up to pass he went rim-riding on the 31-degree second turn, charged down the bank to pick up an extra mile an hour and then used the draft to slingshot by.

The same nine-car train was at it again, but everyone except Andretti was fueled and most had fresh tires. Mario couldn't possibly stay in as the laps completed mounted—no way.

He didn't have to.

As he came down the back straight on lap 39, he motioned Goldsmith by and Darel Dieringer came right with him. The three entered the third turn in tight echelon with Mario taking the low line and Darel the outside—and Goldsmith lost it in a wild screaming, howling spin. Cale Yarborough, right behind, dove into the infield, damaging his front suspension and putting him out, but Goldie only flat-spotted his tires and came right in for a change. Meanwhile, Mario was trying to pit, his fuel pressure gauge fluctuating menacingly. But Curtis Turner, wailing down the inside of the dogleg front chute, put his door up against the H&M Fairlane and kept Andretti from darting into the pits. Another lap and Mario made it—42 laps completed, 105 miles at 170–180 mph on 22 gallons of gas.

The second yellow occasioned another rash of stops, including one by Petty to change a flat left rear tire and one by Don White, second-place man in the '66 USAC standings, to try and stanch a flow of oil. . . .

SERIOUS BUSINESS

Things were getting down to the point where it mattered, and it mattered so much to Curtis Turner that Pops blew his engine trying.

Just before, a National Airlines Electra landed at the adjacent Daytona airport, its landing pattern taking it in parallel to the back chute and in full sight of the grandstand. Andretti pulled it easy, and some wag suggested that Lorenzen tried to pick up the draft.

Out came the green, Pearson, Andretti and Lorenzen charged for the lead, which Mario snaffled, and David blew his cool and his engine at the same time. No yellow for two laps until a report came to NASCAR chief steward John Bruner Sr. of debris all over the track, and the starter was at it again, waving the big yellow with practiced grace.

It was here, according to the press box experts, that the race would be won or lost as Andretti and Lorenzen came into the pits nose to tail. Tires for both, fuel for both, and the winner of the pit race was Freddy by a solid two seconds.

It was the last thing he won all day.

Off the caution, Andretti jumped Tiny Lund (a lap back, but running with the leaders) and Lorenzen, broke the draft and was gone. Freddy was still drafting when Mario started to pull away, saw his mistake, tried to break away from Lund and couldn't.

On lap 85 it was 4.5 sec between the two Fairlanes. Mario opened to 5.2 sec over Lorenzen the next lap around; 6.8 on lap 187, 10 on lap 189, 13 by 191, 18 by 193, and the announcer wowed the crowd by saying, "Freddy's letting Andretti set the pace." By lap 197 Mario had opened to 22 seconds.

There were only two laps, but the yellow wouldn't leave well enough alone. Richard Petty blew in a big big way out of turn 4,

Jerry Grant and Jim Hurtubise spun in his oil, and the race finished on the caution light.

"You never really have the situation in hand here," said Andretti that night. "You can never tell, they hang behind you and slingshot on the last lap."

Unless you open 22 sec on the man behind.

"When Freddy pulled in behind Tiny, it was all over," Mario said. "It was his mistake. I broke Tiny's draft and left them."

Lorenzen joins an increasingly large group who realizes you don't make mistakes when you are running against Andretti.

Airfoil Foils Texas Flyers

Las Vegas
Nov. 13, 1966

IT MAY NOT HAVE BEEN THE ONLY GAME in town, but it was one of the biggest, and John Surtees, taking his action where he found it, won the Stardust GP, the Can-Am series, the thorough approval of Lola builder Eric Broadley and almost $50,000.

Surtees finished the race 59 seconds up on Bruce McLaren's McLaren-Chevy, the only car he failed to lap, and crossed the line a lap plus two seconds over third-place man Mark Donohue in the Sunoco Lola-Chevy.

Phil Hill, tied for the Can-Am lead going in, fell victim to a flapping flipper on his Chaparral (the same thing retired teammate Jim Hall after only four laps), finally finished seventh after a quick wing-ectomy had been performed and saw Donohue take second in the series and McLaren third as a result.

Only 12 cars of the 33 starters finished, and one of the DNFs, Norm Smith's, was a heart-stopper.

Smith, one of the five drivers dropped from the grid two weeks previous at Riverside, lost control of his Lola-Chevy on the very fast turn seven, went off into the dirt, through a spectator fence and 100 feet inside a spectator area, totalling his own car and a spectator car, injuring one person slightly and putting himself in the hospital with superficial injuries.

Smith's accident came with four laps to go, and by then, the issue of the race had long since been settled.

Surtees won every dollar of the $3,500 lap money, finishing the race in 1.55:27.5 at an average of 112.84 mph for the 210 miles. His fast lap of 1:35.7 was a full second faster than either of the Team McLarens and a little more than that over the Chaparrals. It was the most convincing win of the series.

Not that the smart money on the Las Vegas Strip had it booked

93

that way. The two Chaparrals had captured the front row with ease, Amon and McLaren in the McLaren Team cars were strong enough to occupy the inside of the second row (Amon) and the outside of the third (McLaren), Surtees was fourth fastest and the remainder of the first four rows were filled with the likes of Jackie Stewart (third row inside), George Follmer (same on the fourth row) and Parnelli Jones with Dan Gurney right behind.

Hill was a trifle slow off the line, but Hall got away smartly and Stewart jumped to the inside and third position in the first turn. But by turn two Surtees had shot the gap to lead, and though no one could know it at the time, that was the beginning and the end of the fight for the championship.

On the very first lap the Chaparral's troubles began with Hill encountering an immovable competitor in turn two and shedding a chunk of the right front of the winged wonder as a result. Worse yet, he dropped to sixth, trailing the remains of a brake cooling duct. . . .

Hall had to retire with the mounting pad for the spoiler actuating rod pulled out from the base of the wing. Unlike Hill, who was to finish the race wingless, Hall gave it up immediately as a bad job. "These cars just don't handle without it [the flipper]. They were designed for a wing," he said from the pits after Hill's appendage had been removed halfway into the race.

And Stewart had to spin in spectacular fashion in turn five and pit for a quick check of externals.

ANDRETTI OUT

To thin the traffic and make everyone's job easier, consolation race winner Andretti had retired with a broken shift linkage in the 427 Lola-Ford, Bud Morley was out with a blown clutch, Skip Scott dropped a ring and pinion, Ed Hamill (Hamill SR3-Chevy) broke a right rear lug bolt, lost his wheel in turn 10, looped it and, quite understandably, decided to call it a day.

That Andretti even started was a mark of courage. He had been right behind Don Branson and Dick Atkins at Ascot the night before when the accident that was to kill both occurred. The USAC champion was clearly deeply disturbed but flew back from Los Angeles nonetheless to meet his commitment to run at Stardust.

CLOSE COMPANY

By now Surtees had settled down to a quick but calculated cruising speed with 15 seconds in hand over McLaren and another five over Gurney. But there was no complacency down a few notches in the field.

George Follmer and Mark Donohue, both Lola-Chevy mounted, were running almost wheel to wheel; Masten Gregory in the Pacesetter McLaren-Chevy and Peter Revson's McLaren-Ford were doing the same thing; Mike Goth's McLaren-Chevy, Sam Posey's McLaren-Ford and Chuck Parsons' McLaren-Chevy were equally intimate, and, back almost a lap, Bill Eve and Hugh Dibley were hooked up— Genie to Lola.

At this point the McLaren express looked to be in near ideal position: Bruce was fourth and running easily and Amon was backing him up in seventh, both obviously within striking distance. But Amon was about to break a left A-arm (on lap 21) and McLaren began falling back to trail Surtees by 40 seconds at halfway.

Mostly, though, the excitement was dimmed by the retirement of Dan Gurney at mid-race.

Gurney had been falling back into the clutches of Jones and Hill and obviously was suffering a serious malaise. Then, on lap 37, having been unresponsive to questions from his pit about the nature of the disease, he rolled into the racing pits and retired with no oil pressure and a fine driveshaft, or fine oil pressure and a diseased driveshaft or fine oil pressure, a splendid driveshaft and a disintegrated fuel cell that came violently adrift.

Which is to say, he wasn't talking.

Stewart was out with a broken fuel line, Hayes lost a wheel right in front of McLaren (who avoided it skillfully but lost even more ground to Surtees) and decided against continuing on three wheels, Hulme's

Lola-Chevy was the victim of a broken gearbox and Parnelli came into the pits stuck in third.

WING REMOVED

But the big news in the racing pits was Phil Hill, whose airfoil had been fluttering for two laps when he finally came in to have it removed. The Chaparral team took four laps to pull off the wing, install a spacer bar and attach a temporary spoiler that ran the full width of the lip on the deck and stuck up about two inches in the air. How the flighty had fallen.

Then, with four laps to go, there was a great cloud of dust at the bend of the back chute, spectators running toward the scene and emergency vehicles screaming off to a clot in the midst of a spectator area.

Norm Smith had lost control of his Lola, gone through the spectator fence, 100 feet inside it, and broken his car into thousands of tiny yellow bits.

The Lola hit a Chevrolet and totaled it, the Chevrolet hit a Mustang and almost did the same, and the Mustang hit a third car, which hit a woman. Injuries to both the woman and Smith were not considered serious, but both were taken to the hospital.

By now, the sun was sinking over the crap tables and attention shifted as Surtees took the checkered, arm raised high, and half a lap later McLaren followed.

Surtees had had no trouble save a slight vibration when a balance weight came off a wheel. Asked if it was his biggest single payday, he smiled hugely and answered, "I should imagine so." His total for the Can-Am series cut and the race was over $40,000.

It may have been that the post-race ceremony was more trying than the race for Surtees. He was mobbed at the finish and couldn't break out of the ring of well-wishers for 20 minutes.

Throughout all he was courteous and obviously happy—his Can-Am wealth clearly not affecting him. And there was only one moment when he seemed even puzzled.

A press type stuck his head through the window and shouted to Can-Am commissioner Stirling Moss and Surtees please to move over so he could get a shot of them "shaking hands with the man from the *Christian Science Monitor.*"

Not even Henry Manney could figure that one.

Dawn of the Turbo Panzers

HULME WINS CAN-AM OPENER
Mosport Park, Ont.
July 1, 1972

"AS OF THIS WEEKEND," said Peter Bryant, designer of the UOP Shadow, "the day of the stock block engine in the Can-Am is over."

Bryant's car, with Jackie Oliver driving, had gone faster at Mosport in qualifying for the new season's first Can-Am than it had ever gone before and the Gulf-McLaren team, which had turned what would have been record times in '71, had gone even faster.

It did none of them any good.

Ahead of all three on the grid, glistening in the bright Canadian sunshine, was the new king of the Can-Am: the Roger Penske L&M Porsche 917/10 sitting arrogantly on the pole attended by a horde of mechanics from Pennsylvania, engineers from Stuttgart and P.R. flacks from every fashionable suburb west of Pago Pago.

It made absolutely no difference at all that Mark Donohue and the Porsche subsequently lost the race to Denny Hulme's M20 McLaren-Chevy. Penske and Porsche made their point by leading the opening Can-Am before an intake valve stuck on the turbo and forced the car to pit for three laps. And just to rub it in, Donohue almost pulled it off when he came back to unlap himself twice from the winning McLaren and wind up 55.5 seconds behind Hulme for a remarkable second-place finish. The Penske Panzer convinced everyone that the McLaren domination of the series is over and that a turbocharged racing engine is the way to go. The result sent the crowd of 52,743 home happy, the Porsche engineers into paroxysms of joy and Teddy Mayer and Tyler Alexander of McLaren back to the drawing boards.

For the record, Hulme finished the 80 laps (197 miles) in 1.46:40.0 for an average speed of 110.655 mph; Donohue was just under a minute behind and Peter Revson, who broke his racer while leading on the 78th lap, was credited with third on the basis of number of laps completed.

Milt Minter's $30,000 (plus engine and transmission) normally aspirated Porsche 917/10 was fourth after a brilliant ride and 25 seconds behind him came Peter Gregg in his $78,000 917/10.

"They're twice as expensive as customer McLarens," said Gregg, "but they're twice as good."

"Then how come we didn't win?" asked Minter, putting an end to the conversation. Lothar Motschenbacher managed a sixth in his last year's McLaren M8D, so that made it three McLarens and three Porsches in the top six.

The first Can-Am of the bright new season was as remarkable for those who weren't there as for those who were. Number 1/2 Gulf McLaren driver Jackie Stewart was home in Switzerland nursing his bleeding ulcer (and Revson was seething all weekend about being called a "substitute driver") and Francois Cevert, who will run the second Gregg Young M8F McLaren, won't appear until Atlanta. John Greenwood with his last year's works Lola T260s was at Le Mans, and this year's Lola, the 310 for David Hobbs, wasn't ready. As the season progresses, there will be the Can-Am Ferrari (the 1971 7-liter Andretti car, now owned by NART), which might just be driven by Gianclaudio Regazzoni; a second Shadow (driver unnamed, but somebody mentioned Ickx or Redman); and the second Penske Porsche, originally planned for Foyt but probably to be driven by Gary Bettenhausen. Don't be surprised if there's also a superstar from NASCAR running the Can-Am before the year is out either.

In sum, what's in store is a super series with dynamite races and at least 10 really competitive cars—including the two Mosport 917/10s that came in behind Donohue but which will get turbo-motors for the next race.

It's going to be spectacular.

Not that Mosport was bad—not at all. As a matter of fact, Mosport was pretty spectacular in its own right. "It's the first time we've had any real competition," said a pensive Teddy Mayer whose years in England have taught him the value of understatement.

Unlike Saturday, which had been cold (a fact that exacerbated the tire/understeer problem), race day was warm and bright. The spectator gates were backed up clear to Nova Scotia and the infield was a sea of tents. By noon, the track announced that 50,000 paid were already in and some 8,500 of those had bought paddock passes and were swarming like frenzied lemmings around the race cars and crews.

The flag dropped, the crowd screamed and Donohue and Revson streaked side-by-side over the brow of the turn one hill. Not for long. "He outdragged me at the start, and he outdragged me out of the hairpin," Revson would say later. There's just no substitute for horsepower—especially 940 of them.

By lap one, Donohue had a two-second lead with the two McLarens a nanosecond apart in second and third. The Shadow was hanging on tenaciously, but the top four already were clear and gone from fifth-place Minter. Well back, Peter Gregg was flying through the field on his way to challenge the sister 917. By lap two, Donohue had another second and dismay had struck the Canadian nationalists. Roger McCaig, running in sixth in his M8FP ("P" for Paul, his crew chief), came up over the turn eight rise, locked his brakes, spun and went off into the underbrush and out of the race with a dented car and bruised ribs.

On the same lap, Gregg Young threw a rod in his Reynolds engine in his M8F (last year's team car) and was out after covering the track with oil. It was an unfortunate end for Young, and it was not much better for Charlie Kemp in the Holiday Inn/Rinzler Racing Lola T222 (Hiroshi Kazato's ex), who hit the oil, spun off the track and collected a few pecks of Canadian soil as well as a bad vibration in the front of the car. Kemp would continue bravely on to finish a respectable ninth despite his wobbly Lola, but it was a disappointment to Rinzler and his crew chief on the superbly prepared racer.

Four laps later it was all over for the Shadow, which lost the rear bearing in its Weismann transaxle. Gearbox trouble had caused the

Bryant crew to change transmissions on Saturday night—a tedious job, and the new one was suspect, but the crew had it down during Sunday morning. While it went, the Shadow went brilliantly. The combination of Jackie Oliver and Peter Bryant, first seen with the Ti22, is a formidable one and now they have the whole-hearted backing of Universal Oil Products which quadrupled its sponsorship to Shadow owner Don Nichols this year in its campaign to convince the world that the rival Ethyl Corp is being capricious and wicked when it tells people cars won't run on unleaded gasoline. The new Shadow is a viciously fast car handsomely turned out. It proved itself a very serious contender indeed at Mosport.

By the 10th lap, Donohue had six seconds on the McLarens, Revson was moving away from Hulme, Minter was 40 seconds back in fourth and Gregg had carved his way by Motschenbacher into fifth. The crowd was loving it and so was Donohue. Until, that is, lap 16. Going by the start/finish line, Donohue moved out to lap Bob Nagel's Lola and found himself without the power to get by. The intake turbo valve had stuck shut, and it looked like *Götterdämmerung* for the Fourth Reich. Unhappily, Mark had to putter around the whole 2.459-mile track before he could get back into his pit and the McLarens swept majestically by.

Donohue was in the pits for four and a half minutes—three laps—until the trouble could be corrected, and when he went back out, no one expected very much of him. They were wrong.

He went out between the two McLarens, behind Revvie and ahead of Hulme, and immediately the Porsche and the lead McLaren began to race. Donohue had been turning 1:16 laps. With Revson leading and Donohue chasing, the times got down to 1:15.6, then 1:15.4 and finally a record-shattering lap of 1:15.2—equal to last year's Formula 1 qualifying mark. But it was set, strangely, not by Donohue but by Revson, who had been passed and was determined to hang onto the Porsche and not allow Donohue to unlap himself even once.

By lap 33, Donohue was back in fifth (he had come out of the pits in ninth), just after the halfway mark he went by Gregg into fourth, and three laps later he passed Minter for third. Hulme was next in line to be passed, and his times had gone from the 1:16s early in the race to 1:23s and 24s as his tires began to vibrate wickedly. Mark took him on lap 55, and he was two laps down on the second-place McLaren.

Revson, who was still hanging on up to that point, seemed to have trouble getting by his teammate until Denny moved way over on the front straight to let him through. At this point, Gregg began to have trouble of his own; a left rear wheel bearing went, and he forgot all about taking Minter and concentrated on holding off Motschenbacher.

Donohue was slicing eight seconds a lap off of Hulme's lead and unlapped himself again with 10 laps to go. Still, it looked hopeless. Revson was still three laps ahead and flying and the very best Mark could hope for was a close third.

On lap 78—with two to go—Revson came steaming up the start/finish straight, slowed, poured smoke and swerved into the pit rail. He had broken a crankshaft. The crowd went berserk and even the imperturbable Penske seemed moved.

Hulme was in the lead with less than a lap on Donohue and Hulme was not going well at all. What had seemed heretofore like hysteria from the P.A. system sounded like morning prayers compared to the way they were screaming now. They loved it in the bleachers, but even in the Penske pit—perhaps especially in the Penske pit—they knew better.

With one lap to go, Denny had 1:14 on Mark. On the last lap the Porsche made up almost 15 seconds, but it was far from enough and 1972's first Can-Am ended as so many have in the past—with a McLaren winning again.

But this time it's different.

It was only bad luck that kept the Porsche out of the winner's circle and everyone knows it. McLaren's turbo-engine, a 430-cid unit, has run on the dyno but never in a car. "We're not more than one second off the Porsche, and we can fix that with handling," said Teddy Mayer wistfully. But isn't he just a little tempted by the turbo engine on McLaren's dyno? "We're definitely not going to do that first," said Mayer. "We've got about 47 other things to try first."

"To be honest with you, it's confusing as hell," mused Tyler Alexander about a minute later. "I just don't know if he (Donohue) was playing with us or not.

"At any rate," he said, turning to Revson with a smile, "you got the fastest lap."

"Terrific," said Revson. "What does that pay?"

On to Road Atlanta, where the McLarens will be the long shots.

Mosport made it clear that as of now at least, Roger Penske is the overdog.

Requiem for a Heavyweight

WHEN DONOHUE WAS DONE WITH THE MID-OHIO CAN-AM, THE RACE—AND MAYBE THE SEASON AND SERIES—WAS OVER
Lexington, Ohio
Sept. 1, 1973

Leon had covered the Can-Am in its first season and resumed when he returned from Car and Driver *in the '70s. In the following race report from September 1973, he announces the death of the series—a year before it actually ended, but the writing was on the wall. It took Mandel to put it in print where everyone could read it.*

CAN-AM TOPOGRAPHY only changes from Edmonton west.

So by now, at Mid-Ohio, the sameness of the land and the familiarity of the lush and humid Eastern/Midwestern summer heighten the feeling that the Can-Am has settled into a hopeless inevitability. From now on, nothing will be new. Not the results, not the people, not even the conversation.

Whatever uncertainty about the outcome has long since been resolved. They were right all the time.

Mark Donohue will not lose another race. Bobby Rinzler's foolish and expensive challenge with last year's cars has been a $750,000 self-indulgence. The Shadow is too little and too late: a ritual joke. Roy Woods and David Hobbs know better now, also. By his absence, [*McLaren's*] Teddy Mayer becomes a prophet second only to Roger Penske in his prescience. Neither is here; neither needs to be. Donohue does not need Penske to win over anemic opposition. It is clear now that Team McLaren's scorn has been apt.

However bored and sure of the outcome the Can-Am repertory company might be, it is certain too that in Ohio, as in Eastern Canada, Georgia and Western New York, the innocent are still there. The posters with the RC cars, the legend of Jody Scheckter, the Andy

Warhol paint job on the Carling M20 have all done their work well. Even to the race workers, the Lake Erie corner people and the Ohio Valley paddock marshals, there remains an air of uncertainty . . . expectancy. In the infield, meanwhile, something has happened to the knowledgeable cynicism of two years ago's crowd. They used to be able to sense when Denny Hulme was dogging it; last month here they booed Jody Scheckter, yesterday they had to look at their programs to identify the Sunoco Porsche.

The paying crowd has lost its elitist cachet; even the white-clad people who work the race are innocently hopeful. Why? No such optimism, no such fresh expectations stand in the way of the complaints and the bitterness of the itinerant Can-Am people. By now they are bored with each other, gray-faced with fatigue and dead-eyed. They have long since conceded the outcome.

Although the series is only four races old, already the memory of four Holiday Inns has blurred into the recollection of a single, monstrous imposition on simple comfort. If this is August, it must be Ohio, but was it Oshawa or Gainesville where Andretti packed up and went home? Is it New York or is it here where you must remember not to eat in the motel? Michigan and Donnybrooke are cancelled or bankrupt; thank God Penske is on his honeymoon, but Rinzler will go home to an empty house. And it is the Rinzler experience which is common (as Penske well knows), but there are no reserves left for a simple word of kindness. The Carling uniforms, so vivid in the promise of Canadian spring, have begun to fray. How can all this seem so fresh, so exciting to the turn marshals and the operating stewards and the race physicians—much less to the crowds, when it all has begun to sound like "Kodachrome" played for the 1,000th time in the same bar in the same evening? Even the good-meets-evil parable of Follmer against Donohue has begun to pall. And Scheckter, who wore the sparkling white of a bride at Mosport, has seen his veil age and turn yellow in the searing heat of the summer.

Les Griebling runs Mid-Ohio as one of the few profitable road racetracks in the country. His penuriousness is famous. Even so his profits are small. So at Mid-Ohio they neither practice nor qualify on Friday; a day's insurance premium saved is a profit earned. That puts the whole weekend out of phase and Friday becomes Thursday, Saturday is Friday. No wonder then that the four full seconds Donohue took off the outright lap record was so difficult to comprehend. Somehow, you can't take four full seconds seriously, especially since it feels like it happened on a Friday. More especially when it shattered everyone's last hopes.

That may have been the moment, somewhere around 3:30 p.m. on a threatening, sticky Saturday in Central Ohio, when the racing establishment decided finally that the Can-Am had lost its vitality and became just another dusty American institution like the Soap Box Derby or a parade by the 40 & Eight.

Until then, everyone was mouthing his lines almost with conviction. Hobbs and Follmer, Kemp and Scheckter were all still giving out their own versions of how Donohue still put his pants on one leg at a time to the few bedraggled daily press guys who weren't senior enough to be traveling to the West Coast with the Browns or covering the Indians or doing golf up north.

Rinzler was figuring this was his weekend. Roy Woods, who had stayed away from the Glen when Hobbs drove his car to second, hurried into Cleveland's sagging airport and drove here hoping to see him win this time. And the turbo Shadow sat in the paddock, wrapped in foil and nestled in hope.

"We're going out and rattle the racetrack with it tomorrow morning," said a grimly smiling Jackie Oliver.

What time tomorrow morning?

"Between 9 a.m. and 9:01 a.m." He laughed. Be serious, someone said to him. "I am," he replied. "We've done some long-distance testing with it. Only last month we did a lap in England." But Oliver was simply yielding to his own black humor. He fully expected to run his car. It never left the paddock.

Unaware of its seat at the right hand of history, the crowd watched as though it was seeing what it had paid to see. As the race

The Porsche 50th anniversary in 1998, with Brumos Porsche co-owners Bob Snodgrass and Hurley Haywood. *AutoWeek Archives*

started, Scheckter, Donohue and Follmer went through the first turn NASCAR-like and came out with Follmer leading a line ahead. The Sunoco Porsche emerged scathed, but not as scathed as Scheckter was to be when he had to spin to avoid a slower car. It finished him after two pit stops. Neither suffered as much as Oliver, who watched Willi Kauhsen, back in the Can-Am with a new paint job, spin at the start/finish line and end up across the track with his nose in the Armco. Oliver, who was behind, did the finest driving of the day to spin with Kauhsen's Porsche as though choreographed. It bent the right outside coolant pipes on the Shadow, and although Oliver finished the heat, he finished it badly.

Donohue was far gone by the seventh lap of the first heat. He finished it just eight seconds from lapping second-place Follmer. As the cars came in for the intermission, Follmer's Porsche staggered in the pit lane and Follmer's head flopped forward. He had passed out from the heat on what seemed an only mildly warm day. He was not alone in the field hospital. Hurley Haywood (fourth), Scooter Patrick (sixth) and Bobby Brown (seventh) were there too. David Hobbs, who was third and airily chatting with his wife and boys in the pits, was astonished to hear about the stricken Follmer and assumed the perfectly baffled facial expression of a basset.

Scheckter didn't restart. Kauhsen didn't restart. Kemp hadn't started at all after breaking his car in Sunday practice. Follmer was not recovered, nor Haywood, Patrick nor Brown. In the pause, they dialed in all the boost in Follmer's car, and Follmer, who won here last year and in the Trans-Am too, kept Donohue at bay for 36 laps. Still, the high-pitched screams from the infield couldn't have been serious. The two were going five full seconds slower than Donohue had gone earlier in the day. They must have known that. And if Donohue couldn't get by . . . really couldn't get by, that was no reason for excitement either, was it?

Is it possible the crowd wasn't listening? Where were they and what were they doing when the man in the bright red jacket, the man with the pipe and the man with the dirty white shoes all agreed the Can-Am was through? There is not much point in talking to them if they turn away instead to watch the parachutes pour out of a transport in the bright Ohio sky.

Mid-Ohio's largest crowd followed Mosport's and Watkins Glen's and maybe even beleaguered Atlanta's. They spread across the vivid green landscape and curled their bare toes in the grass, listening to the bark and the rumble of the cars and watching Oliver's remarkable moment of brilliance, and stubborn Follmer, and Donohue's extraordinary afternoon.

They didn't hear the stage whisper from the self-important figure who insinuated himself along the pit rail next to David Hobbs between the heats as he stood with his wife and young sons to say that Larry Smith had just been killed in a single-car accident at Talladega. Smith was a Carling teammate of Hobbs'. Thirty-five minutes later Hobbs broke—still holding third behind Follmer and Donohue. McLarens are perishable too, he said . . . and nothing else.

An hour's drive north on I-71 at Canterbury in Cleveland, the PGA has come to town. All across the dial, the radio drones with the names like Tommy Weiskopf, Al Geiberger and Arnold Palmer—who didn't even make the cut. The *Plain Dealer* has no space for people like Oliver and Hobbs on page one of the sports section.

Palmer, after all, is still a legend. Palmer can still win next week in Des Moines. Who would say the same about David Hobbs?

Circus in the City

CAN CAR-HATING NEW YORKERS
LEARN TO LOVE INDY RACING?
Dec. 5, 1983

CONVENTIONAL NEW YORK WISDOM on the subject of the automobile does not consider it one of the noble artifacts fashioned by man. To a New Yorker, the car's greatest monument is a crosstown Manhattan street at 5:30 p.m. on any given weekday—three feet in three hours. If you own a car in the City, you've been in town an hour, maximum, from Iowa City and the corn is still growing out of your eyebrows. Only troglodytes like racing, and every Friday night they troop out of their Long Island cave cities, knuckles dragging on the ground as they walk, to Islip Speedway where they watch Figure Eight automotive roller ball, occasionally reaching over to pluck lice out of the pelts of their neighbors. Printers at the *New York Times* are as familiar with the phrases "auto racing" and "motorsports" as they are with the Egyptian alphabet.

Give or take a day, a month ago the New Jersey Sports and Exposition Authority, a.k.a. the Meadowlands, home of Howard Cosell's New York Football Giants, agreed to stage the United States Grand Prix for Indianapolis-type cars eight miles from the Empire State Building.

The race date is July 1, 1984. New York is about to be driven into the 20th century.

Since the Meadowlands was an Ordovician swamp, it served as the Potter's Field of the New York brotherhood. By rough guess, Manhattan Homicide might as well bury half its files on unsolved murders in the Meadowlands to go with the remains of their subjects. Industrial neighboring Jersey was never, er, savory. The Meadowlands must have been so named by one of the century's great practitioners of black humor.

Understand that New Jerseyites are used to this kind of characterization: New Jersey is the Rodney Dangerfield of the Union.

Aching for respect, New Jersey has reconstituted Atlantic City, transforming it from an empty, weather-beaten, sagging slum to a seething, chrome-and-sequined, silicon-injected slum. If Jersey could tackle Atlantic City, it could take on the Meadowlands.

The first step was to create a unique entity: the Sports Authority. It is not a state agency. It is unlike any other bureaucratic creature in the United States. It has no analog. Three members of the state's executive branch sit on its nine-man board of commissioners and the governor must sign the minutes of the meetings.

But the Authority is privately financed (through tax-free bonds) and, initially, there was the rub. No sooner had New Jersey announced its intentions of bringing the Meadowlands to a state of grace than hated enemy Nelson Rockefeller, the governor of New York, leaped in with an echo that he would spearhead a similar venture on Long Island, not an hour away. There went all of the Meadowlands' carefully cultivated New York banks and underwriters—off to curry favor with a home-state governor with that magic name and a brother who was the head of Chase Manhattan.

Start all over, Meadowlands.

There is an infuriating persistence about stepsiblings that frequently propels them to accomplishments beyond those achieved by their more favored natural brethren. Seeing the snub to a Jersey enterprise by the entire financial community of New York, Jersey banks and money marts rallied 'round.

The initial underwriting was not highly thought of by the rating services: Bonds were BB, three steps down from the chosen AAA. But in the mid-'70s work was begun, eventually to total $450 million worth.

Everything New Jersey did wrong in Atlantic City, it did right in the Meadowlands. State moles and ferrets are everywhere in the Vegas of the East. They are nowhere at the Meadowlands. Atlantic City—admittedly a municipality with endlessly complex social problems no 750-acre sports enclave would ever have to contemplate—is a patchwork of glitz and wheeze; monuments of glamour intermixed with tragic back alleys filled with pain and poverty. Despite its huge gaming handle,

Atlantic City teeters on some endless financial brink; the Meadowlands has returned over $100 million to the state in taxes and surplus revenue since it opened with a horse racing track in 1976. Its stadia (an arena, the track and Giants Stadium) are immaculate and handsome. The analogy with Atlantic City, however irresistible, is probably unfair; it is better to think of the Meadowlands as some dedicated sports mall on the order of the Great Shopping Centers of the Southwest.

"Perhaps you could think of this part of New Jersey as a heretofore underprivileged corridor," says Meadowlands chief executive officer Bob Mulcahy, a compact, elegantly dressed man with a face that, however much you try to dismiss the thought, reminds you of a very bright, very determined basset hound. "We are between the two big cities (Philadelphia and New York). Maybe what we've done more than anything is bring a sense of pride and identity to this part of New Jersey."

Yes indeed. The Meadowlands could hardly do otherwise if it tried these days; it is the sports center of the globe so far as the biggest population clot in North America is concerned. Football (three professional teams, a college preseason game last August between Nebraska and Penn State), professional and amateur (including high school) basketball, outdoor soccer and indoor soccer, a rumored American League baseball franchise to come (a site is being examined as we speak—a team wooed) and that ain't all.

Tractor pulls. Rock concerts. The circus.

One day last year, the Meadowlands held the Super Bowl of harness racing, the Hambletonian, in the afternoon and a FIFA World Cup all-star soccer match as well as a Doobie Brothers rock concert at night. One hundred and thirty thousand people on the first weekend in August.

All very well, wonderful as a matter of fact.

But the first weekend in July in 1984, the Meadowlands is talking CART.

You can't bring cars to New Yorkers. How come the Meadowlands is so sure it can bring New Yorkers to cars?

• • •

The Meadowlands did a study. Naturally. The study's conclusions were predictably fascinating: "From the financial aspect, World Championship of Makes and Endurance provides the least return to a Promoter . . ."

There was another international event proposed: "Formula One is still the strongest, although if the attendance were on the low side, a loss would be generated." And finally, "Financially, the Indy Car World Series is by far the better investment. . . . Initial capital costs for improvement of street surfaces and the safety systems are less, and returns to the promoter are immediate. The marketing of an Indy Car World Series event would be somewhat easier [than Formula One] inasmuch that the names of the participants are well known to the American public and thus have greater acceptability. Of importance to note is the added attraction of the ability to negotiate directly with the sanctioning organization—Championship Auto Racing Teams—whereas with international events there is a series of diplomatic channels that have to be accomplished before a final sanction can be granted."

Equally, correct that, far more fascinating is the man behind the study. His name is Christopher Robin Pook, variously thought of as the savior of international racing in the United States, the assassin of international racing in the United States, inventor of urban racing, Rasputin of downtown speed ghettos, high-binding huckster who tap dances so fast you see neither the brass on his Ballys nor the hand picking your pocket, or the man who finally brought business sense to top-level motor racing. Probably, all of the above.

Pook looks as purposeful as a Porsche; his fringe beard is spoiler-like, both in the sense of being a cosmetic add-on and in the literal sense of contradicting his open expression with a theatrically sinister cast. He is an Englishman whose accent is almost totally diluted by the inflections and expressions of his adopted home, Southern California.

In 1975, Pook, a total unknown in the racing world, announced he was about to stage a Formula One event through the streets of Long Beach, Calif.

Bad enough that Pook was anonymous. Worse that Long Beach was a kind of West Coast pre-gambling version of Atlantic City—exhausted, shabby, all but abandoned—and a service town to boot.

In the fall of that year, Pook staged a preliminary event as then required by the international body that approves world championship events; the next spring came the for-real, honest-to-God, Ferrari-to-Lotus complete with strutting jockey drivers who were there racing through the streets of Long Beach just as though they thought they were at Monaco.

This, of course, infuriated the established racing promoters who had never been able to do anything near so bold. It outraged traditionalists who knew that in the testament of truth it was written that the United States Grand Prix was held annually at Watkins Glen, N.Y., and stood alone as the one and the only righteous grand prix.

Essentially, Pook's coup angered just about everybody in racing—except maybe the people who pay racing's tab: the spectators and the sponsors.

Inevitably, Pook's success brought him consultancies with cities that wanted in on this spectacular international action and all the publicity it generated. Equally inevitably, such consultancies set him face-to-face with the international puppet master of race promotion, Bernie Ecclestone, who was then and is now convinced that he is the man who is to be consulted by potential race organizers be they cities or sheiks.

Some people were calling the Pook/Ecclestone confrontation a "fleece-off."

Whatever it was, no matter the shape it took, its results were clear. Ecclestone had done a contract with Las Vegas to hold a downtown Formula One race—and Pook slid in under him and put the thing on for the organizing hotel. After a pair of years of loss, Vegas opted to drop the international show and replace it with a CART event.

So did Long Beach.

And Long Beach was Christopher Robin Pook.

"It's simple," said Ecclestone. "Pook thinks he runs Formula One racing in the United States. He doesn't." Unspoken was that Ecclestone ran Formula One racing not only in the United States but all over the world. And so he does. And so, at least as far as Chris Pook is concerned, he may.

Because, despite Pook's current consultancy with the promoters of the proposed Dallas F1 event next July, Christopher Robin has his CART race in Long Beach and he is the godfather to the CART race at the Meadowlands, which in addition to providing him with a widened power base, and a no-doubt handsome fee, coincidentally seems to finesse the much-discussed rival New York Grand Prix for Formula One cars which was to be held on—oh, if Nelson Rockefeller were still alive—Long Island. So Pook's accomplishment in Long Beach gives Meadowlands CEO Mulcahy and its president, Loris Smith, much encouragement that what shabby Long Beach could do, the glistening Meadowlands can do better.

A skeptic might rightly suggest that such reasoning belongs in the category of faith, and the businessman who uses faith as his marketing plan would do well to turn his collar around and take up another calling.

Mulcahy, Smith and Pook would certainly agree.

Drive into Manhattan on the approach that uses the George Washington Bridge as entry to the island and you pass industrial park after industrial park. Each cleaner than the next. Each newer. Each more chockablock with low-lying, turnkey one- and two-stories with pastel logos that say "Gould" or "Penske" or "Detroit Diesel" or a hundred, hell, a thousand names familiar to those who use the *Wall Street Journal* as a go-to-work St. Christopher's medal. These are the very same corporations that have paid mega-thousands in annual rent for corporate suites in Giants Stadium, in the Meadowlands Arena. These are the corporations the high-powered management of the great sports complex in East Rutherford have trained and taught in the ways of profits through hospitality through sports.

And these are the bulwarks and the bollards of any Meadowlands sports construct, of whatever event it chooses to stage, however weird.

You say New York hates cars? You want us all to hear that motor racing is as strange to the denizens of the Apple as grape-rolling? And about as appealing?

Never mind. Never mind because anything the Meadowlands puts on will be supported by its corporate allies. They have seen the light. They understand. They want in. All they ask is a little piece of the action.

To be precise, a little piece of what totals somewhere between $2.7 million and $3 million worth of action to do a bit of reconstruction for the "temporary" road circuit of 1.8 miles on which Mario Andretti, Unser *pere* and Unser *fils*, Bobby Rahal, Teo Fabi and, for all anyone knows, the actual A.J. Foyt will race. In front of NBC live cameras, flag to flag, rain or shine, with the New York City skyline in the background and the Cosworths howling and the people screaming, praise the Lord, you think the corporados don't want a part of that?

To the tune of—total—maybe a couple of million. Added to the TV rights. And the gate. And the major sponsor that might, just might, do business out of a big glass house in Dearborn, Mich., according to an advertising agency whose employees, if they're high enough up, drive cars with the "SVO" logo discreetly emblazoned upon them.

"Look," says Pook's marketing director, Brian Turner, "here's the way it is. You put on an event, it's what the real estate people say: Location, location, location.

"A race is a show, isn't it? It's a circus. You make enough noise, you call enough attention to yourself, you're successful. Simple as that."

Not quite.

Because in addition to everything else, there's the Meadowlands, and nobody's ever seen anything quite like the Meadowlands before. It is the ultimate expression of corporate sport. It has absolutely nothing to do with the playing fields of Eton. It is General Motors.

And you remember who sold the Chevette to an entire nation.

Remembering the Bridge

Nov. 8, 1999

THE LINGERING MEMORY OF BRIDGEHAMPTON is the endless drive there from Manhattan. One hundred thirty-five miles of Long Island Expressway that was invariably constipated. Endless.

The other memory is how astonishing it was to find a major league circuit that close.

And finally the Perils of Pauline adventures the Bridge put us all through—it was variously vibrant, then deathly ill, then on life support, then back to being merely deathly ill.

I went there first in its Can-Am days, when the racing was glorious. At first as a journalist, then a Steward of the Meet, the place confronted me in both incarnations with absolutely extraordinary experiences. I took my son (not yet by half a lifetime the editor), where he saw the motorsports writer for a great metropolitan newspaper lean over to the correspondent for a local rag and ask for—and then file—the other man's carbons. "Should he have done that, Dad?" he asked me. What better life lesson could I have asked for a boy preparing for a career in journalism?

My steward moment of memory was vastly less innocent. The particular race had been over for half an hour or so, the crowd was leaving via the circuit, and one of the spectators who had been drinking hit and killed a turn worker, infuriating his fellows. Until the police arrived, it was necessary to somehow protect him, as odious as that job was. The task fell to several of us and we chose to put him in a small building just off the track.

I have a photo of my then-eight-year-old daughter at Bridge-hampton lying on the top bunk of a motor home reading *Mad* as her mother babysat her, Roger Penske Jr. and, if I remember correctly, one or another Donohue. It was a lovely warm scene, but it could not begin to overcome the horror of the weekend.

Dan Gurney, Scooter Patrick, Denny Hulme—the names ring in

memory—the Can-Am days at Bridgehampton were as wonderful as that wonderful series got at any track in the land.

The other day a publication called *Wheels* arrived on my desk courtesy of a local Southampton architect named Guy Frost. He founded an organization called the Friends of Bridgehampton and is fighting a rear guard action against the Forces of Evil that are trying to put an end to the Bridge.

Since the Can-Am went away, and during the years that the Trans-Am and then the Atlantic Series pumped life blood into Bridgehampton, real estate developers chewed away at the edges of the property on which the Bridge stood. In the manner these things happen, in the decade during the last pro race at the circuit, the developers came to outnumber the racers and certainly in the halls of decision their voices were louder. "Your racket is polluting our neighborhood," they said to the track. At which point a financier and car collector named Bob Rubin stepped in and snatched the track and the land on which it stood out from under a plan to put a 114-house subdivision on the property.

Not the first threat to Bridgehampton, but close to the last. Bob Rubin, after more than a decade of trying to make it work as a racetrack, is set on converting his property into a golf course. His example could point a cautionary way to others, Don Panoz and Jim France for instance, both of whom have allegedly expressed interest in the Bridge. After all, Gotham has seduced such remarkable promoters as Chip Ganassi, emptied their pockets and then thrown them away.

But don't think the golf course is a laydown either. "No you don't," says the town council, a golf course would pollute the water.

Ain't it always the way.

Tuned Out

JUST BEING THERE IS NOT ENOUGH
Feb. 21, 2000

LAST WEEK ESPN2 COVERED DAYTONA to the bitter end with only a mild slice taken out of the middle. I should be grateful, but I'm not. It made me angry.

In the beginning there was a *Competition Press* because there was almost nothing else. No newspaper covered racing. There was never a mention of results on radio. Television? What television? This journal was begun in 1958 because our club—our collection of enthusiasts—was parched for information about motorsports. We reported some on Formula One, on international sports car racing, but mostly on what was happening in this country. During Denise McCluggage's very early stewardship we did this well, thereafter increasingly badly. More enthusiasts than journalists, we failed both in understanding and in objectivity. Like many who followed us in motorsports reportage, and particularly (it says here) with coverage of the Rolex 24, we thought it was enough just to be there.

But soon it became more and more evident that motorsports was engaging the attention of an increasingly large audience. Result? Newspapers began to cover racing as an almost legitimate sport. Was this a matter of satisfaction to those of us who had been aching for institutional recognition for years? Not in the least. They got it wrong, they buried it in the hemorrhoid ads, they covered the inconsequential and ignored the important. Nonetheless, many of us were pathetically grateful that the race reports were there at all even as it became clearer and clearer they weren't any good. The more frustrating it was, the more puzzled I was at my reaction. After all, weren't *ComPress* and the newspapers competitors? And wasn't it good for us that our daily antagonists were so inept? No it wasn't. Then and now, I thought, motor racing would never come out of the closet until it was treated like the serious, important sport it clearly was becoming.

Since those days, the world of coverage has changed enormously. NASCAR has made the point that racing is a major league American sport. Formula One is treated on television with the seriousness it deserves, albeit still it is consigned to the limbo of lesser cable. CART is big time, but its presentation is so weak it teeters on the edge of rodeo-like share. Newspapers now assign real reporters to cover major races.

This is all hugely satisfying because it gives our sport proper respect. It is no longer a poor second to cod fishing. It is covered by people who are both knowledgeable in the sport and journalistically excellent.

Which is what infuriated me about ESPN2's coverage of Daytona. With the exception of the camera work, which was often remarkable, it might as well have been 1975 for all the thoughtfulness its commentators brought to it. Cars were not referred to by chassis and engine but by car number. Who cared?

Drivers were mentioned as though we all knew them intimately. We didn't. And only at the end was the dramatic battle between Corvette and Viper put onto the forefront of the commentary. Why should this be so annoying when *AutoWeek* stands ready to take advantage of television's shabby coverage? Same reason it's always been. It is critical, we believe, that coverage not be exclusionary but inclusionary. We are now, as we have always been, missionaries. When reporting is sloppy and smug, assuming everyone knows intimately the cast of characters on the racetrack and in the pits, commentary turns into mystery theater or inside baseball.

That's all we need, 10 hours of coverage that invites the audience to tune out.

Hail to the Chiefs

March 15, 1999

IT'S ABOUT TIME that somebody glorified the great American crew chief. But it does seem odd that Hendrick Racing has gone to all that trouble to convince us that the combination of Ray Evernham and Jeff Gordon is an evil partnership of Rasputin and Dan Quayle.

All successful driver/crew chief combinations are.

Used to be we immortalized drivers. We cast them in the image of great American Western Heroes: tough, contrary mavericks. They didn't shave, not all of them drove sober. Of course, those were days before two-way radios; you put the driver out on the track and hoped he'd drive in the right direction. Nowadays, a race driver is like a quarterback who doesn't even call his own plays. He's got a spotter on top of the stands. He's got a team manager in the pits. He's got an engineer in the timing and scoring stand. He's got an owner out at the wall. He's got a wife watching him on television in the motor home. And this is the guy you expect to be a legend?

No, Hendrick and Co. are right: The time of the crew chief is here. You could see it coming 25 years ago. The great prototype was Tyler Alexander of McLaren. Tyler summed up his view of the world, particularly the racing world, in one brisk aphorism: "Don't turn around," he'd say. "You might get stabbed in the face."

He was also the ultimate realist. I was standing in the pits at the Speedway during practice one afternoon when Peter Revson blasted a truly evil-handling car up to Tyler, ripped off his helmet and demanded, "What in the hell are you going to do to keep this s - - - box from killing me?"

"Don't ever ask a question you don't want to hear the answer to," said Tyler.

There was then and is now a super Tyler: Roger Bailey began his career with Sir John Whitmore, racing Minis, and then as one half of the Cooper Mini team, for Ken Tyrrell. Now understand it was a simpler world. You built your own car, you roomed with your wrench, you traveled together and, more important, you went together to the pub in the evening. We use the word team now but I wonder how sure we are that we know what it means. Roger did. Over time he worked with a wonderment of drivers, including Chris Amon at Ferrari, David Hobbs at BMW and George Follmer at Penske (where his apprentice was a kid named Al Holbert).

In every case, there was a partnership. The fierce, independent artisan with his tools always ready to be packed. The ferociously freelance driver, always prepared to go his own way, loyal to his mate the mechanic and nobody else.

In time, Roger went to work alongside the legendary Indy engine builder Herb Porter—Herbie Horsepower—to learn the dark secrets of the Offenhauser, and there I met him. His nickname then was "Boost" because he would dial three digits into McLaren's qualifying motors knowing they had to live for only four laps. It was a time he and Tyler worked together and John Rutherford and Peter drove the cars. I don't expect to see the likes of them again.

Roger's managerial and technical competence carried him beyond the dyno room; he became technical director of IMSA and then co-founder of Indy Lights. With the Lights series sold to CART, Roger was finally rewarded.

There's a lesson here for Ray Evernham. Even in a time of software and marketing, the role of the crew chief remains unique. He is the last of the great artisans, the indispensable alter ego of one of the few daredevil adventurers who remain. What Evernham brings to his team is uniquely his. More than a skill, it is an attitude and a way of looking at the world. It's in shorter and shorter supply, and it's becoming very clear that you can't buy it; you can only reward it.

Cadillac's Will

June 5, 2000

WE ARE POISED ON THE BRINK of another Le Mans and things don't look good. For Cadillac that is. They look fine for Audi. In prequalifying everybody is holding everyone else's chin up and saying that if Caddy fails it will either be a gearbox problem or God's will. Mind you, I can't fault Cadillac's courage in being there. An American presence in international racing deserves applause no matter what happens. Forgive me if I don't understand it. (I do understand the Evoq and Imaj, and I wish Cadillac was spending its time and money on them.)

To the racing point: Cadillac sells 7 cars a year in Switzerland, 11 in Sweden; so if that's the reason it's racing—and even if it wins Le Mans (and how would you book that?)—it might double its sales. On the other hand, there's the ugly possibility that Cadillac actually expects the Sarthe results to affect sales in the United States. Let's hope not.

(By the way, I'm fairly sure I know why Corvette races. Corvette's a sports car and it should race. Just as Porsche should. *L'affaire* Porsche is another matter and one this department will get around to in due time.)

Anyway, there's Cadillac, a marque (these days we say "brand," saints preserve us) claiming to be renewing a racing heritage of 50 years and doing nothing of the sort—it was Briggs Cunningham, Denise reminds us, who had to go to a Cadillac dealership to buy his cars for Le Mans. Nonetheless, Cadillac does indeed have a strong past to draw upon, even a brilliant one. Let's not forget two Dewar's Trophies, let's not forget the marvelous multi-cylinder engines of the 1930s. But instead of glorifying its past with, say, a museum, it's going racing. And I fear for it. A wonderfully experienced endurance racer we all know wonders if Cadillac is exhibiting the commitment a successful effort requires: every race with every car every year over the full term of a project that must be a minimum of three to five years. It must draw from the best and most experienced people available. For the Cadillac program, the preliminary inquiries of household-name American racers consisted of a superficial sent-out-in-the-mail questionnaire that many of them considered insulting and ignored. (What is your background, Mr. Foyt?) And that was the end of it. No follow-up phone calls. Nothing. Does this sound like commitment to you?

GM has a racing boss for whom I have a lot of respect. His name is Herb Fishel, and he has seen it all, done it all. As with people in racing who have many miles on their odos, sometimes you can tell what he's up to and sometimes you can't. His job is not an easy one. Dragons dwell in the pits and paddocks of the racing world, but they're nothing compared to the dragons that stalk the halls of GM. There doesn't seem to be much reason Herb can't eventually win Le Mans for Cadillac. On the other hand, that's looking at it from the outside.

It's Over

July 9, 2001

This column, published years before the division in American open-wheel racing really was "over," infuriated CART loyalists. Like Leon's Can-Am story nearly 30 years earlier, though, it was simply acknowledging what the smart insiders were saying in private.

NEVER MIND THE EXTRAORDINARY accommodation the IRL made for CART at the Indianapolis Motor Speedway last month, not even its gracious by-your-leave to the rival sanctioning body's first six finishing cars. What really counted was the melding of cultures. At least that's what it looked like to an outsider. To someone inside Gasoline Alley, it was more the continuing separation thereof.

One of the absolutely great Indy icons said about the Speedway this year that it was a perpetuation of Indianapolis 10 years ago. The IRL, in his view, was formed to make it comfortable for everyone who wanted to live in the past to do so. He was answering the question about why the CART invaders finished at the top of the field: There are two levels of professionalism, he said, today's and yesterday's.

It went far to explain what happened. But it would be an enormous mistake to take it as a signal for what is to come between the two sanctioning bodies. Far better to look at the comity in the relationship between Roger Penske and Tony George. Both have understood the need for reconciliation in the race series; both have watched the two come closer together at the 500 over the last two years. This year Tony was truly happy that Roger was at the Speedway but no happier than Roger was.

Now IRL is becoming muscular. As this is written, Michigan International Speedway either will have announced or will be about to announce it will become an IRL venue. Fontana too. The league is about to make clear its own feeder series. Indy Lights, before it expires, will run three races in conjunction with three IRL events. Whatever

CART does with its engine formula, IRL has been bolstered by Chevrolet announcing that it will replace Aurora as its engine supplier, which means far greater funding and support.

What all this says is that once again racing has practiced the law of unintended consequences. The Indy Racing League was formed to bring back the old days. And it did. CART split off to glorify the best and the brightest and the newest and the best. And it did. When the best and the brightest and the newest and the best met the old days at the Indianapolis Motor Speedway in a 500-mile race, guess who finished in the top six places? Right.

Everything and everybody predicted that the course of racing would be in favor of the new. But also guess which one's prevailing on some kind of perverse survival scales? It is a matter of momentum. No matter how new the new, it's the old that has the momentum and it's the new that's being swept along with it.

Which is to say that it may not be today and it may not be tomorrow, but it's over.

Of Cars and Racing and Friendship

March 9, 1998

I RECEIVED A NICE LETTER from the Detroit Region of the Sports Car Club of America—would I come and say a word at their 50th anniversary celebration next November?

These are serious people in Detroit and they contribute much. For example, they staff the FedEx Championship race (did I really say that?) on Belle Isle every year. Trouble is, I never had much to do with the SCCA here. What would I say?

Then I began to remember. I went to my first SCCA event 45 years ago: Watkins Glen. Not much later, when I moved with my new wife to California, the destination was Pebble Beach—Nirvana. Over the decades, she and I spent most free weekends at Cotati or Stockton, standing on corners and jumping behind haybales. The point was to be around cars. But there was a larger reason. We were strangers in a strange land. California in the 1950s was hospitable— but as a place of immigrants, there was no established society to reach out and welcome newcomers.

But there was a car culture, which was its own community. So weekend after weekend, all over Northern California, and later Southern California, my wife and I shared the car experience with others of like mind. And values. And disposition.

We found ourselves a part of an exciting world filled with people whose decision to go racing or rallying marked them, particularly in those times, as adventurous and interesting.

It's not too much to say that the friends we made then are the core of my circle of friends still, even though I may not have seen some of them in years.

Jack Dalton was a factory MG driver (in the sense that there was such a thing) whose talents today might have put him in the high

127

ranks of the elite. Jack's spontaneous joy in racing, the relish that was so obvious when he climbed into the car on the grid, said enough to me about the fierce pleasure of competition for racers and workers too. I never again wondered why people on flag stations or working a grid wanted to help make racing possible and safe.

Ted Rothermel defined the new quasi-science of racetrack safety before there was a Laguna Seca circuit. He taught me, simply, that without the people behind the scenes within the SCCA there'd be no sport. His wife, Mary Jane, chief of communications in the San Francisco Region, took my wife in hand and brought her inside both the club and racing with a marvelous generosity of spirit.

I would talk about my friend Leo Bourke, who with Merle Brennan and Harry Banta founded the Reno Racing Team. Or Rod Carveth, who played in the big leagues with his Aston DB3S and considered racers and workers part of one shared community.

Waving at cars during the *AW* Road Show and Driveable Feast in front of the Grosse Pointe Historical Society building. Olivia was active in the GPHS.
AutoWeek Archives

Mainly, perhaps, Jack Flaherty, a one-time California Sprint Car champion and, like Jack Dalton, factory BMC road racer, whose hard-headed, clear-eyed approach to racing gave me a framework to make later judgments when I would travel with Peter Revson and Danny Sullivan and write books about them both.

My point? It seems that as I look back at a misspent life in cars, much of it at the track, the foundation of my knowledge and understanding came from the friends I made in the SCCA and the hours and days I spent at weed-strewn, sunbaked racetracks all over summertime America.

As a flagman and later steward from Lime Rock to Mid-Ohio.

As a dreadfully slow and tentative racer in Northern California and Nevada.

As a race reporter at Watkins Glen and Road Atlanta, and later a book writer from Mosport to Indianapolis.

What will I say to the gathering of the Detroit Region's 50th anniversary? That perhaps I may not have shared the specific moments of their own experience, that perhaps many of us are meeting for the very first time, but that nonetheless I know them well. And I thank them for being there and making possible a special life.

I Miss My People

Jan. 4, 1999

IT'S BEEN ALMOST THREE YEARS since the racing community was my neighborhood, and I miss it. I grew up in the SCCA as a corner worker, drove some, stewarded a little bit in a few distant places and then presumed to think I knew enough to report. I didn't, of course, but if you act as though you do, more and more people come to believe you.

Race writing in the days of the Can-Am required only primitive skill. The most technically demanding requirements were: (1) spelling Donohue right, (2) likewise Chaparral. Press rooms were filled with local writers from the dailies, and then as now, the absolute junior reporter was given the motorsports beat. You wouldn't believe how many ways they invented to spell either or both.

And yet out of the morass of these clusters of the inept came some remarkable talents: the delightful Eoin Young, Jim MacQueen, Gordon Kirby and that *nonpareil*, Pete Lyons.

The motorsports community then, as now, was a loosely woven (and sometimes equally loosely wrapped) group of brave, funny, treacherous risk-takers. And then there were the drivers. They were, however loathsome their behavior, the most attractive and admirable people I knew.

Simply being with them was an adventure. May I tell you about Charlie Fox, the Mission Inn and Les Richter in the guise of Guardian Angel? The scene: Riverside, specifically Highway 15 in front of the Mission Inn, a beautiful, old-time mission-style hotel at which this weekend Dan Blocker, team owner and "Hoss" on *Bonanza*, is giving a 72-hour party complete with a variety of, er, debutantes. It doesn't take long for the party to get rough with people of every sort and stripe bouncing off walls and out of windows. The management, despairing of the locals, calls the Highway Patrol. But the Highway Patrol has other things on its mind. Charles Fox, motorsports writer and car

Chatting with Carroll Shelby at the Pebble Beach Concours d'Elegance.
AutoWeek Archives

evaluator, at this very moment evaluating a KR500 loaned to him by his pal Carroll Shelby, is blasting down the hill outside town at warp speed, unaware that his every move has been tracked by the CHP. It is a challenge, it is a dare, it is an outrage, and the CHP is up to it.

Totally ignoring the orgy at the Mission Inn, the Highway Patrol blocks off both ends of the freeway and lies in wait. In the meantime,

131

the CHP division chief is on the phone to the exec director of the Raceway, complaining about the behavior of . . . not the gang at the Mission Inn, but the dimwit in the KR500. Richter, who has been on the receiving end of several desperate calls from the Mission Inn management, is delighted. So long as the Highway Patrol can be diverted. . . .

Richter went bail. Blocker's car broke in the race. Some very deep pockets paid for the damage at the Mission Inn, which shortly closed. Years later it opened again, graceful and beautiful. Les the Wise is at California Speedway. There's still a Highway Patrol.

Perhaps you have the patience to hear about the prominently dentured woman car owner ("There she is now, standing behind her teeth," said William Jeanes one day at Watkins Glen), who interrupted a semi-formal dinner in what was very much a family dining spot at Riverside by disappearing under the table and anticipating Paula Jones with a 12-year-old adjunct reporter.

Or even about the novice motorsports writer who was dispatched to bring Bruce McLaren up to the PA tower at Laguna Seca, and who didn't find out he'd been cruelly victimized by a Kiwi public relations guy, who had passed off an incredibly foul-mouthed wrench instead, until the guy actually got on the air. It remains one of the greatest embarrassments of my life.

Never mind. I want to go back. Wouldn't you?

American Heroes

June 7, 1999

IT SEEMS LIKE ONLY YESTERDAY Ray Harroun won at the Speedway and now next racing season will be the first of the new millennium. Clearly the time has come to look at the century about to be past and anoint our American heroes.

Roger Penske, Pat Patrick, Carl Haas: I cluster them not because they're alike but because of what they represent: the hard, unyielding principles of progressive racing. Each has his own peculiarities, each his difficult side. But you want them on your side if you go to war.

Steve Horne: The next generation of the same.

Tyler Alexander: The exemplar of the independent artisan crew chief. Nasty, clever, sarcastic, demanding, obsessive. The best of his kind there ever was.

Roger Bailey: Also began with a wrench in his hands, became powerful, respected and rich because he deserved to be.

Leo Mehl: As Goodyear's F1 impresario and then its racing chief, he presided over as thorny a cast of characters as ever existed. By cajoling, bullying, shaping and resolving in the ever-shifting world of Grand Prix racing, he accomplished so much behind the scenes he might have become—and should have been—the first secretary-general of the United Nations.

Chris Economaki: Lots of people know Chris' public face; few are aware of what a personally elegant man he is in his manners, tastes, standards and ethics.

Les Richter: Yes, he's a master of the malaprop, but you'll go a very long way before you hear as much sense from the mouth of anyone in racing.

Bill Brodrick: Retired at last to the stud farm where he belongs, Brodrick established the benchmark of sublime hucksterism others have tried and failed to emulate.

Leon with Roger Bailey. *AutoWeek Archives*

Carroll Shelby: I doubt that most of us have any memory of how talented he was, or how fiercely stubborn he was, or how all-around competitive he was, but how come we celebrate Jackie Stewart for what he's accomplished after racing and don't also mention Carroll?

Bob Tullius: Very early took amateur then professional racing into the world of business and profit. At the same time his cars were the exemplars of superb preparation. As a driver he was remarkable. As an entrepreneur he was even more so.

Jack Dalton: A straight-from-stock amateur. Drove some of the factory's cars, but was unsubsidized and uncontaminated. As much pure talent as anyone of his epoch.

George Follmer: Before he got in a race car, George was always underestimated. After he got out, he never was again.

Dan Gurney: Nobody showed us the way like Dan. Sometimes it was a headstrong way, but we would have followed him anywhere.

Phil Hill: Is it me or have we been extraordinarily lucky in our world champions?

Mario Andretti: See above.

Sam Posey: At a time when it was important to have a spokesman for racing who was urbane, thoughtful and cosmopolitan along came Sam. For all the reasons he brought benefit, he was bitterly criticized. Not by me.

Brian Redman: Once upon a time I was furiously critical of Brian for being a lesser talent than those against whom he was competing. That's how much I knew. Besides which, these days Brian is among us tending to the vintage flame.

Jim Haynes: Somewhere, sometime, some incorruptible someone had to be our living archive. Not only our institutional memory, our institutional conscience. Nobody better.

Peter Revson: Yes, he was selfish. Yes, he was petty. Yes, he could be more difficult to deal with than even Jackie Stewart. But he gave us our sense of national self, he justified our pride, he fulfilled our dreams.

And, of course, Denise.

Legends of Can-Am

CAN-AM'S GREAT RACING PEOPLE
MADE IT OUR GREATEST SPECTACLE
Aug. 13, 1990

This column was published in conjunction with a cover story about the original Can-Am racing series.

I OPEN AN OLD *AutoWeek* and read the names: Bruce McLaren, John Surtees, Dan Gurney, Jackie Stewart, Jim Hall, Denny Hulme, Phil Hill, Mario Andretti, Peter Revson. Graham Hill, Patrick Tambay, Keke Rosberg, Danny Sullivan, Al Unser Jr.—and the small hairs rise at the base of my neck.

Some ran against one another, some raced for the same teams a decade later; but considered as a whole, never again will such a blazing array of drivers form up on a grid staring into the waiting afternoon.

That was the Can-Am, American racing in my formative years as a journalist. When I look back, it seems to me if the Can-Am was to racing as the Battle of Britain to world history, I had the Edward R. Murrow seat. By the sheer good luck of working for this magazine, I was right in the middle of it, and the sound of battle was all around.

As the Can-Am grew in stature and American racing coalesced and matured in its world view, a concomitant maturity overtook *AutoWeek*. In some ways, the story of the growth of the Can-Am—evolution of technology, influx of consequential contributors, availability of greater and greater resources—is the story of the growth of this publication.

It's a quarter of a century later; that sense of identification hasn't diminished. In fact, it has increased as motorsports and marketing have come closer and closer together. With the American industry adopting racing as a part of its development and sales programs, the logical direction of growth of both the sport and this magazine has been to embrace the larger landscape.

Which does not mean that the Great Names of the Can-Am are any smaller on the map of cardom than they were in the glory days of the racing series. The regard I feel at encountering one or another of them is renewed every time I run into a Carl Haas or a Roger Penske or a Tyler Alexander, they are still event makers, they are history shapers to this day.

It is hard to remember a time when Roger Penske was mortal. But he was only one of a band of equals in the Can-Am, although already his standards were becoming the standards of an entire community. His voice was heard clearly in the councils of the owners. But in the early years, he was not the Penske of the all-conquering Porsches. These days, American racing bears the imprint of the Penske vision. In terms of the industrialization of the sport, no one's contributions even come close.

Dan Gurney had his own car, the McLeagle, in the Can-Am; no surprise, Dan Gurney always has his own car everywhere. But having his own car was symbolic of something much larger with Dan. It was his insistence on doing things his own way. What's more, Dan's way was always the honorable, even if it wasn't the most expedient. That exasperated many of his fans and some of his supporters. But it's what Dan stood for then and what he stands for now. Dan Gurney is the conscience of American racing.

Jim Hall, of course, is the Can-Am's exemplar of inventiveness. Whatever racing represents in terms of American ingenuity, Jim Hall exemplified 10 times over. Was the unlimited sports car the ultimate race car on the planet? The arguments in favor were based largely on what Hall devised and employed and what Hall—and his underground cadre of wizards at GM—managed to bestow on his marvelous Chaparral. Next season Hall reappears in racing with an Indy car. Does anybody really think Hall will revert to store-bought ideas?

Once during the Can-Am years, at a time when the wanna-but-never-would-be insiders were busy crafting Carl Haas cheapskate jokes as the trend of the moment, I eavesdropped on him as he stood toe-to-toe with a promoter who was insisting on cutting a purse for one of the legendary events. Mind you this was after all the teams had arrived, coming from as far away as Australia, and already begun practice. The promoter, certain he had the racers at his mercy, was smug and intractable. Haas was outraged, but, as always, pragmatic. Representing no one but himself, and interested only in seeing that the race proceed, Haas went surety for the entire amount. Let me say that again; he guaranteed the purse for his competitors. Today, still often alone, Carl fights frequently losing battles in CART's committee-of-the-whole owners' group in behalf of retaining the classic old tracks: Mid-Ohio, Elkhart Lake, Laguna Seca. They are the tracks he raced on in the Can-Am, one in fact is the track for which he guaranteed that purse. Carl Haas is a loyal man.

Pete Lyons never raced a car, never owned one, never promoted an event; all he did was redefine the way racing was written and understood in America. Writers who do that come along in sports very rarely. I think of Red Smith and Jim Murray. They excelled not so much as recounters of events but as interpreters. Smith and Murray let the players speak for themselves; upon their special dialogue, their attitudes and their arguments, both men picketed signposts of clarity and understanding. But never so clever as to take attention away from the players. As he traveled with the series, Lyons wrote the races for *AutoWeek* as though they were acts in a summer-long drama. He set stages. He wrote program notes. He prepared his audience for the action and then stood aside and let the drama unfold. There's never been a race reporter like Lyons; there never is likely to be again.

Unless it was Charlie Fox. He came to the Can-Am Series from England and the editorial assistant's job at *AutoWeek,* and he came upon it as though he knew it was historic and the Can-Am was there for the very purpose of providing him an opportunity to chronicle grand events. Fox had in common with Lyons that he dealt with the great as though they were players in a complex theatrical. But Fox wrote the Can-Am as though he were its playwright and it was his own production.

See for yourself [*in the cover story for this week's issue*]. There is Charlie Fox presenting the opening year of the Can-Am, 1966—

Leon totes a tire for Danny Sullivan's Can-Am race car during the season he was researching the book *Fast Lane Summer*. *Baron Wolman/Mandel Family Archive*

brought to you with Tyler Alexander photos; starring John Surtees, Mark Donohue, Jim Hall, Teddy Mayer, Roger Penske—the whole wonderful, glorious cast.

Lord, it's good to revisit them all. And wonderful to see them through the eye of Tyler. But most of all to hear Charlie's grand chords roll out once again.

Fast Lane Summer

May 28, 2001

BARON WOLMAN IS SENDING ME the entire backlog of documents for *Fast Lane Summer*. An explanation: *Fast Lane Summer* is the book I wrote and he photographed in 1981 about a summer on the Can-Am circuit focusing on Garvin Brown Racing and Danny Sullivan. Having the film for the book will represent more than just owning what it would take to reproduce *Fast Lane Summer*; it will mean being able to go back in time to relive that extraordinary summer.

While it seemed to me then that this second iteration of the Can-Am was weak tea in comparison to the ferocious original, when I look at the drivers and the cars it was nothing of the sort. There was Al Holbert, Mario Andretti, Patrick Tambay, Geoff Brabham, Elliott Forbes-Robinson and Bobby Rahal. There were car owners Brown, Paul Newman, Carl Haas and Holbert. And the cars, while developments of Formula 5000 instead of the unlimited sports racers of the original Can-Am, were sufficiently formidable for anyone.

At any rate, there we were at the beginning of the season at Sears Point with an unproven car of home design, a demanding series and a first-year owner whose credentials were less than impressive. Even so, almost everyone was a seemingly better bet for success than the moderately accomplished open-wheel driver whose achievements were mainly counted on the pages of some obscure overseas calendar of a minor race series.

Baron and I were along for the summer because Garvin wanted a chronicle of the year, all unknowing what might happen—which was a measure of his insouciance. As the series traveled its course from track to track across the Midwest—Mid-Ohio to Mosport—it became clear that the homemade car was an atrocity. Its designers, brothers who were also the crew, pointed fingers directly at Sullivan and the atmosphere became poisonous. Brown, inexperienced in the politics of team management, was at his wits' end.

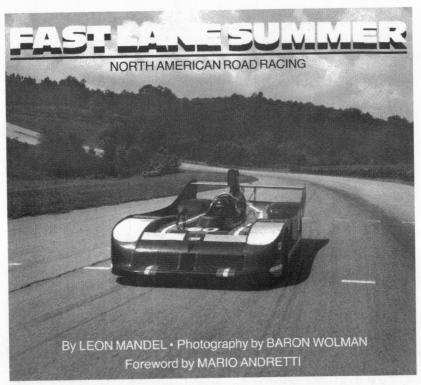

FAST LANE SUMMER
NORTH AMERICAN ROAD RACING

By LEON MANDEL • Photography by BARON WOLMAN
Foreword by MARIO ANDRETTI

Cover of *Fast Lane Summer,* published by Van Nostrand Reinhold,
October 1981.

At Elkhart Lake, Garvin made his decision. He chose Sullivan over his crew, packed them up, junked their car and sent them away; $100,000 later, Brown had invested in a new Lola T530, Sullivan had called in a new crew chief, and a week later at Brainerd, Minnesota, Danny was on the front row. The question of where the problem lay was solved. It was really solved four years later at Indianapolis, when, driving for Roger Penske, Danny put himself in the record book as Mr. Spin and Win.

When the 60 pounds of film on which the book is recorded gets here, I'll store it carefully because it's very much a part of my life. There are not many things you do that remain vivid in your memory. That summer is one of mine. It's not entirely bright. But what remains extraordinary for me is how the story told itself as though preordained. Its rhythms were there. Its highs were there, and its lows; it was there for me to tell.

How Dare We?

Oct. 15, 2001

SIMPLE QUESTION: HOW DARE WE? Given all the expertise and all the exhaustive research and conscientious effort to find the truth in the matter of Dale Earnhardt's death, what on earth possesses us to question NASCAR's conclusion that it's none of our business?

How dare we question the results of an investigation reported in 324 pages, presented in two bound volumes, led by Dr. James Raddin and Dr. Dean Sicking and backed up by more than 50 doctors, engineers and physicists retained by NASCAR?

After the results were presented there was an hour's Q&A during which it was clear that NASCAR doesn't plan any immediate changes to its safety procedures. The rationale? "Nothing we can do can bring back those who we've lost," said NASCAR's president Mike Helton, so who are we to be asking questions?

After all, there are going to be black boxes. And in a major change from the past, the sanctioning body will hire a medical liaison to deal with on-track injuries. But no traveling medical teams as in CART and the IRL. "Local physicians are good enough," said Helton. And, he said, a driver-led safety committee sounds too much like a union. "We already have a safety committee. It's 43 drivers every Sunday."

Now, about restraint systems. Drivers and owners say the sanctioning body shouldn't mandate systems, nor how belts and seats are installed. And this despite evidence Earnhardt's belt failed because it was improperly anchored. Bill Simpson said he repeatedly warned Earnhardt about his failure to secure the belt properly, but that's the way Dale liked it. Moreover, Earnhardt's shoulder harnesses were secured too low behind his seat, his lap belts too far behind his hips, and his crotch belt was secured too far in front of his seat.

So now some questions: If NASCAR is not a public company, what is its obligation to provide traveling medical teams to its participants if they're not asking for them? If the sanctioning body is not hearing from the people who make up the full-time players, why should it worry about rules and regulations for safety systems?

Which brings us back to the original question: How dare we? If the summer soldiers are complacent, looking at racing safety as motorcyclists look at helmet laws, what makes us think we shouldn't be able to do the same? The simple fact is that we are stakeholders, too. It's our sport as much as it is theirs. Yes, they built it, but so did we. As we've seen, they can give us the back of their hand when we come to them for understanding. It took NASCAR six months to produce an all but impenetrable two-volume report that does not serve anyone. Our job is to be sure that the sun shines on NASCAR's deliberations. It hasn't thus far. It has to from now on.

True Heroes Revisited

March 1, 1999

This story appeared in print two weeks short of the 25th anniversary of Peter Revson's death.

JULIE REVSON, PETER'S SISTER, called the other day to tell me that after all these years she was going down to Homestead. She's reconciled at last to the loss of her brother. Pat Patrick's a friend and she wants to see him and test the waters as well as her own feelings. Good for her.

I haven't seen or talked to Julie in a quarter-century. Just think how racing's changed in that time. Used to be that an incident like Peter's, killed in testing at Kyalami, was expectable. Now it's so rare we're paralyzed with shock when it happens. Denny Hulme once told me that he'd rushed over to try to help Peter, but there was nothing to be done. That afternoon, he said, when he showered, Peter's blood streamed off his hands. It was then he decided to retire.

Mind you this was maybe the toughest-minded driver in F1. Someone who, like so many of his era, had seen and managed to put aside the deaths of many of his competitors. By the way, Denny too would die on the racetrack. But of a heart attack while in a kind of recreational event. Denny had style.

Anyway, Denny's story. It's highly improbable we would hear such today and much of our progress is thanks to Jackie [*Stewart*], toward whom Peter felt both antipathy and admiration. Antipathy because no Grand Prix driver is predisposed to embrace any other, admiration because Jackie was, after all, the exemplar.

"I don't care how many copies of our book we sell," Peter said when we shipped the manuscript to Doubleday, "so long as we sell one more than Jackie's." We did.

At any rate, much of the truly remarkable progress in race car safety since Peter's death has happened because Jackie defined it and pushed for it.

The results come not only in Grand Prix cars, but CART cars too. CART is the beneficiary of research by GM and Ford into driver safety, and if this, in some remote way, is a legacy of Peter's death I'm sure he'd be glad to know it, although he certainly wouldn't have volunteered for the job.

When all the horrendous head injuries were happening one after another in the IRL, I spoke to John Barnes, crew chief for Panther Racing and an ex-member of the USAC safety committee, and asked him what he thought about it all. He pointed out the changes to the cockpit of his car meant to cosset the driver and then he said something I shall never forget. "When you get down to it, it's the driver's responsibility when he hits the wall to protect himself, to know what to do."

That was so callous, so primitive, so shockingly unenlightened that I came away stunned. I still am.

It isn't the IRL that promotes such feelings, I know. Leo Mehl is as sophisticated a race overseer as exists anywhere in the world, with huge experience in Formula One. He has seen it all, he has been as devastated by its dark side as anyone, and he has worked with Jackie to change what needed to be changed.

It's not Leo, it's John Barnes who's the out-of-step member of the community. The other day my friend Robbie Buhl announced he and Scott Brayton's widow Becky were to be married. I'm very glad for them. Becky understands the world through the racer's eyes, she is courageous enough to embrace a life for her and her seven-year-old daughter that takes her again into the world of the race driver. She and, of course, Robbie have an enormous advantage that Peter Revson and his family never had. They are guarded by a barrier of safety on the racetracks built by people dedicated to achieving it. I would hope Julie Revson understands some of this when she goes down to Homestead and understands too that in a real way her brother made his own contribution to it.

Speed with Style

EXCERPT FROM
THE AUTOBIOGRAPHY OF PETER REVSON
Doubleday, 1974

For the book Speed with Style, *Leon followed American racing driver Peter Revson through the 1973 Formula One season, during which Revson was racing with the McLaren team. The men became close and the entire Mandel family was devastated when Revson was killed in a fiery accident while testing at the Kyalami track in South Africa just as the book was going to print in 1974. Although the book subtitle is "The Autobiography of Peter Revson," it bears a dual byline. In form, chapters written by Revson about events of the 1973 season alternate with chapters of biography written by Mandel.*

I never heard him say as much directly, but I think this look into the psyche of a rich kid with a famous name—excerpted from both the introduction to the book and the first of the chapters Leon wrote—was something Leon could relate to directly. Although the Mandel family was not nearly as wealthy or prominent as Revson's, it was well known as the founders of Chicago's Mandel Department Store. And both men went to college at Cornell.

In a section (not reproduced here) of the first chapter, Leon tells how Revson cashed in stocks meant to support his college fund and a batch of 21st birthday presents to buy a race car—it would be the last one he had to pay for himself because he was successful enough with it that he became a paid professional driver. Leon himself once used an inheritance to buy his Porsche 356—in a speech at the Porsche Rennsport Reunion in 2001, he said his parents had expected him to invest the money in "something like IBM" and that if he had, he would have become very wealthy himself. Instead, Leon said, "I bought a Porsche, and got a life." These parallels in their life experiences no doubt explain why Revson and Mandel understood each other—the rest of the friendship was the product of what came after that. Mandel's writing reflected a resolute professionalism in the face of this fact—in the foreword to the book, he even denies there was a friendship, as

*such, bemoaning that their jobs required some emotional distance—and he
sees and reports Revson's character weaknesses and blind spots as resolutely
as he does his strengths. It's an honest and unflinching portrayal, but they
worked on it together, and the result bespeaks both intimacy and trust. Is
there a better definition of friendship?*

FROM THE INTRODUCTION

After eight months of following Peter Revson around the world, I
finally discovered his real name.

For eight months I stared at him over his platter of sea bass
(Weight Watchers style) in New York restaurants, hung around the
pits at Watkins Glen and Indianapolis wondering whether his driving
suit was tailored by the same London people who cut his slightly flared
flannels, and watched him ease his executive chair back to full rake in
his office in Harbor City, California ... all this thinking his name was
merely Peter Revson. It isn't. It's Peter Jeffrey Revlon Revson.

In all his 14 years as a race driver, he had reacted in the same,
predictable, outraged way whenever he read newspaper stories referring
to him as "Peter Revson, the Revlon heir." It was as though they were
calling him some kind of faggot. Now, I discovered, "Revlon" was his
middle name.

Even two years ago, the words above would have pissed off P.J.
Revlon Revson almost beyond calculation. But something's happened
to him since he won the Canadian-American championship, won his
Grand Prix, almost tied ex-heavyweight champion Joe Frazier in a
coast-to-coast-TV weight-lifting contest, and became recognized in
Brazil, South Africa, Sweden and England (if not quite yet in the
United States) as one of the three absolutely top drivers in the world—
not to say one of the great international sports presences at 21 or on
the beach at Juan-les-Pins. He laughs a great deal more, and now that
he's rich by his own hand he's openly boastful about being careful with
money, even as the Kennedys and the Rockefellers.

As for the lipstick connection, well, if it's there it's there. Is it his
fault that his father Martin and his uncles Charles and Joseph were

compulsive empire builders? Besides, more people in supermarkets in Belgium recognize the name Peter Revson than the name of either his father or his surviving uncle. In France and Germany and Italy too. Perspective has come to Peter Jeffrey R. Revson. Moreover, he's pretty busy these days, not really enough time left for petulance. . . .

FROM CHAPTER ONE

If 1973 came as a nasty surprise to Peter Revson, 1967 had come as an even nastier one to his brother Douglas, although perhaps he never knew it. It killed him.

Doug Revson died in a small single-seater race car in the rain in Denmark. The news of his death saddened the racing community for the obligatory moment, but it didn't distract them much from whatever they were doing at the time. After all, Douglas Revson was another rich kid playing at racing, and that kind of thing can be expected to happen. Too bad, of course, but Denmark is far away and the race wasn't an important one. Not much of an opportunity for dipping into a little self-importance by letting people know what a good guy Douglas had been. Few people outside sports-car racing on the East Coast knew Douglas. When someone is killed, the least he can have done is to have provided the survivors with something to say to their friends in the bar at the Holiday Inn in Speedway, Indiana, or at the monthly meeting of the San Francisco Region of the Sports Car Club of America at the boathouse in Oakland. Doug Revson hadn't had the consideration to do even that.

Now Peter could have killed himself in 1967 and that would have been worthwhile. People knew Peter. He had already made his mark. Peter was a rich kid in the minds of the racing people too, and if by the year of his younger brother's death he hadn't exactly become a superstar, there was still something about him and something about his driving that demanded he be taken seriously. Well, at least not completely written off as just another preppie making noises about being a race driver instead of going into his father's business. "Yes," those people tend to say at Southampton and Pebble Beach somewhere between

Leon with Peter Revson gal pal Marji Wallace. *Mandel Family Archive*

races no one has ever heard of, "actually, I'm a racing driver. A professional." By their languid manner and the cut of their J. Press madras, they're denying it at the same time.

Douglas Revson never quite escaped that. He was an intense, moderately good-looking young man. His rides were at least acceptable, but the problem was they were his rides, which is to say he owned the cars he drove. If you're any good at all, if you even promise to be any good, you don't have to buy a car to go racing. Did Johnny Longden or Willie Shoemaker ever have to own their own horses? In '68, when his legs and his eyes and his reputation were still intact, did Willie Mays have to have a piece of the Giants franchise to play ball?

It's damn near as cut and dried in racing. But of course a race car is a lot cheaper than a National League ball club or even a small piece

151

of one. So to get a leg up the ladder, sometimes you buy your ride. But Doug Revson owned everything he drove, even the red, white and blue Porsche 906 that he surprised everyone with at Laguna Seca.

By then, though, his elder brother was being paid to race somebody else's cars and was very much a man of his own.

Not everyone gets to "co-author" an autobiography. Revson and Mandel alternated chapters in *Speed with Style*. The final galleys had just been finished on this 1974 Doubleday book when Revson was killed in a fiery F1 testing crash in South Africa.

152

That surprised a lot of people. At least the ones who were willing to look and see a real race driver beneath the tailored jackets and the transatlantic accent. CIA directors may come from the Ivy League, even the occasional New York Knickerbocker or Minnesota Viking, but race drivers don't. Ask A.J. Foyt about the Ivy Leagues and he'll probably think you're getting around to calling him a flaming faggot and punch you in the mouth just in case.

So Cornell would have been explanation enough for Peter Revson's truculence from time to time among his fellow racers. It could also be that if everybody in the pits thought that the profits from 100 million tubes of Orange Flip lipstick were buying your car, you'd tend to be a little testy too.

Whether they thought that or not didn't matter. Because, at the time, Revson was convinced they did, that everyone figured he was floating to his successes on a sea of Intimate.

For example, it is true that Martin Revson, Peter's father, is one of the three Revson brothers who founded Revlon. And surely Revlon is one of the extraordinary postwar business phenomena and made an astonishing amount of money for its major stockholders.

But after these two facts, matters begin to get a little confusing: The people involved start to have a curious way of appearing in one context and reappearing in another; the paths of truth and the zigzags of legend begin overlapping until tracing the course of Revson history is as difficult as mapping the Bridger Range.

Take something as innocent as the appearance of RevUp (The Vitamin for Men), "something they've asked me to endorse," according to Peter, who spent four days before the Indianapolis 500 wandering from shopping-center drug store to shopping-center drug store smiling and autographing glossies. The deal was put together by the number two man in the office of Revson's business manager, Mark McCormack. It looked like any other deal that any other of McCormack's athlete-clients (who include Jackie Stewart, Rod Laver, Evonne Goolagong, Arnold Palmer, Larry Csonka) might have had. Give a slightly commercial nod in favor of Wilkinson Sword Blades

Leon with Marji and Peter in the motor home, 1974. *Mandel Family Archive*

or Oleg Cassini sunglasses. What it is supposed to do is double your sports earnings in any given year. Mark McCormack's organization is very, very good at that sort of thing.

Except . . . the number two man in Motormarketing International, which is the automobile racing division of McCormack's International Management, is Peter Revson's longtime friend George Lysle. Nothing very strange about that, of course. It's reasonable that McCormack might hire a qualified friend of one of his big earners. We make some money, you make some money, right?

On the other hand, RevUp (The Vitamin for Men) is marketed by Commerce Drug, makers of Detain (numby dummy as Revson calls it—"First a RevUp, then a little Detain"). And Detain is marketed by Commerce, and Commerce is a subsidiary of Del Laboratories, a toiletry and chemicals company. And Del Laboratories' major stockholder is . . . Martin Revson.

Nowadays, [Peter] Revson remembers 1963, his first year in Europe, as the time that racing was sweetest. He spoke no foreign language; he lived like a gypsy. Everything was an adventure: travelling, ordering in restaurants, going through customs in the Thames bread van with Walter Boyd. The results of 1963 were mixed, but at least by the end of the season everyone knew who Peter Revson was.

These days when he goes to a race at Monte Carlo he doesn't camp on the beach; he stands on a balcony in the Hotel de Paris, a place he very much doubted he'd be.

Those are clear memories for Revson. The difference between 1963 and 1973, the balcony and the beach, marks a clear path of accomplishment to him now.

He also remembers, but does not talk about, a moment in 1967. That was the year, as mentioned, that his brother Douglas was killed, and he and his friend George Lysle changed from their dinner suits to go to the funeral. Afterwards, Lysle drove him to Bryar Motorsports Park in New Hampshire, where, expressionless, he won the second [Trans-Am] race in a row for the Cougar racing team.

WILLIAM FISK HARRAH

THE LIFE AND TIMES OF A GAMBLING MAGNATE

BY LEON MANDEL

Chapter Four

Historic Perspectives

" Henry Ford was chief engineer of the company that was to become Cadillac before it built its first car by that name. By the time it did, it was owned by the man who would leave Cadillac to start Lincoln. Henry M. Leland started Cadillac because he had built an engine for Ransom Eli Olds that was too good for the curved dash Olds, then America's most popular car. It was 1902. **"**

Leon's automotive fascinations predated the rather late arrival of Competition Press *(later to become* AutoWeek*) in 1958, so it was well before the century turned that he was drawing on memory as the starting point to write authentic history. But he'd also done much deeper research, evident not only in his book* American Cars *but also in the perspective and context he brought to everything he wrote. In this chapter, the long view predominates.*

A Not-So-Quiet Revolution

July 13, 1998

Published as the lead essay in the 40th anniversary issue of AutoWeek, *this capsule history of four decades in automotive America weaves together numerous repeating themes from Mandel's work over the years. It's also a narrative, a story that makes sense of diverse influences and changes and gives the reader perspective and context by which he or she may come not only to understand this snapshot of a moment in time but also to apply those understandings to what's happening more than a decade later.*

WELCOME TO A COOL JULY DAY on the Bayshore Freeway between San Jose and San Francisco in the year of our Oldsmobile 1958. It is prime commuting time. The cars are mainly American (yes, there are a few VWs but nothing Japanese; if the Euro-Influence flavors the mix at all, it is courtesy of some square and slow MG-TDs.

There is no Candlestick Park. The entire village of Foster City has yet to be filled in, perhaps even conceived. Broderick Crawford lookalikes patrol the 101 in giant Black and Whites without radar.

And we are headed for a thriving metropolitan auto row on Van Ness Avenue to talk about trading our Dynamic 88 in on something perhaps a little more flamboyant, which would be hard to conceive.

. . .

Consumer bard John Keats wrote a book called *The Insolent Chariots* that year that called the 88 and its big brother the 98 "a Chinese love junk, or perpetual Wurlitzer, [a] vast neon lit pin-ball machine with chromium schmaltz, pushbuttons, multiple batteries of headlamps and the glitter of tailfins that Detroit calls the Luxury automobile."

If you were driving the 88 you were likely content with your choice; it was, after all, a decade of contentment.

You were able to accelerate to your 65 mph legal speed in about 11 seconds, and you rumbled along there without much strain, courtesy of an oversquare 371-cid V-8 with a 10.1:1 compression ratio, making an advertised 265 horsepower at 4400 rpm and 390 lb-ft of torque at 2400 rpm. The car cost $3,510 West Coast, including the automatic and a single two-barrel carburetor. You might have been a little annoyed by what one contemporary tester called a "burble" sound from the open wind-wing at more than 40 mph. (Good thing you didn't have any railroad tracks on the way to Van Ness because the car was prone to pitch as it went over them.) It leaned on corners. It was typically tippy at speeds in light turns. It had a lot of space inside, but heaven help you if you ran out of gas and didn't know where the filler cap was: behind the taillight on the left side.

By and large you liked your car; the people who made it liked it a lot since it generated a big profit for Oldsmobile. They saw only Sloanist reasons for change. They thought of themselves as mobility benefactors to a nation that would be well advised to leave design specification choice and price to them. Festung Detroit. The fortress of insularity. Said one contemporary observer: "Detroit was convinced that Detroit and only Detroit was able to understand consumer needs. Any questioning of the way it went about its business was not just presumptuous, it was heretical." The great GM innovator Charles H. Kettering famously said: "It isn't that we are such lousy car builders, as that they are such lousy car customers."

Keats thought it was the Midwesterner's immemorial custom of attending agricultural fairs that led him to want to grow the biggest pumpkins, dig the world's deepest sunken gardens and build the world's biggest and gaudiest cars.

Into this town, into this mindset, into this outpouring of pot metal, tiptoed a tiny, tabloid fortnightly of sports car racing called *Competition Press* midwived by two local advertising men. *Compress* was soon to become a wanderer, migrating first to Greenwich Village in the hands of a future icon, Denise McCluggage, then to Los Angeles under the guardianship of *Road & Track* and finally to Northern California where it became *Auto Week* (two words); and thence to Reno, because its owners were publishing libertarians and Reno's Stead Industrial

Park was a free port. It would return to its roots in 1978, to Detroit, where it thrives today.

Compress was far too preoccupied with its tiny concerns at birth to open its eyes to what was going on in the larger world. And what was going on would shake Detroit to its foundations, increase in Richter Scale magnitude until those foundations themselves would be imperiled and, finally, challenge the industry and perhaps even the nation to reinvent themselves or come tumbling down, which is the point to this story.

. . .

As the '50s closed, the problems seemed parochial and manageable. For example, the country's dealers were in quasi-revolt; part of that revolt was the manufacturers' fault, but whoever's fault it was, it was further alienating a consumer body, which was just waiting to be unfaithful. These were the buyers, after all, who were forced to pay the dealer extortion money under the table to get any kind of new car right after the war. They were seething.

Now, onto the dealers, and from the dealers to the customers, poured a giant waterfall of excess production. This was the inevitable result of a bloated wartime capacity. It wasn't a new problem; in fact, it went as far back as the dawn of the '30s, when REO's sales manager had warned that "this greatest of all industries has built up a capacity for building and selling approximately twice as many automobiles as the market can absorb." Almost 30 years later, the problem had been multiplied 100-fold. Here's how one automotive historian saw it: "The evidence is unequivocal that the shoddy treatment of customers by dealers emanated from long-standing policies of the manufacturers.

"They forced their franchised dealers to accept too many cars [which] came off the assembly line with too many flaws."

High volume "stimulator" dealerships were franchised in territories where competition was already ruinous. Phantom freight rates were charged. Franchises were arbitrarily canceled.

What resulted was the "System," a method devised by a Ford-sponsored management company called Hull Dobbs that processed the customer as though he were a carcass at a meat packing plant. He was "unhorsed" (his car keys taken away); he was whipsawed by closers and turnover men; he was bewildered by adding machine sleight of hand ("Okie Charmers"); his private conversations were wiretapped, he was wrapped in price packs, outrageous finance charges, credit life insurance and ghost accessories like undercoating. In other words, he became as much of a victim as the dealer was of the manufacturer.

It couldn't last. It didn't.

What neither the dealer nor the manufacturer recognized was that it was dealing with a new kind of customer, one who had been educated by the GI bill and achieved a rising degree of worldliness as both he and his country moved increasingly into the world.

Television may have served the local dealer wonderfully in his snake oil pitch, but it also was a marvelous educator of the masses in terms of what they should begin to expect. A new interstate highway system was beginning to reach across the entire nation, making it easier and easier for more and more people to shop farther and farther away from home.

And, as the '50s came to a close, a whole new automotive phenomenon was appearing. The imported car offered choice, it offered alternative technology, it offered low price, low maintenance and high mileage, it offered a whole new perspective on something that was about to be called "fit and finish" even in the heartland, home of the big pumpkin. Did the doors fit?

. . .

If you walked into a metropolitan VW dealership in the middle '60s, you were saying a lot of things about yourself. Not as much about how old you were as Detroit wanted to believe, by the way, but you were more likely to be younger than older. You were what the new psychographic wizards at the increasingly important think tanks were calling "inner directed," by which they meant you cared more about what you thought than what others thought of you. You were probably college educated. You could be earning anywhere from $10,000 a year (not as bad a wage as it sounds today) to $100,000 (*lots* of money then). You were traveled, almost certainly overseas. You were aware of a social revolution occurring mainly in Northern California, but you were not necessarily a part of it. You'd never owned a foreign car before. When you went into the dealership, you were surprised to be allowed to look at the only VW on the floor and, only later, to be addressed courteously by a salesperson who not only didn't look at all like a snake oil salesman but wanted to talk about the car, not the deal. As a matter of fact, it came as no small shock to you that the price was the price: no haggling. And in many cases the dealer didn't even want your trade or valued it at such a low price that you were clearly being discouraged from trading it in at all.

Today, with the New Beetle taking the world by storm, we tend to forget the old Beetle driving experience. It was borderline dreadful. The VW was slow and it was moderately perilous (Cornell Aeronautical Labs, soon to be CalSpan, called it the second most likely car to experience a single-car accident; only the Renault Dauphine was worse). But it was wonderfully well put together. It was utterly unpretentious. It worked and it didn't cost a fortune to fix. Best of all, it took its owner off the Sloanist merry-go-round; VW owners never had to lust after next year's model again.

The numbers were by no means as great, but cars sold by Jaguar, Austin-Healey and Porsche in particular—even by MG—were at the same time educating American buyers about handling. About the notion that performance should include stopping power and the agility that enables a car to *avoid* accidents. And of all things, about fun. That a car could once again be what it was at the beginning of the century, a device of pleasure.

As a foreign car buyer, it is likely you were aware of the new environmentalism. Rachel Carson had published her landmark work, *Silent Spring*, about the devastating effects of pesticides in 1962. In 1959, a California biochemist called Arlie Haagen-Smit had discovered the link between auto exhaust and photochemical smog. Not surprisingly, California took the lead in proposing changes to the car (the catalytic converter had been invented in 1952) under the aegis of an Air Resources Board. It would take a while, but when California's pioneer work was clearly irrefutable, the result was the Motor Vehicle Air Pollution and Control Act of 1965, which promulgated national standards for 1968 comparable to California's.

What it all said was that the public was becoming more and more concerned with the broad social impact of the car. And if American manufacturers were not yet prepared to accept a consumer group that wanted alternatives, that was educating itself about what was good and bad in car design, it for sure wasn't ready for an activist government that would poke its nose even further into Detroit's business.

But why now? Why after decades of partnership in the national consensus on highway building and funding should the middle '60s see such a profound rupture in the relationship between government and industry that they were at each other's throat?

. . .

Part of it, of course, came from the combination of enlightenment and abuse of the consumer body—a rising cry of complaint with a concomitant abandoning of the love affair; fewer car swains, fewer lovers, fewer of the car-committed to go to the barricades in defense of the product and the industry.

And this: America in the middle of the decade was suffering 16 million traffic accidents a year. In terms of violent death, the car led all other causes. Counting *all* causes, death by car was the fourth-ranked killer in the States at 50,000 a year. Of everyone in the hospital, a staggering one-third were there because of something that had happened with a car. Detroit's response to this was a total of $9 million spent among all safety groups, and a general agreement that it wasn't the car, but it was the "nut behind the wheel."

Provocation upon provocation, and in Washington—in the Age of the New Frontier—dwelt just the men to respond. Sen. Abraham Ribicoff of Connecticut had become chairman of something called the Subcommittee on Executive Reorganization of the Senate Committee on Government Operations. As governor of Connecticut, Ribicoff had been a highway-offender terror and the fever of that crusade was still upon him. Ribicoff had a chief counsel called Jerry Sonosky and Jerry Sonosky hired a young lawyer as a consultant by the name of Ralph Nader.

Ribicoff, no doubt prompted by Sonosky, decided that in one of their hearings they would call in the heads of the car companies. Now, this was unprecedented. The way it worked, the way it *always* had worked, was that the ineffectual little committee would call the Washington lobbyist for the car company who would duly report with a sanitized and approved answer to a previously submitted question.

Ribicoff wanted more. Ribicoff wanted the Top Guys at the table in front of him. And that thrilled the TV people, so that one day, with the bright lights shining, and GM's elite on stage, Bobby Kennedy— who sat on Ribicoff's committee but was rarely there—wandered into the hearing by chance. GM's president James Roche had just revealed that his company had spent about $1 million on safety in the previous year. That immediately caught Sen. Kennedy's interest.

Sen. Kennedy: What was the profit of General Motors last year?

Mr. Roche: I don't think that has anything to do . . .

Kennedy: I would like to have an answer to that if I may. . . . You spent a million and a quarter dollars . . . on this aspect of safety. I would like to know what the profit is.

GM chairman Frederick Donner: The one aspect we are talking about is safety.

Kennedy: What was the profit of General Motors last year!

Donner: I will have to ask one of my associates.

Kennedy: Would you please?

Roche: $1,700,000,000.

Kennedy: What?

Donner: About a billion and a half.

Kennedy: About a billion and a half?

Donner: Yes.

Kennedy: Or $1.7 billion. You made $1.7 billion last year?

Donner: That is correct.

Kennedy: And spent one million on this?

That was in July 1965. In November, a small publishing house in New York called Grossman published *Unsafe at Any Speed,* a devastating indictment of the American car focusing on the Corvair. It was the making of its author, Ralph Nader. It was also the making of the National Traffic and Motor Safety Act of 1966, which at last made the interior of the car protective to the occupants instead of lethal to them.

But not because the book was so persuasive. Rather, because it so infuriated GM that the company put a private investigator on Nader hoping to find something, *anything,* to discredit him. One night as Sonosky was working late in his office in the New Senate Office Building, a knock came on his door. It was a security guard; did Mr. Sonosky know that the consultant to the committee, Ralph Nader, was being followed? Sonosky politely thanked the guard, picked up the phone and called Ribicoff. "Senator," he said. "I think we have a bill."

• • •

When Alan Loufbourrow, chief engineer of Chrysler Corp., announced to the world, "They've moved our design departments to Washington and they're holding our feet to the fire," he was talking about the Energy Policy and Conservation Act of 1973. The act came about as a result of the turning off of the OPEC oil tap, the rise in the price of gas at the pump and two-hour waits for gasoline, and it mandated something called CAFE, which stood for Corporate Average Fuel Economy.

Loufbourrow could have been prejudiced. The line of Chrysler cars, three years in the planning and making, introduced that fall of the Great Embargo—cars that had the fingerprints of Alan Loufbourrow all over them—consisted of the largest cars it had ever built. Names like Polara, Gran Fury and Monaco rang with their immensity and pretentiousness at exactly the time the market demanded—no, insisted on—small, fuel-efficient economy cars, which the Japanese were happily supplying in quantity and quality.

Emissions, safety, fuel economy of the car had clearly become domesticated. Detroit, with no choice but to conform to the new emissions control restrictions, to the new safety mandates, to the new requirements of CAFE (which meant downsizing), was first bewildered. Then it was resentful. Then it put all its engineering resources to work on these problems, depriving all other areas of development of the necessary expertise, and, of course, the expected happened. The cars that resulted didn't work. They stalled crossing intersections. They ran like asthmatic nursing home residents. They offered neither performance nor reliability. All Detroit could think of to do by way of compensating was to tack on huge price increases to "cover the cost of government-mandated equipment." Thus the public was being asked to pay more for cars that offered vastly less. Hardly the way to induce the buyer, increasingly lured by the beautifully finished Japanese and European product, to come home.

AutoWeek, increasingly concerned with everyday cars and consumer angst, spoke from its Reno headquarters about the virtues of the Japanese and European products. Mainly, though, by reporting more and more on competition, it was underscoring the achievements of the participating manufacturers, principally Porsche.

By the '70s, a domestic industry that had been so self-confident it could blame its buyers for its own deficiencies had been beaten to the ground. Its customers had abandoned it in favor of new svelte *houris* from overseas; its dealers (the real customers) were no longer even pretending to be part and parcel of the industry's solid front; the very design of its cars was being dictated by bureaucrats instead of white-suited stylists. An array of social critics who could bedevil the archangel Gabriel himself was daily firing darts to remind the car-buying public how primitive the industry's views were, how shabby its products, how, in fact, it had betrayed its purpose and its people and was doomed.

It seemed as though the mighty had been laid as low as possible.

And just when the night seemed darkest, there was darker to come. Chrysler went down.

In the middle of the decade of the '70s few would have predicted it. Sales had rebounded from the '73 Embargo days. Full-size cars in particular were selling well, and toward the end of the decade, light trucks were beginning to outsell cars in many parts of the country. In fact, when it came to unloading inventory, it was the Japanese dealers who were under pressure. Detroit was making money again from large cars, which would stand it well as it prepared to meet tough new government-mandated fuel-economy standards coming in 1979. But for the time being, GM was doing well, even Ford was slightly up. Ominously, only Chrysler still suffered.

All this was happening against a background of skyrocketing inflation, at least in good part the result of the seven-fold increase in the price of oil (from $2.35 a barrel in 1973 to $15.77 in January of 1974).

As new car introductions drew nearer, everyone's attention was taken by a personnel change at Ford. Henry II fired his president Lee Iacocca, ostensibly in a difference of opinion over the need for small cars sooner rather than later, but probably simply in a clash of strong personalities.

At which point Chrysler introduced its critical, indispensable-to-success '79 Disasters. In particular, the New Yorker and the St. Regis were abominable, and as if to rub salt into the wound, Michigan governor William Milliken and Detroit mayor Coleman Young, on hand to drive them off the assembly line of the plant, newly renovated to the tune of $57 million, took the green flag and just sat there with dead batteries. (Not the first embarrassment in recent memory: The previous February, at Chrysler's Warren, Mich., tank plant, the company unveiled the first new battle tank in 19 years, the XM-1, and promptly got it stuck in reverse.)

Not everything was Chrysler's fault. In the beginning of the year, OPEC had again raised prices; Iran had undergone revolution, and its oil production and exports had been interrupted. Spot gas shortages appeared, prices went up, gas guzzlers were once again anathema to the market, and what was Chrysler selling? Of course. On July 31, 1979, with an inventory of 80,000 unsold cars, passenger car sales down 15 percent and a commitment to capital expenditures of $100 million a month to convert to small cars, Chrysler held a news conference in which it appealed for government aid. Foreign car penetration was just over 21 percent, a 15 percent increase over the year before. It was everything that the doomsayers had predicted. Insularity and arrogance, a disregard for end user and immediate consumer, contempt for competition and a profound underestimation of the intelligence of the buyer; plus an infernal federal government, the lure of alternative pleasures to the car and a determined insistence on doing things as they had always been done had produced the inevitable. Fortress Detroit was tottering.

. . .

All the while that the consumerist legions were assaulting the temple, the Greens carefully making their reasoned cases and the chattering classes pronouncing the end of the automobile, a bedrock fact was being overlooked. Even, it seemed, by Detroit.

The car and the highway, in combination with a body of owners who *liked* cars and was utterly reliant on the mobility the car bestowed, had become the principal transportation infrastructure in America. Simply said by Barry Bruce-Briggs in his book *The War against the Automobile:* "Car, owner/drivers and the highway combined made up the unique American mass transportation system and not much out there threatened to replace it either by being cheaper or more efficient or because it was more appealing to its users."

Perhaps Bruce-Briggs' most telling point was the one about choice.

Use of the system was the choice of the people most affected: the car owner/driver, the same people who elected those who would perpetuate the system, and who chose to keep buying in record numbers the product the carmakers offered.

So even during the times of the most egregious behavior on the part of the makers, even when the cars on offer were shoddy objects that performed disgracefully, America bought because cars were the fundamental element in our mass transportation system.

But why should this mean domestic cars when there was an alternative? ("It's not that we are such lousy car builders, it's that they are such lousy car customers.") VW taught us choice. Toyota, Nissan, Mitsubishi, Mazda and most especially Honda institutionalized that

169

choice. And at the top end of the pyramid, Mercedes-Benz and BMW established the benchmark for automotive excellence. What's more, Americans were paying attention and aspiring to their ownership. Cadillac was no longer the Cadillac of cars, Mercedes-Benz and BMW were. Nothing would ever be the same again.

. . .

Sometime in the late '80s, in an impossibly Old World restaurant in Geneva, Switzerland, Robert Eaton, then-president of GM Europe, was dining with a small group of industry observers-cum-friends. He had just been asked about a recently published MIT study of how cars were made all over the globe called *The Machine That Changed the World*. It was a book that challenged conventional production wisdom in America and Europe. Over five years, funded by many of the large car companies, its researchers and writers had looked at the ways cars were made and concluded that we had passed from the era of Mass Production to something they chose to call Lean Production. Mass Production assigned one man to one endlessly repeating task along a moving line, concerned with mistakes only at the end of the line in the rework bay. Employees were considered a variable cost, to be discarded when business turned bad. Huge stockpiles of parts needed to be kept on hand, many of them made by the company that made the car itself. The relationship between the workers and the people who supervised them was adversarial.

Lean Production, on the other hand, sought to make the worker part of the process by giving him authority to identify a problem, stop a line and join a group dedicated to solving the problem so it would not repeat itself endlessly only to have to be rectified in a rework bay. Parts and pieces were not stored but delivered when needed, saving millions. Subcontractors, instead of being pitted against one another, were given the chance to become part of the design team on a new car and to supply their component over the life of the project. But perhaps most important, any new design on its way to becoming a car was created by a cross-functional team, working synchronously under a leader who had enormous authority.

Lean Production, in other words, threatened to change not only the way a company did business, but the way it thought about how it did business. Chrysler, fresh from its near-death experience, was almost compelled to look at this curious system of making cars that produced cheaper products, that were better built and that could be changed to suit the market in just over three years.

On the other hand, Eaton, who bought 300 copies of *The Machine That Changed the World* with his own money and required his senior managers to read it, was watching an exactly contrary experience back home in GM land. There, the heavily automated (at great expense) assembly lines were about to spew out the GM-10 cars. The robots were inflexibly devoted to production of that one platform, and there were enough of them to build much larger numbers of these cars than the market would ever desire—this was the antithesis of Lean Production.

Robert Eaton, of course, would return to the United States, not with GM, but as the CEO of Chrysler. He and his team would make Chrysler a world-class example of production efficiency, very much on the Toyota Lean Production model.

. . .

Nor were Eaton and Chrysler alone. Both Mercedes-Benz and Porsche, each in its own way, stared into the chasm, as had Chrysler. Porsche because it had seemed to lose an understanding of its *raison d'etre* as a car company, because it forgot what a Porsche should be. Mercedes because it had come so utterly under the sway of its internal values, primarily those of the dominant clique of engineers, that it was ignoring the customer in terms of price and value. Both companies were fat and lazy. Both were making cars that no longer represented what their buyers wanted.

The prices of both companies' products were utterly out of touch with their competitors'; in Mercedes' case particularly, with the new generations of Japanese luxury cars, Lexus and Infiniti.

It is too much to say that the MIT study so changed attitudes in America and Europe that it caused a revolution, but most revolutions, ready to happen, are ignited by a manifesto. *The Machine That Changed the World* was the manifesto of the Great Industrial Revolution in the car industry; it did not cause change, it simply helped ignite it.

. . .

It is a lovely summer day two years before the end of the Century of the Automobile. We are cruising along Metropolitan Detroit's Chrysler Freeway toward a small club racing circuit where this weekend they will race vintage cars in conjunction with one of the country's great concours d'elegance at Meadow Brook Hall.

The pleasure of the day comes both from anticipation and from the car we're driving: an Oldsmobile Intrigue with the new Northstar-derived 3.5-liter V-6. The Intrigue may be a linear descendant of the Dynamic 88, but it almost seems as though it was constructed on another planet.

It is no bigger than it absolutely has to be, but it has more room in it than the 88. It is faster. Its four-speed automatic responds to the way the driver uses it and adjusts shift points accordingly. Steering is speed-sensitive and as quick and precise as only could be found on a sports car four decades ago. The car's interior is carefully designed to protect its occupants against the Second Collision, that of the occupant with the inside of his own car. Brakes are all-disc, ABS-assisted. The engine compartment is a laboratory of microprocessors that not only tame the internal-combustion engine but bring it into the 21st century as a sufficiently efficient device to meet emissions standards and provide the kind of acceleration and top end unheard of 40 years ago. At least as important, the styling is classic, not meant to be replaced in response to a Sloanist marketing imperative later in the year, or next year or even for five years to come.

The fact of our destination is as interesting as the car we're driving. For in the staging of historic races and concours, we are underscoring the fact that attitudinally we have shifted in our view of the car. Where 20 years ago, car enthusiasts hid behind a curtain of social correctness in the face of a storm of criticism, car love is not only out of the closet but thriving. There is a whole new population of collectors. "Orphan cars" are being given their own shows, so even mundane Studebakers and, gasp, Corvairs are brought out for display. Motorsports attendance is rocketing. Huge new tracks are being opened practically monthly. And cars are getting better and better.

What's going on? What has seemingly so suddenly happened? First of all, after decades of refusal to respond to the marketplace, automakers have come to understand that it is their customer who ultimately determines the shape and characteristics of the product. Build what they want and they will come. Ironically, as the century turned toward its end, what the customer increasingly wanted was the largest vehicle, the largest profit margin vehicle Detroit could build: the light truck, mainly in its SUV form. To accomplish this profound shift in attitude toward the customer required a generational change in management of the car companies. Bright young people with experience overseas and an understanding of the world beyond the Great Pumpkin have moved into the executive offices of the car companies, wearing not dark blue suits, but khakis and shirts open at the neck. Finally, worldwide competition has given no choice to those who wish to compete globally. Of all the markets in the world, the American is the most open, the most combative, the most Darwinian, the most rewarding of excellence and brutal to failure. Still, a singular aspect of the American character has utterly confounded all those who predicted doom for the domestic industry: a willingness and an ability to change the way things are done. The great automotive economist Emma Rothschild predicted for the auto industry the fate of the British railroads; she was right about her native industry, but she was wrong about ours.

In many ways, this is the most important fact of the four decades since the founding of *Competition Press*, the social and industrial phenomenon that *AutoWeek* has watched and reported on all its life: the remarkable American genius for change. Utter and complete. The ability to remake the molecular structure of an industry. To abandon old ideas. To devise new ones. To put them in place. To start over with vigor and optimism. It has been one of the great stories of the last half of the century, one of the most thrilling, and it has gone largely unreported by the mass press.

Now we enter yet another new phase. Global merger. Change in the retail distribution system. The onset of practical alternative powerplants. Now we see enormous new problems: highway congestion, increasing costs, a revival of the safety problem, a need for the automobile to bear its share of reduction in the greenhouse gas problem.

Forty years ago had we all been suddenly told these would be our challenges at the end of the century, the industry would have scoffed and buried its head in the sand. But it has demonstrated an ability to meet equally demanding problems and solve them. We have good reason to believe it will resolve these.

And that the private car will continue to be a central fact of American middle-class automobile life well into the next century.

AutoWeek too.

The Ultimate Artifact

AND YOU SOLD YOURS IN '59 FOR $3,000!
March 17, 1972

OF COURSE, THERE WAS this merest hint that something extraordinary might be forthcoming from Mercedes-Benz in the way of sports cars.

Two very curious-looking, bubble-topped, gull-winged coupes showed up at the Mille Miglia in 1952 with Carraciola and Kling driving and placed second and fourth overall . . . after surviving the incredulity of the Italian scrutineers who insisted that those things that folded upward weren't doors at all but some kind of hatches and that real sports cars had real doors that swung in and out like doors in a wild west saloon. "Who said doors couldn't open upwards?" asked Mercedes, and the Italians shrugged their Latin shrugs and walked away.

The cars appeared again in the Carrera Panamericana and at Le Mans where they finished one-two. But the racers were almost accidents. Rudolf Uhlenhaut had persisted in building them against the strong sentiment of the Daimler-Benz board, built them almost in his garage at home, and Karl Wilfert had done the bodies in much the same way. They went like hell, because they were, after all, from Uhlenhaut's basement, the best damn garage in town, but they were cobbled up cars nonetheless.

And then, two years later, there they were. Brutal, low, crouching teutonic menaces, sitting right there on the showroom floor for sale to anyone at somewhere near $7,000. And the doors still swung up like hatches, and Americans, who were not as sophisticated in 1954 about cars as they were to become a decade later, wandered into the Mercedes showrooms, took one look and went into shock. The hardcore sports car people, those pioneers who had been reading *Road & Track*, knew immediately what they were looking at, and those who could afford them wrote their checks on the spot. But there weren't many of those, and even among them were the unreconstructed reactionaries who insisted that a sports car had to be a roadster or it was not a sports car.

Along with Porsche, the 300SL introduced the Grand Touring concept to the world (before the war, and immediately after, all sports car were open topped), and there were many, even among the knowledgeable, who were unprepared to accept it.

As for the rest of the enlightened, they looked at the coupe and saw an evocation of the 540K. Mercedes was back in the big, brutal sports car business, and they couldn't have been happier.

But they were cultists, avant garde cultists at that, and America was not ready for a gullwing coupe that surrounded its driver like a primitive space capsule, had a slanted six-cylinder, three-liter fuel injected engine, was dressed in an outrageous and utterly incongruous plaid upholstery (leather optional) and could suck the doors off anything in sight. No way would they climb over the great, wide sill, tilt the wheel down to slide under it and look out from the Apollo-like slit windows. And it was probably a good thing they resisted. The 300SL was a bitch to drive, unpredictable in oversteer and up on the cam all the time if you wanted anything at all (if you bought the thing, you had to order the high lift cam). And there were no pieces to be had for it if it broke, no one understood the fuel injection and no one could do any bodywork on it.

So they sat. And (although the story may be apocryphal) Max Hoffman (Karl Ludvigsen calls him the "Baron of Park Avenue"), who is said to have guaranteed the first 1,000 cars into the United States if only Mercedes would build them, must have had sweaty Bavarian palms. Because why would any American in his right mind want one of those strange things for $7,000 when he could buy a perfectly good Chevy for about $1,950, or if he was some kind of weirdo, an MG for about the same?

Fourteen hundred of the things were built from August '54 until '57 (when only 76 were made), and then Mercedes switched to the 300SL roadster (not the 300SLR) and most of the people who bought the coupes were the faithful. They bought them, they kept them a while and then they sold them for $3,000 to $4,000 and went on to XK150s and Aston Martin DB4s and the Ferrari of the month.

Meanwhile, a pair of curious things were happening. Paul O'Shea, in an allegedly independent 300SL, was cleaning house in SCCA racing. In fact, the car was no more and no less than a full factory entry with about 25 hp more than any other 300SL around and with an axle ratio for every track in the U.S. The legend began to build. And then the roadster appeared—at $11,000 plus hardtop which was another several hundred dollars. The roadster was in every way an easier and pleasanter car to drive than the coupe; it had low pivot swing axles, disc brakes and more luggage space. Furthermore, you could get in and out of it without a dockside crane to assist. In sum, it was perfect for the dilettante, and the dilettante bought it on sight. Built from April '57 to '63, the roadster sold only about 458 cars more than the coupe, but it sold to entirely different people. Gone was the stark, mean, vicious handling loveliness of the coupe; in its place was a meek and civilized car.

It took a while, but even among skeptics in their upwardly mobile 20s and 30s, truth has a way of penetrating. By the end of the '60s the fact had been established. The 300SL (and make no mistake, you may call it Gullwing if you wish, but as the one and only original 300SL, the coupe has claim to that name and only the coupe) had become the most desirable collector's car in the country.

The trouble was there were damn few to be found anymore. And especially the really good ones, one of those 29 with aluminum bodies and knock-off wheels with fitted luggage, a 37-gallon gas tank and full belly pan. Prices soared and the irony was complete. The cars that had sat new and pristine on the dealer's floor for $7,000 and gone begging for customers were now in such demand that a perfect 15-year-old specimen would bring double its original figure.

And among the faithful—especially those who had sold their cars for $3,000 because, for example, the fuel injection pump diaphragm was made of leather and punctured easily, which usually meant replacing the whole pump for $200—there was a deep sickness in the pit of the stomach. If only they had been more patient. If only they had been willing to cope with a little inconvenience.

The ones who grew up with the car, the ones who were 13 or 14 or 15 when the 300SL appeared and who were the vanguard of the real car generation, knew all the time what the car was all about. At 13 you cannot afford a $7,000 car. Not even at 15. But when you are 33 or 34 and you remember going into the showroom alone and just standing there and knowing what you were seeing, even if those others with their sober faces and their tight pocketbooks and their Buicks did not, you have a legacy. And if there is a 300SL to be found, you will buy it because, after all, you were right 20 years ago, and you are even more right today.

Because whatever else happens, however strongly Mercedes or Jaguar or Ferrari feels about it, however overwhelming the demand might be, in 1973, the Department of Transportation stands at the gates and tells you "no more." And theirs is the final word. There will never be another 300SL.

Only Yesterday

REMEMBERING WHEN IT WAS "US," THE
SPORTS CAR SAVVY CLAN, VS. "THEM"
July 24, 2000

THESE DAYS SPORTS CAR RACING at the weekend, club level is a carefully nurtured activity. Aware or not, its participants are benefiting from a tradition that flourished in the country at the end of World War II. It all began, according to one account, in the middle '40s with a self-timed speed run between tunnels on the Pennsylvania Turnpike, calculated on the honor system, as road racing shaped itself into something we could recognize easily now. It set our traditions and determined how we were going to do things. Not that we even suspected it then.

Consider the times: In 1957, when the San Francisco Region of the Sports Car Club of America opened its season in Stockton with the Fifth Annual races, the same company that would make Indy Racing League engines half a century later was building a car that was large, ugly and bore a designation—98—that could have stood for its tonnage. The same year's MGA was svelte, sleek and so seductive it simply didn't allow its owner to leave it, or his life, alone. Even by then, the Sports Car Club of America had 8,500 members (compared with 50,000 today), was 13 years old and was bringing actual road racing to the back provinces of the country.

Jim Kimberly was the national president of the SCCA in 1957, Kjell Qvale activities chairman, when the San Francisco Region played to 17,000 spectators in Stockton. That's 17,000. The self-same IRL doesn't get 17,000 in the stands at any place other than Indianapolis. No matter what CART says, it's lucky to do a crowd like that at Mid-Ohio or Elkhart Lake. What was going on?

It was the blossoming of sports cars in postwar America. The San Francisco Region's activities chairman had begun bringing MGs into the country in 1947. Ten years later there was a total of almost 1,500 foreign car dealers in the United States, among them 34 MG and Austin-Healey points selling about 1,000 cars a month. By the year of the fifth Stockton race, U.S. imports numbered about 260,000 of total vehicle sales of just under six million. You could buy an MGA with disc wheels (called a standard) for $2,269 while a Chevy 150 would cost you $1,885. No wonder MG drivers waved to one another. They were a besieged minority.

Besieged but proud. The whole idea of buying and owning a foreign car—from Healey 100-6 to VW—was to stand out from the pot metal crowd.

Moreover, buying an MG was a very different experience from going into a dealership for a Ford or a Chevy. In fact, '57 was a year in which the so-called System House selling process thrived in America. Devised by a Ford consulting firm called Hull Dobbs, it was what the retail side of the industry considered a solution to the massive overproduction of the postwar industry. Once the pent-up demand for cars was satisfied, then almost oversatisfied, then saturated, someone somehow had to invent a way to sell cars to people who didn't want them, didn't need them and couldn't afford them. The result was a process that treated customers like carcasses in a slaughterhouse. More often than not, the transaction led to bitterness from buyer toward seller. There is a residue of resentment that lingers to this day.

In contrast, Qvale, and, for that matter VW, sold cars at list price (there was no such thing as a Monroney window sticker yet), took trades in at legitimate value and talked not deal, deal, deal, but car, car, car. Obviously, the foreign makes attracted people who could not only afford to buy their choice, but legitimately knew and wanted what they bought.

So it was a pleasure to sell the cars, a pleasure to buy them, and often buyer and seller became friends. What's more, what was being sold was not just the car, but a lifestyle. Those who bought MGs weren't buying a car, they were buying an adventure.

"When was the first race," goes the old saying, "when the second car was made?" Much the same held true for sports car activity in

America after the Second World War. As the Brits began to export, because unless they earned hard dollars they couldn't get scarce material allocations, SCCA regions began to pop up like sprouts across the country, and not just the regions, but local sports car clubs. While everyone began using sports cars for rallying (spelled "rallyeing" in a ghastly colonial imitation of what we thought was British), gymkhanas and poker runs, actual racing was limited. Of course there were such glorious events as Watkins Glen, Elkhart Lake and Golden Gate Park, but they were grand institutions planted in our midst like monuments.

What counted then was not so much what you did with your car but the simple fact of ownership. If you had an Austin A40 sports or a Triumph, you were a member of an elite. Not necessarily a rich elite, but an elite of taste and choice. And you banded together, and met every third Thursday or so at the local boat club or Y, rallied and had social events, and then tentatively, very tentatively, held a club race. It would be the race, and the participation in the race, that would mark you as a bona fide clan member. And by the way, it was not only the drivers who became the anointed, that distinction also included the race personnel. Local clubs would man individual turns or specialties and, at a time when licensing wasn't even contemplated, it was the dedication of such people and their high morale that provided a decent level of expertise for the drivers.

By 1957, the San Francisco Region's Golden Gate Park race was long gone and the tree-lined race through the Del Monte Forest at Pebble Beach was halted as being too dangerous when a prominent driver was killed there. So until Laguna Seca (whose moving force was the region's activities chairman, only reluctantly grandfathered into the club despite being an auto dealer because he had joined in 1949 at Watkins Glen) was completed later that year, Stockton was the region's opening event. Nineteen fifty-seven was Stockton's fifth running, and for two years it had banded with the Stockton Lions Club for the benefit of both. Seventeen thousand spectators made for a lot of benefit.

When you drove to Stockton in March that year, it was at least even money you got there by driving the car you were going to race. In the first place, the vast majority of the 181 entries were production cars (there were three categories of racers: Production Sports, Sports and Unrestricted), and production cars were required to be almost exactly as they came off the showroom floor. Defined as having to be "as purchased new," they could have a .030-inch overbore (to account for wear), alternative gear and rear axle ratios so long as they were specified as optional by the manufacturer, and the engines could be balanced. Straight pipes were permitted so long as there were no modifications forward of the muffler.

Since these were cars their entrants could and did drive every day, what reason could they have had for trailering them just to go to a race?

Of course there were cars that were far too ferocious to try to drive on the highway. In addition to John Edgar's 4.9 Ferrari for Carroll Shelby to drive, and Lou Brero Sr.'s D-Jag, Bill Murphy brought a Kurtis-Buick up from Southern California, Rod Carveth had an Aston Martin DB3S, and Merle Brennan drove the Brennan Beast, which represented, particularly in comparison to the Ferrari, American impertinence at its most outrageous.

It was entered by the Reno Racing Team comprising not only Brennan but also Harry Banta and Leo Bourke. Bourke remembers the car as having been built on a sprint car chassis and powered by a flathead Mercury engine breathing through Stromberg 97s. The car weighed only 1,500 pounds, so it went "like an SOB in a straight line, but it had no diff so you had to dirt track it around a corner."

Bourke also remembers pushing the car through technical inspection ("a limited number of cars may be inspected according to the entry"), where officials checked the mandatory-for-modified-cars roll bar only for the integrity of the welds, but not for the quality of the material used. Preceding tech, prudent entrants of English cars drained their vehicles of fluids, so that they wouldn't be seen to leak. Bourke remembers wearing a McHal steel helmet and later a

Cromwell Korker, lined in cork and covered in white. Today's club racer would have been at least bemused by the protocols of the day. If a 1957-era driver had never raced before he arrived at the track, he would have a temporary permit. That was gotten from his regional contest board by having presented to them a state driver's license, having taken a written test to demonstrate knowledge of the 23-page competition regulations and giving them the satisfactory results of a physical examination. Those things and $3.

Once at the circuit, he, along with the other novices, drove his car (with a big "N" on the side) to a section of the track and "schooled"— by and large, a chalk-talk process. If he looked around, he would see that the corners were marked with haybales. Period. And to keep the crowds contained, inside and outside the turns, there was only snow fencing.

Besides that everyone was required to drive under his own name. "The practice of racing under an assumed name will not be allowed [as] the reason would be to deceive someone and the Club cannot be made a party to such deception."

Commercialism was anathema. "No advertising or trade sign shall be carried on or distributed from any car during an SCCA event. No car shall be entered in the name of any dealer or organization."

More than that. "No person shall receive ... valuable remuneration for participating in events ... except the usual cups and trophies and must at all times maintain their status as bona fide amateurs.

"[Nor shall anyone] accept wages or other compensation for driving another person's car.

"[Nor] accept ... transportation or food, lodging or other expenses."

While modified and unrestricted cars had long since been required to carry roll bars, the great debate of the hour was roll bars or no roll bars for series production vehicles. The argument against was that they spoiled the looks of the car. On the other side, "The national/contest board concedes ... that the fitting of a roll bar may involve sums as large as sixty dollars. It is conscious that when trading in a car impeccably maintained and driven only on weekends, the presence of two inconspicuous sockets on the frame may arouse suspicion [but] a little roll bar never hurt anyone.

"Our sport is at a crossroads. . . . In five states there is legislation pending which has as its avowed object the total abolition of racing.

"A nation capable of enacting Prohibition is fully capable of enacting anything! The contest board does not like roll bars. It does not like death and taxes either. All three are with us."

In 1957 roll bars were not required at Stockton in production cars. By at least 1962 at last they were.

There was another quiet problem nobody was talking about. Paid drivers.

In fact, Carroll Shelby had been to Europe in 1954 and 1955 and returned only to be with his family, but he could not be expected to play in the minor leagues without compensation. John Edgar was picking up his expenses and paying him $1,000 a month to drive.

It's likely that only Stirling Moss and Juan Manuel Fangio—and perhaps a handful of oval track drivers in this country—were making more.

But the rest of the drivers that year at Stockton couldn't have been further from hired guns.

Which is not to say that drivers at Stockton did not make their contributions. Particularly to racing safety, which was in a profoundly primitive state in 1957. Case in point: Dr. George Snively who was entered at Stockton in his Austin-Healey. With Rod Aya, the San Francisco Region's treasurer, Snively had gone far down the path of research into helmet safety that would result in the Snell standards, the first important head-protection criteria for racing drivers.

Other than Snively's presence, not much about the race at the Stockton airport was much different from most events in California or, for that matter, across the country. In every area, people were making progress in car preparation. And—because of the brutal toll on drivers in the late '50s and early '60s—particularly in safety. Engine and suspension efficiencies were the subjects of increasing attention everywhere, all of which marginalized the Austin A40 sports and

Borgwards that were barely hanging on in the marketplace. It was a Darwinian world made all the more so because of results at the racetrack. Moreover, 1957 racing clearly reinforced the conviction on everyone's part that participation extended the notion of membership in a club, racers and officials alike.

For better or for worse, George Snively would not go down alone in the history books.

Bob Winkelmann, who was entered at Stockton in his MG-TC, would go on to build an eponymous formula car that had tremendous success. Kjell Qvale, already by Stockton a hugely successful importer, would become a somewhat less successful manufacturer of Jensen-Healeys and is today embarked on a similar venture making Mangustas.

Carroll Shelby, driver of John Edgar's 4.9-liter Ferrari, became America's most important sports car constructor. Bill Murphy, Kurtis-Buick, is today at 90 years old Carroll Shelby's partner in a Dodge dealership in Los Angeles' San Fernando Valley. Merle Brennan would become a highly successful factory driver for Jaguar, appearing mainly on the West Coast but also in races at Sebring.

Lou Brero Sr., who would win the main event at Stockton in his D-type Jaguar, would be killed almost immediately thereafter in a race in Hawaii. Jimmy Hughes, entered at Stockton in a Lotus 11, would be killed at Sebring. Dave Ridenour, entered at Stockton in his Austin-Healey 100M, would be killed racing at Calistoga, Calif., in a sprint car accident.

In those days it was club racing, and the camaraderie that it engendered, that produced the bond that exists today among sports car enthusiasts. The Reno Racing Team's Leo Bourke remembers especially the spirit of helpfulness between competitors that so clearly marked the early racers; he believes it underlined the difference between sports car owners and everybody else. He believes it carried over into everyday interchange among MG owners and MG owners, Porsche people and Porsche people. If he is right, he is saying we have become what we are because of what we have been.

Selling Off the Standard of the World

GM—AND CADILLAC—TURNED A
BLIND EYE TO THEIR OWN HISTORY
WITH NO INTENTION OF LOOKING BACK
Nov. 3, 1986

This piece was published behind a cover line that read "The Decline and Fall of Cadillac." In the wake of recent events, it's interesting to read into it an analysis of what happened to General Motors overall. The prescribed "fixes" for Cadillac's woes came more than 20 years later and are still just beginning to bear the desired fruits.

NOT SINCE HENRY FORD II gave his elder daughter Charlotte a $250,000 debutante ball at the Country Club of Detroit in 1959 had there been such an elaborate society introduction. This one would have made Charlotte's affair look like a ladies society afternoon tea. GM was giving its newest car a coming out party in, of all places, a factory. GM Hamtramck (a.k.a. Poletown) was the facility the company brags about as the newest of its new GM superautomated factories. Allante was here.

And here, too, was tall, distinguished John O. Grettenberger, general manager of Cadillac, standing beside a huge motion picture screen on which an enormous image of John O. Grettenberger talked about Allante, telling the crowd of 400-plus: "We won't be making the Allante in pink, but you're going to see one that looks pink, with someone who has made pink Cadillacs famous." Out rolled Aretha Franklin in a white Allante tinged by a pink spot. She was singing "Freeway of Love" with its line about ridin' on the freeway in "a pink Cadillac."

The car knowledgeable found it hard to look at the Hamtramck plant through a rose-colored haze. This was the plant, after all, which had given GM fits. Its fully robotic modular paint shop generated so much heat at first that the plastic taillights on the cars made here—Eldorado, Seville, Toronado and Riviera—melted. Backup systems were so deficient cars had to be trucked to the ancient Clark Avenue Cadillac plant for painting. Poletown, vision of the future, lost a vision system meant to inspect gaps between body panels because "it was in the wrong place in the manufacturing process." As late as the end of May, a fleet of AGVs, automated guided vehicles, to be used for materials handling, sat idle and unprogrammed. All this not only put the Just-In-Time delivery system into the realm of the unthinkable, it shook the foundations of GM's whole philosophy of attacking the American industry's slipping world competitiveness through the use of high tech.

Nor was that the worst of it. Even if everything here worked perfectly, Poletown would still be turning out cars, the latest iterations of Seville and Eldorado, Toronado and Riviera, that Goldman Sachs financial analyst Philip K. Fricke pointed out comprised GM's highest profit margin group and whose failure to sell was disastrous to the ledger book. "We believe that gross profits [of GM] have been reduced almost $500 million [by the] market failure of its most profitable cars. The cars are simply not selling well, and the problem will be very difficult to solve quickly."

As of the end of September, Cadillac Division was particularly hard hit with Seville in its new, smaller shape down 40.5 percent from the old model of the year previous and the equally new, equally changed Eldorado off a devastating 61.8 percent, a six-months sales drop from 97,000 to 33,000. Certainly the division was maintaining sales at a healthy rate, some 300,000 units annually, and returning about $1 billion to its corporate parent. So it was not generation of current revenue that was worrying Cadillac. What was bothersome was the fact that the size of the luxury market was increasing, but Cadillac sales most definitely were not. Until now, not only were Seville and Eldorado the big profit cars, but they had been positioned as the cutting-edge cars, the new cars, the sexy cars—the cars Cadillac looked to for image in order to sell its less-alluring products. In many ways, Seville and Eldorado for years had played the "lead horse" role that General Motors expected of Cadillac. Now there would be Allante, about which General Manager Grettenberger would later say, "Cadillac is to GM as Allante is to Cadillac. The car is there to create an aura to begin [the] climb in the luxury market." It would be a virtual affirmation of the failure of Seville and Eldorado to perform their traditional job. It would also be an admission that a "climb in the luxury market" was a first order of priority for Cadillac for clearly all was not well with the division.

How did a marque with so distinguished a past as Cadillac find itself in so parlous a state? Said one high executive in a competing GM division: "I think they just forgot who the hell they are." More tactful was the comment by Sir John Egan, chairman of Jaguar: "I don't think there are any shortcuts to our business, you have to put your foundations in deep and make yourself a really beautiful system to create luxury cars, and you have got to have some history doing it."

So far as the last part of Sir John's comment was concerned, Cadillac would seem to have had nothing to worry about. This side of Daimler Benz and Rolls-Royce, nobody in the world could touch Cadillac for history. . . .

. . .

Henry Ford was chief engineer of the company that was to become Cadillac before it built its first car by that name. By the time it did, it was owned by the man who would leave Cadillac to start Lincoln. Henry M. Leland started Cadillac because he had built an engine for Ransom Eli Olds that was too good for the curved dash Olds, then America's most popular car. It was 1902. Olds had taken a giant step in what we now call mass production by inventing subcontracting when the factory in which he was building his curved dash burned down. One of his engine contractors was Leland and Faulconer, considered the finest machinists in Detroit if not the world. L and F's guiding spirit was Leland, about whom a biography was written titled *Master of Precision*. In Leland's case, the title was modest. Leland had taken one of the engines he was building for Olds and hotted it up. By the time he was finished, it was making almost three times the horsepower of the motor he was selling Olds, but the Olds people were selling everything they could make and saw no point in fixing something that wasn't broken. When the financial backers of the Detroit Automobile Company (Henry Ford, chief engineer) came to Leland for an appraisal of plant and equipment for purposes of liquidation, Leland saw a chance to use the improved engine. Thus was born Cadillac, begun on the 200th anniversary of the discovery of Detroit and named for its discoverer, Antoine de la Mothe Cadillac.

By 1908, Cadillac had built such momentum and reputation that it was ready to win the first of its towering engineering achievements: the Dewar Trophy for technical progress. That first Dewar Trophy came when the Royal Automobile Club selected three cars of a random shipment of eight, had them disassembled, then reassembled randomly. All three ran flawlessly for 500 miles at Brooklands. It was an unheard of achievement in that time of taking a car back to the factory for repairs.

Cadillac won its second Dewar Trophy in 1912 for introduction of coil ignition and the self starter.

By now, Cadillac was part of William Crapo Durant's General Motors, but Henry Leland was running it. In 1910, GM had brought aboard an engineer every bit Leland's equal, Charles Kettering. The self starter was a Kettering invention as was coil ignition, both products of the Dayton Engineering Laboratory Company (DELCO).

By 1925, Lawrence Fisher had become general manager of Cadillac. He was a man of elegant—perhaps even sporting—tastes, and on one of his trips to California came upon a man styling cars at a dealership in Hollywood. Styling was an unpracticed art in Detroit— left to specialist coach builders who charged enormous prices—until Harley Earl was persuaded to leave California, come to Detroit and begin what was to be known first as Art and Color, then Styling and Design at GM.

Earl's first car was the '27 LaSalle, his second the remarkable '27 341 Cadillac, which made 90 hp at 3,000 rpm, had under-slung springs, a low and handsome body as a result, and a V-8 engine. It was not Cadillac's first V-8. The company had introduced the V-8 to America in 1914.

From the V-8, it was not a long step to the V-16, considered now one of the great American engines in one of the great American cars. The 452-cid engine was introduced in 1929, the first car with hydraulic valve adjusters.

On July 30, 1930, Cadillac introduced its V-12, a V-16 with four cylinders taken off. It was a fertile time in the division, a division being run in the same tradition as it was founded, by engineers. Francis Davis began work on a power steering unit in the '20s and had it ready by 1933. It was delayed for almost two decades, because of cost, then rushed to production a year after Chrysler introduced its virtual equivalent in 1951.

Earl Thompson and Oliver K. Kelly started work on a fully automatic transmission in 1932. By 1935 they had pilot models ready, but they went to Oldsmobile by corporate order. In 1941, Cadillac introduced factory air conditioning. After war's interruption, Cadillac offered the world its stunning 331 V-8 high compression, short-stroke engine, the so-called Kettering, but actually done by three others: John Gordon, Harry Barr and Ed Cole.

All of these achievements, and more, began with Cadillac. They were the work of great men. And they were world recognized. What Mercedes is to the U.S. today, Cadillac was to France and Switzerland and Germany before 1939. Cadillac was being modest when it called itself the Standard of the World.

By comparison with its early history, Cadillac's postwar achievements seem hardly worthy of mention. Most memorable were tailfins. Most useful was cruise control. In between came such things as vinyl roof and quadruple headlights.

What had happened to the Standard of the World?

Erosion of the standard had many causes: The Great Depression ended much of the demand for complex, expensive cars from mass producers. A coming war would expand industry capacity to meet its needs and then leave Detroit with enormous peacetime overcapacity. That would be solved by something called "Sloanism" after its creator, which was, among other things, a system of management and marketing that put a premium on economy of scale and sameness. Sloanist principles would guide management in a huge sales success made necessary to cope with overcapacity, and that sales success would feed on itself to encourage continued sameness and it would do worse. It would induce arrogance, parochialism and an almost religious belief in the worth of a system that would make that system virtually immune from change. All these would come to haunt Cadillac.

Cadillac's Depression casualties were its wonderful engines. Both the V-16 and V-12 were introduced with uncannily bad timing. In its total 10-year run, the V-16 sold only 4,377 units; the V-12 in its seven-year life did a little better, 7,500.

Far more dynamic in inducing change was the increasing influence of what would come to be known as Sloanist marketing. Alfred P. Sloan Jr. had ascended to the chairmanship of GM after two chaotic periods of stewardship by founder Durant and interim control by banks and mega-stockholder DuPont. He became a GM man when Durant acquired his company, Hyatt Roller Bearing. Sloan's organizational genius took him quickly to the top.

Sloan is known as the great rationalizer of GM. Enunciating his principles, he set forth that markets were segmented. GM would be a participant in each segment. It would be at or near the top of each segment. It would, moreover, encourage change of ownership by annual change of style. Thus was born planned obsolescence, thus was born the Age of the Stylist, thus was ushered out the Reign of the Engineer, thus, ultimately, was initiated the practice of "badge engineering": the use of one platform around which to build several makes of cars.

Sloanism also introduced something called economy of scale, based on the commercial success of shared componentry.

So blame Sloanism for chipping away at the Standard of the World. Blame too, if you will, postwar prosperity and industry over-capacity. There were no limits on what the American consumer was willing, able and hungry to buy. Of all things, the most desirable was a new car. The most desirable new car was Cadillac, and so everyone, particularly competing divisions within GM, tried to look as much like Cadillac as possible. Throughout, Cadillac was so successful it sold everything it could make. "We were capacity constrained until 1973," says Cadillac chief engineer Warren Hirschfield, who has spent his career with the division.

. . .

None of these things had a devastating effect on Cadillac in the public's view. In fact, there is strong argument that they had little effect on the car. Surely fit and finish suffered somewhat as sales volume grew. But, until the very late '60s, an American boasting about the virtues of his premier marque could point to its enormous durability, its infinite luxury, its incredibly low price.

At which point came the legislation that changed the industry. The National Highway Safety Act of 1966. The Clean Air Act of 1970 and amendments. The Energy Policy and Conservation Act of 1973. CAFE. Downsizing. Emissions controls. While Hirschfield is willing to admit "[federal legislation's] overall direction has produced far better handling cars that are also more crash worthy and have better fuel economy," failure of Seville and Eldorado continue to be blamed on decisions having to do with making the cars smaller and more efficient. Both were designed for a world of $30 a barrel crude. Both are accused of being too small and too plain.

But downsizing wasn't the only ill effect of federal legislation. If Cadillac engineering had gone from the sublime to the merely adequate, in the late '70s it turned abysmal. In pursuit of fuel economy, GM converted its 350 gas engine to a diesel. The hybrid was so bad it resulted in class-action suits. Whereupon Cadillac marketed its notorious 8-6-4 V-8 engine, which led to even more consumer distress. Next? The successor 4.1-liter aluminum V-8, which suffered severe oil leak problems initially. Added to that was a transmission almost as deficient. "All of a sudden," says new Cadillac general sales manager Peter Gerosa, "the cars that used to be perfect [weren't] perfect." Gerosa's litany is repeated by Grettenberger. It is accurate but also incomplete. It does not reflect the legacy of arrogance bestowed by all that sales success for all those years. Sheri Perelli, Cadillac's public relations chief, harks back to a dark age of Detroit parochialism and arrogance when she responds to a question about why Cadillac is no longer viewed as the world's standard. "You've got it backwards," she says, "it's the market that changed." The trouble is, Cadillac did not change with it.

One market shift came in the black community, where Cadillac is no longer the force it used to be. "If you go into urban black communities, and I do," says George Edwards, president of the National Black Network and marketing director of the World Institute of Black Communications, "you will see a proliferation of European cars like BMWs and Audis and Mercedes . . . every one of those owners could have been a Cadillac buyer. Many are former Cadillac owners." Edwards attributes much of this to what is being called, even in-house, the look-alike syndrome: "The ElRivado has turned off the current segment of black prestige car buyers." Edwards says he believes GM is working with the basic assumption that black consumers do not have enough discretionary income to buy luxury cars. Then he adds that GM has never understood "that the underprivileged consumer in any society always seeks instant gratification" as he moves up, "showing his new prosperity in the form of highly visible, status automobiles."

Cadillac seems to be proving him at least partially wrong. The division has a substantial ad campaign aimed at Hispanics predicated on that very assumption. Moreover, Cadillac runs a significant schedule of print ads in black publications.

Yet it is not just the black buyer Cadillac seems to misunderstand, it is the far more important age cohort called variously Boomers and Yuppies.

The argument for failure of market understanding here begins with Cadillac's outdated assumption of continued owner loyalty. Added to that is clearly a massive misunderstanding of the impact of foreign cars on a group of people who were themselves holders of what Hirschfield now calls "new values." In reality, it was the new value system that accepted the imports and then ownership of the imports that reinforced the new values. Closed loop change.

In the understanding of the psycho-graphers, and in particular a cutting-edge group at a think tank called the Stanford Research Institute (now SRI International), car buyers who might be in the market for the traditional Cadillac belonged to three groups. They classified these as "belongers," "emulators" and "achievers." The last is self-explanatory, the middle group consists simply of strivers to achievement, and the first the traditional, establishment-accepting, relatively conservative consumer. All three were considered "outer-directed." In translation: Members of the three groups sought rewards from things owned or acquired, or status and achievement defined by others.

In contrast new value people were "inner-directed." Their own experiences, social consciousness, self-, not society-, defined achievement were their satisfactions. And it was this group that was not only buying the imports, but learning its car lessons from them. Says one former member of SRI's Values and Lifestyles Group (VALS), "For the most part, the inner-directeds spent the late 1970s and early 1980s cruising around in well-made, efficient, little Japanese pocket cars: Hondas, Toyotas and Datsuns, as well as a few econo-performance Euro-cars like the VW Rabbit.

"Detroit, particularly GM, was convinced it would get back all those buyers when they grew up, made lots of money and embarked on the Great American Status Trip. They didn't."

When the boomers grew up, found real jobs and started the trek to affluence, they took their experiences and values right along with them. A Carter administration recession ended, prosperity returned, and car sales took off. Right into the arms of the Japanese, who had moved upscale in anticipation of the Boomers' new affluence, and the

Germans who had been there all along. Says the SRI man: "Cadillac, the glorious Cadillac of earlier generations, foundered in a storm of social change, foreign competition and lack of vision."

. . .

Allante's elaborate debut was the first step in what GM's executive vice president for North American Car Operations, Lloyd Reuss, calls the effort to "restore Cadillac products and image to where they are the standard of the world." Reuss' deputy, and chief of the armies of Buick, Oldsmobile and Cadillac, characterizes what Reuss has said as "The Vision." His name is Bill Hoglund, and he is widely regarded as the best product man in GM.

"Step one is the vision," he says. "Is the goal up there? Our job [at Buick Olds Cadillac: BOC] is to be sure that the marketing division [Cadillac] has the vision."

The vision, according to the book of John O. Grettenberger, can be seen in its macro-outline in the shape of a triangle. *Advertising Age* talked to Grettenberger last March and heard about that triangle. At the apex, the magazine paraphrased, are the world-class cars: ultra-luxury vehicles like Rolls-Royce, some Mercedes-Benzes, Jaguar, some BMWs and the exotics. Below come the traditional luxury cars: Cadillac, Lincoln, Chrysler, Buick, Olds and other Mercedeses. At the bottom are the near luxury cars, including Alfa Romeo, Audi, Peugeot, Saab, Volvo and, among others, the Cadillac Cimarron. Grettenberger told *Advertising Age* that growth in the total segment would be in the top part of the market and at the bottom, ultra-luxury and near luxury. He estimated total sales of 1.9 million units in the whole segment by 1990 compared to 1.6 million now. In other words, an increase equivalent to the same number of cars (total) that Cadillac sells today. At the moment, he said, the ultras took 12.4 percent of the business, the traditionals 55.4 percent and the near luxury 38.2 percent. In his forecast, he predicted sales of traditional luxury cars would be flat, but there would be a 68 percent gain among the ultras and a 60 percent increase in the near luxury market.

What did all that mean in terms of the Vision Translated? Simply said, it meant that to achieve Reuss' mandate of becoming again the standard of the world, Cadillac would have to grow in the ultra segment and in the near segment as a result of products that would be competitive against specific targets. It would not do merely to continue selling 300,000 traditional luxury cars a year (which *Forbes* magazine quoted a GM insider as saying, in terms of profitability, was virtually the equivalent of selling 300,000 Buicks) because in Grettenberger's words "if we concentrate [on doing that] our share will erode."

First things first, then. What is the shape of the near luxury car that will lead Cadillac out of the wilderness? Hoglund says any new product from the division must start with the powerplant "made by people who know cars. It must have comfort and convenience: Do the seats mold to the body? How about the [instrument] panel look and feel? Are the controls precise and crisp?" He goes on: "The car has to have design themes and cues that mean Cadillac-ness. [It] has to be a complete car. It has to get . . . good fuel economy and it has to have responsiveness. It must be reliable and fit and finish are important."

But what does this *mean* exactly? And how does Cadillac Division translate it into hardware? "The Datsun [Nissan] Maxima and Toyota Cressida are about where I'd like to be," says Grettenberger. "At the top of the near luxury car segment. It is leading edge technology." He does not mention Saab. He does not speak the name Volvo. He ignores Mercedes 190 and BMW Three Series. If you begin to get a feeling that the current management of Cadillac is insular, you can also begin to make preliminary judgments about prospects for change, as well as for the division's chances for success in its self-defined task.

Chief engineer Hirschfield adds: "These are not so much near luxury cars as new value cars. [They must have] functional performance, a total absence of phoniness. They must have traction, cornering power, [impressive] powertrains."

Wait, though. Doesn't Cadillac already have an entry in the near luxury market, the Cimarron? Hasn't Cadillac said publicly it intends to continue marketing the Cimarron? And wouldn't that mean Cimarron meets the Grettenberger/Hirschfield criteria?

Here, a strong answer comes not so much from Cadillac management but from Cadillac's greatest remaining strength, its dealer body. Cadillac knows exactly what those dealers mean in its drive to regain status. It knows why as well. Sales manager Gerosa calls their facilities "magnificent." Grettenberger says their score on product satisfaction (service and warranty) "equals or is higher than the product scores." Cadillac mega-dealer Roger Penske says the dealer council for Cadillac is the strongest in the country. Owner of the nation's largest dealership in Longo Toyota (12,000 cars a year or more), Penske nevertheless maintains that the most valuable franchise in America in the future will be Cadillac, although he does not say why.

And yet it is Penske, along with mega-dealer Potamkin and about 42 other Cadillac franchise holders, who have taken on Sterling, Austin Rover's entry in the near luxury market. (Adding insult: Norman Braman, principal in ARCONA, Austin Rover Cars of North America—the importer—is a Cadillac mega-dealer himself.) "I think [a dealer taking on Sterling] is a comment on Cimarron," says Grettenberger. "They're unhappy with what's been positioned as an import fighter, and I'm unhappy too. If we can't come up with the right mix in the near luxury [segment] I'd rather not be there."

So the Cimarron is not the car to gain what Cadillac needs in the near luxury market. Which means that the division will have to get the right car or abandon one of the two segments Grettenberger has already defined as critical to Cadillac's renewal.

What then of the ultra-luxury cars, the second of the two subsegments in which, according to Cadillac's general manager, the division absolutely must succeed? What is the UltraVision? Allante is one of its incarnations. It has been very well received by reviewers. Penske's Bakersfield dealership has "40 or 50 people definitely interested. We just don't have any cars." But Allante is a limited edition aura car. How do general manager, chief engineer and sales manager see the mainstream entry? Grettenberger is nearly unable to articulate his image and so he falls back on what he knows, what is already there to boast about. "You have to set yourself some standards that are higher than ever set before. . . . When you look at durability, we still hold the advantage. [We lead] in interiors, comfort and convenience." Gerosa, who came to the division only 70 days ago with a reputation as a tough, hard-headed, no-nonsense man, can't be expected to add much. But he gives perspective nonetheless: "When the dude drives up in front of the place, he wants 'em to look. He wants 'em to look because he's paid big bucks for the car. [But the ultra?] We're still looking at it."

It is, predictably, the chief engineer who comes the closest to crossing t's and dotting i's. "We've been shown by Allante that we can reach for the finest. [At present] we've got this Sears thing: 'this is our regular, this is our better, this is our best.' We've got to stop that." Then, as if suddenly realizing the implications of what he's said, he becomes deferential to his current customers. "We can't turn off the Sun City buyer. They want good chair height. They want easy ingress and egress." But what about the vision, specifically what about those cars Grettenberger has specified as belonging to the ultra-luxury segment, how does the vision compare to them? Hirschfield takes refuge in the same cove as his general manager. When he is asked to put his vision and the Mercedes 560SEL side by side, he answers as though he were contrasting what he has today with the Mercedes, not what he hopes to have: "Is it [the 560SEL] as quiet as us? Is it as soft riding as us? How about noise? Vibration? How about air conditioning systems?"

It may not seem that much of this spells out the shape and kind of car Cadillac wants and needs. Grettenberger and his top people are uncomfortably vague.

At least as troublesome is the system for achieving the product. No matter how grand the vision, it is and will remain a simple fact of life that Cadillac does not design its own cars. BOC does.

The outline of the car Cadillac wants becomes clearer and clearer when its top people are asked about the system for achieving the product when it is defined. It does not seem very much different from what it has been since the end of World War Two; it does not seem like a way of arriving at the best and the brightest. In fact it seems like, it is, a casebook study in how to build a car that will be the quintessential product of an exercise in economy of scale.

Describing the process, Hirschfield descends into the jargon of the industry. He begins with a reminder that under GM chairman Roger Smith's reorganization, the divisions have become the marketing arms of the company. Subtitle: Cadillac no longer manufactures, no longer designs. Everything significant is done by BOC. If this says "sameness," that would be your conclusion, not Cadillac's. Cadillac believes it more than embellishes the basic design that it shares with the B and the O. Cadillac believes it can make the shared platform into a truly unique automobile.

Perhaps this is so ingrained in men like Hirschfield, heirs to the people who made cars according to the Book of Sloan, they seem hardly conscious of what they are saying. But listen now as he describes the way he allocates the hours of his days.

While he does not admit as much, Hirschfield concedes Cadillac's forced relinquishment of control of its own destiny by saying his engineering group, a total of 25 people including himself, spends half its time "understanding what the markets need and 50 percent defining that to the platform groups and then ensuring that the products are what [we've defined]." Subtitle: We ask the people designing the replacement for (say) the current Eldorado/Seville/Toronado/Riviera if we can have such and such a variation on the theme according to what we think our people can best sell as a Cadillac distinct from a Buick or an Oldsmobile.

"The chief engineer draws up a Level One specification," he says. "It starts with the demographics of the buyer, the target market and includes such things as the theme of the car.

"It outlines fuel economy, performance, styling accents and general price." Subtitle: We make our case for a differentiation.

"The specifications in Level One go to the Platform Group, which returns a Level Two 'Plan Book' from the product team." Subtitle:

The BOC and styling department people take our wishes into consideration when they make their decisions. Sometimes, as in future C bodies (Cadillac DeVille/Olds 98/Buick Electra), the decision is made to offer very different sheet metal on cars for Cadillac in order to combat the look-alike syndrome. Sometimes, as will be the case, the decision is implemented in conjunction with another decision to give Cadillac the new car a full year ahead of its sister divisions in BOC.

"From this come compromises and specific decisions in light of the specific problems posed [Subtitle: The product team answers a request for something big, 'are you anxious enough to have it that you'll pay a lot of money?'], and from that comes the final blueprint, complete in every detail: Level Three."

Remembering that Grettenberger has said if Cadillac can't have the best car in the near luxury group he will abandon it, and that he has also reached for a definition of ultra-luxury and only come as close as "more upscale, more exclusive, and if it's more expensive, so be it," and that both groups represent the future of Cadillac; the process of creation needs more concrete definition. Hirschfield supplies details.

"Level One might say we want larger all-season radials for the Eldorado; another example would be we want a storage tray put inside the front seat armrest . . . or we want a 0-60 time of X seconds."

The Level Two or product team answer "might say you can have the tire, but you need the inclusion of spring rate changes and different shocks to accommodate [them]. It might say the storage tray [will be practical] only on cars with individual seats and only leather, not bench and not cloth. On the 0-60 times it might say, 'We can't unless you want a tuned intake with port instead of throttle body injection and do you want a cost study done?'"

Hirschfield's walk through the GM paper jungle can be seen in three ways. When the leadership of Cadillac says it wants to build the best car in the ultra-luxury segment, and mentions Rolls-Royce, Mercedes and Jaguar as potential competitors, it is truly prepared to spend what it takes to design and make an automobile unique from everything else in GM. Mercedes, for example, builds three distinct passenger cars and sells worldwide in approximately the same numbers as does Cadillac. Second: The leadership of Cadillac believes that it can build a competitive car within the GM system. Third: The leadership is so completely indoctrinated as GM/Sloanists they don't understand their own myopia.

From as far into GM's past as Alfred Sloan, the words come echoing: We will be at the top of each segment. Added is Grettenberger's caveat: Or we will abandon it. Hirschfield has said earlier, "We were out in front. We became conservative. The competition took risks and put us in a tough spot. Now we have to take risks."

When Cadillac takes the step beyond Allante, will it have to share a platform and then suffer sheet metal that is so much like its siblings' that when Hoglund says "each body panel on the C body [Cadillac] is unique to that car," it comes as a shock?

How will Cadillac use its Sloanist economy of scale approach to build an ultra-luxury car, even with the technical help of new GM addition Lotus and new partner Pininfarina? How important is it to GM that the goal be reached?

Only this important, says Bill Hoglund: "If GM is to be the finest car company in the world, it has to sell the finest car in the world."

Once upon a time it did.

There is a very real question whether it can ever do so again.

Edward Lapham, Thomas F. Mandel and Kevin A. Wilson contributed to this story.

The Long Road Back

RENO REKINDLES THE FLAME OF
WILLIAM HARRAH'S AUTOMOTIVE PASSION,
BUT ONLY AFTER A SERIES OF
PERILS OF PAULINE MISADVENTURES
Dec. 18, 1989

THE SCENE WAS STRAIGHT from a latter-day medicine show: A scattering of men, in boots and leather vests and big hats surrounded by women clinging to squalling children, stood expectantly in front of a temporary wooden platform. A large man wearing an Eastern suit and hand-painted tie stepped to an old-fashioned stand-up microphone, blew into it and counted backwards from five.

"We got a tight schedule here. . . . We gotta open this museum in short order here," he said, looking behind him to a row of men seated on folding chairs and behind them to the low-lying, pink-and-chrome building gleaming in the cold Sunday morning sunlight.

"I'm gonna be after all of you to keep right on your timin' here," he said. All of them? Including even the mayor? The man from the governor's office? The head of the chamber, the museum director, too? Well, why not? For eight long years, through a series of Perils of Pauline adventures that charted like a massive coronary occlusion, the project to save Bill Harrah's wonderful car collection stayed miraculously on course. Came, in fact, to this very moment when a $36 million knockout of a museum containing the 220-car core of the collection was opening this November 5th morning in downtown Reno, more or less on schedule.

The miracle lay as much in the shape of the museum as the fact of it; a place designed by the people who did the Freedom Train and California's Railroad Museum, it displayed the cars in a fresh, vivid and creative way, setting them down in time and place complete with contemporary storefronts and paraphernalia in contrast to the cheek-by-jowl clutter and confusion of the old collection.

In this town of professional oddsmakers, nobody involved would have booked the outcome at any time during those long years. Nobody. Not the man who started the whole thing, nor the man who shepherded it along the entire way, nor even the man who seized the project when it seemed to be dead and revived it at the last possible moment.

When William Fisk Harrah, founder and sole proprietor of a hotel/casino empire that defined the genre, died in 1978, the nature of his estate and the specifics of his will guaranteed two things: His company would have to be sold to pay inheritance taxes and his 1,400-car collection would be left in limbo. Bill Harrah's Mayo Clinic doctors lost their 68-year-old patient after five hours of heart surgery unaware that his cash on hand would hardly have paid their medical bills.

He had $10,000 in a checking account. A Reno bank held his personal note for $13 million. His massive apartment complex in Florida had a stiff mortgage against it, and he had pledged half his stock in Harrah's Tahoe and Reno Hotels to a New York bank. Says his executor, Mead Dixon: "We had taxes and we had debt, and we had no money to pay them with.

"Bill had two minor children [John Adam and Tony] and a widow [Verna] whose interests had to be protected.

"We had no choice. We had to sell control in the company."

With the company went the cars. More important, with the company also went the right to disperse the collection, to sell the cars. And what cars! Even the two Bugatti Royales didn't hint at the scope of what Harrah himself considered primarily an American car collection. There were, for example, 18 Duesenbergs—many of them, like the ex-George Whittell, Gordon Buehrig-designed Weymann S.J. Boattail Speedster of 1933, absolutely brilliant examples. Franklins and Fords were Harrah's particular passion, and they were represented not just exhaustively but passionately. There were Packards to delight the most discriminating, but not to the exclusion of Marmons and Wintons and Stanleys and Thomases—including a 1907 Model 36 Touring (Harrah's favorite, affectionately nicknamed "Blondie") and the magnificent and famous 1907 Flyer that won the New York-to-Paris race in 1908. There was even a Jeep Wagoneer with a Ferrari 365 engine and transmission that Harrah had his restoration shop build, among the 1,400 cars.

Why so many? The closest Harrah could come to answering was "You [buy] two [collectible] cars. Then four cars. All I can tell you [is] the cars came real fast. I was makin' money, so I could afford to buy a car here and there."

The reasons for bringing that staggering number of cars together were casual enough; the rationale for not preserving them was even more offhand. The curious fact, little known and not at all remembered, was that Harrah, America's foremost car fanatic, had deliberately refused to make provision for the preservation of his magnificent collection.

"I asked him," recalls Verna Harrah, his sixth and last wife, "why don't you put in your will that the company *can't* sell the ears? 'I'd never do that,' he answered. 'That's my thing, not theirs. They should be able to do whatever they want.'"

Says Dixon, "Bill was interested in collecting, assembling and restoring those cars much more than in displaying or preserving them. He didn't need to keep his collection in any kind of public perspective."

The practical result was that when Holiday Inns completed its acquisition of Harrah's in 1980 and began to look around to see what it had gotten for its $364 million, it discovered three huge warehouses of "non-revenue producing assets."

"Holiday Inns was and is a very capital-conscious company," says Dixon, a white-haired, tanned man in his 70s who left H.I.'s new subsidiary, Harrah's, as its chairman and CEO in 1986 and now is a full-time executor of the Harrah estate. "When they realized the value of the collection compared to the difficulty of making it go commercially, they decided to sell."

The day was June 9, 1981. It began a remarkable saga that would only end on a bright, cold Sunday eight years later.

Almost certainly Holiday was unprepared for the reaction to the announcement of sale. Ever since H.I. was founded in 1952, taking the name of a Bing Crosby movie for its corporate persona, it has put itself forward as one of the country's good-guy companies. It took a while before Holiday chairman Roy Weingartner, deep inside the corporate headquarters in Memphis, Tenn., heard the outcry. He was surprised and distressed.

For at least a week after the announcement, all three Reno network-affiliate TV stations led their nightly news with expressions of outrage by a curious collection of people. There were the altruistic civic-minded, the self-interested tourist and convention people, and there was a small group of car fanatics composed of collectors and auto writers, who felt personally assaulted and who reacted with fury. These last formed a group called Friends of the Cars and threw themselves at any and everybody who would listen. The publisher of the Reno newspaper had a ready ear. Editorialized the *Nevada State Journal:* "Harrah's Auto Collection is too precious to lose. Too unique to be sold. Too much at the very heart of American history to dismantle. . . . Holiday Inns [must] give us the time to save this collection for ourselves and our posterity."

The piece was written for the June 11 edition. H.I. had already set a deadline of Oct. 1.

That they delayed at all somewhat surprised Mead Dixon: "I don't believe they anticipated the public outcry. The resounding voices made them look very carefully at what they were doing."

Announcing the sale of the collection—valued at the time at $30 million—began a sequence of frenzied events that transfixed the city and utterly captivated the press.

On July 1, the *Journal* printed a report that the collection had been sold to San Francisco venture capitalist Tom Perkins.

On July 2, Nevada Gov. Robert List asked the state's congressional delegation to look into possible tax credits for H.I. if it kept the cars.

Eight days later, Bill "Wildcat" Morris of Las Vegas' Convention and Visitor's Authority outraged the northern part of the state by threatening to kidnap the collection from its Reno rival for the hated south.

Exactly one month later, on Aug. 10, Nevada's senators and congressmen reported back to List that the idea of tax credits would never fly.

On Labor Day, the paper reported Perkins turned down the collection.

The long weekend over, List got back to work requesting a delay in the Oct. 1 deadline. A week later, Nevada Sen. Paul Laxalt weighed in with a telegram to H.I. chairman Weingartner asking for the same thing.

Much sound, much fury. But little apparent action.

The operative word is apparent. Nevada, given its principal industry, operates best quietly, in private and through an old boys' network. The chief old boy at work to save the collection was Mead Dixon. He was CEO of a company he knew relied in significant measure on the approbation of the community; he was a man who appreciated the cars. And so he lobbied and harangued and sweet-talked and tough-talked, and finally he persuaded the Holiday Inns board to accept a compromise. H.I. would agree to donate 300 cars and the huge reference library to the community through a charitable foundation to be set up by Harrah's *if* the community would raise the money to buy a site and build a museum.

This deal, which was to be the basis for all that followed, was relatively straightforward. The balance of the cars, 1,100 of them, would be disposed of. Holiday Inns began liquidating its non-revenue-producing assets through private sale. Soon enough, though, it would become apparent that selling off the cars individually would produce rumor and resentment as news got out of first this jewel disposed of and then that gem sacrificed. Eventually, the company would decide to assign collection general manager Clyde Wade to list the cars to be donated and would then put the rest up for auction. As it turned out, that would cause even more upset in the Reno community.

The William F. Harrah Foundation's legal structure was to be left to Harrah's general counsel Phil Satre. Foundation trustees would be drawn from the public sector and, at least initially, from Harrah's management. Sooner or later, a foundation chairman would be found in the person of a civic-minded Renoite named Benedict Dasher. In the meantime, disaster had been averted. Perhaps the entire collection had not been saved. But its core had been—more accurately could be—given the will of the community.

Seeing all this, one man who had been very much in the background sighed with relief. Mark Curtis, friend and advisor and public relations counsel to Bill Harrah, inspiration for the formation of the friends, and orchestrator of what had turned out to be one of the most effective P.R. campaigns of his career, thought to himself that the job of saving what he had called a national cultural heritage was over the hump.

Little did he know.

The rub lay in the conditions of the donation. H.I. was true to its word. It did indeed give 100 cars immediately to the new foundation. It gave the research library worth, many experts agreed, some $3.7 million. But the rest of the cars the company had promised, 200, for a total of 300, were only to be given piecemeal over five years. The reason was simple and explicit: H.I. did not intend to make a corporate gift of what was turning out to be somewhere near $25 million if the community—the citizenry of Reno—was not willing to respond in kind. Land and a museum; that was the deal, and Holiday, relying on Mead Dixon's assurances, expected that deal to be met.

That first tumultuous year of the Battle to Save the Collection, 1981, came to what seemed an auspicious close with a city council resolution to consider anchoring a downtown development plan with a car museum.

If there were those who expected land to be acquired and a building to be built relying only on resolutions, proposals and like expressions of intent on the part of the politicians, they were profoundly wrong. Over the following years, a series of nasty fights would be waged within the community by the city council, by real estate interests, by the casino industry, by the tourist and convention people, by *everybody*.

The first of these fights, predictably, involved land. Where to put a multi-million-dollar museum was a question that went straight to the hearts of businessmen, land speculators, the civic-minded. For most of the second year of the Battle to Save the Collection, the debate raged over proposals to build in town, out of town, even in a high-rise over the downtown railroad tracks.

Mead Dixon, general counsel Phil Satre and the Holiday Inns board looked on in what must have been exasperation. All the while, however, much of the collection was being liquidated.

While this was happening, a formidable figure was emerging through the mists of greed, the fog of municipal confusion and the veils of corporate impatience. He was Benedict Dasher—6 feet, 5 inches of civic-minded retiree and trusted member of the business community. A quiet man, he would prove to be the Great Savior. A low-key, worthy doer was just exactly what the museum project needed in 1983, when Dasher became executive director of the William Fisk Harrah Foundation. In the next years the patience of any project leader would be sorely tried. Why did Dasher volunteer for such an aggravating task?

"I accepted the job because it promised to be a pleasant, satisfying project to help ease me out of full-time work," he says. "But then it started falling apart, and I found myself challenged—a really inadequate word given the fury of the whole thing." The fact was that Dasher was likely the only man in the city who was qualified by experience and disposition for the job.

His first real achievement, the Great Land Acquisition Episode, was typical of his tactics. H.I. was becoming insistent that progress be tangible. Once more the city council dilly-dallied. H.I. reacted with anger. So Dasher told the council that if it wanted the museum inside the city limits and not out near the California border where Harrah's owned some land, it had better offer more than gestures. "Option land," demanded Dasher. That got the council's attention. While it did not accede to the demand, it agreed to an almost equivalent step: It issued a letter of commitment.

"We needed [and got] a commitment from the city to put some kind of lock I felt was necessary to give the community a sense of involvement and a sense that the project was a permanent one," he says.

Early in February of '83 the city went even further than the commitment letter. It agreed to acquire property if the Harrah

Automobile Foundation would guarantee the purchase price. "The 100 cars we already had represented value in terms of a loan on their worth that could be used to buy land or build a building, but not both," Dasher says. He decided to reserve the loan value of the cars for the building fund, so he went out into the community and came back with guarantees on loans for the land from bankers and businessmen. Among the guarantors, in fact the two principal ones, were familiar names: Verna Harrah Levin was the first. The other came from Bill and Scherry Harrah's two teen-age sons: John Adam and Tony. The result of all this was that everyone came to agreement on a site: land downtown bordering the Truckee River.

Of course there was still the problem of the money. Security for borrowing had been found, but how was the money to be paid back? For starters, there was the Gala. From somewhere—no one can quite remember where—came the notion of a national television show and a grand, black-tie banquet; someone had mentioned a $10 million fundraising effort and this seemed to be a perfect kickoff toward that goal. To everyone's surprise, the TV show and the black-tie banquet happened. The $10 million did not, but nobody noticed. Dick Clark produced the syndicated show, and it starred some of Bill Harrah's favorite entertainers, including Debbie Reynolds, Wayne Newton, Bill Cosby and Jim Nabors (other celebs in attendance included Lisa Hartman and her escort, Danny Sullivan).

Twelve hundred tuxedoed and long-gowned paying guests appeared at the MGM Grand for the taping. It was the event of the fall season. News reporters from Reno print and TV covered it, of course, but so did entertainment and gossip press from Sacramento and San Francisco. Not until a year later, when all the arithmetic was sorted and the mysterious accounting of Hollywood deciphered, did Dasher announce the proceeds: $50,000. By then, of course, everyone had long since assumed the Gala had been a smash.

The Gala over, the collection and its troubles were out of mind to almost everybody in Reno. The cars—most of them still being displayed as they were during Bill Harrah's lifetime, clustered together almost willy-nilly in three enormous warehouses in Reno-adjacent Sparks—were playing to fewer and fewer visitors. Once more, the city assumed all was well and turned its mind to more immediate affairs.

Silence seemed to settle over the Collection Battle, but it was a stillness that would not last. Nevada's summers are hot and dry. This August in '84 turned explosive when an impatient Holiday Inns decided to auction the Harrah cars. The company had waited long enough. Cars were not being sold fast enough. Moreover, the community was doing very little to meet the terms of the donation agreement. No complete land package existed; there was nothing resembling a building. Enough was enough.

Cars up for auction included some that were at the heart of what was admirable in the Harrah collection: a Bugatti Royale (the Berline de Voyage), a Type 50 Bugatti, the Ethel Mars Duesenberg Town Car, a Ford Model K and an 812 Cord. No sooner was the auction announced than attendance at the Sparks site of the collection soared to record numbers; at last, people in the community were beginning to realize that what had been the largest, most magnificent collection of cars in the world would soon be gone.

Trouble is, they still were serenely certain 300 cars would be left, land to build on would be theirs, and a museum to house the cars would rise as if by magic.

After three auctions (concluding with a 240-car one in '86) and many private sales—and a resultant last spasm of outrage by the remaining collection-saving activists in Reno—came a paradoxical turning away from the whole problem, even by those who'd been most concerned. The battle to save the cars was in its fifth year; too long for the philanthropic attention span of Renoites. The stage was set for the last act of the morality play. More accurately, in the mind of the new CEO of Harrah's, the time had come for the end game. He was none other than Phil Satre, the legal architect of the foundation itself.

By now the twists and turns of the collection story were almost so convoluted as to be beyond unravelling. The original donation of 100 cars and the library still represented the whole of the Foundation's gift;

the remaining 200 cars had been withheld pending acquisition of land and assurance of enough money to construct a museum. Worse, the 200 cars which the Harrah's Foundation thought of as its own had been quietly pared to 75 as prospects for a successful museum seemed to dim. Including the 75 "earmarked" for the foundation, only 159 vehicles from Harrah's 1,400-plus were still in Holiday's possession by late 1986.

Although foundation executive director Dasher had persuaded the city of Reno to buy and own the land identified as the museum site, thereby relieving the private guarantors of their obligations, the city had not completed negotiations.

Nor had money for the museum been raised, and so, the last 75 cars were still being withheld from the foundation.

What's more, a much-ignored deadline for final settlement of conditions, June 30, 1987, was approaching. When it had been set, way back then, nobody dreamed anything other than that the museum would have been up and operating long since by the time that date would come. Now June 30, 1987, stared grimly at Dasher.

If the people in Reno had not been paying attention to the deadline, the people in Memphis had. Mike Rose had succeeded Roy Weingartner as CEO of Holiday Inns. He had been president when Harrah's was acquired. He had been all through the years of starts and stops. He was flat out of patience. Rose told the man running Harrah's that Reno had been given every opportunity and it wouldn't or couldn't respond. The last parcels of land were still missing; the money to build was not in the bank. Let the foundation keep the 100 cars and the library—not enough for a museum, of course, but worth enough at sale that at the very least H.I. would have given the city an important gift. H.I. would sell the remaining cars, including the promised 75. The man to whom Rose gave what amounted to a museum ultimatum is an out-of-the-ordinary manager. Lawyer, hotelier, former Pac-8 linebacker, Phil Satre is also very much a man of his time. Case in point: No sooner did he become president of Harrah's than he evicted the Prospectors Club from the Reno hotel. The Prospectors was made up of a small group of men who ran Northern Nevada by winks, grins, backslaps and handshakes and who refused, even after Satre's insistence, to accept women members. That made them ex-tenants. This was the man being issued sell orders by Memphis. Walking away from battle is not Satre's style, so he devised a plan that was part lawyer, part linebacker, part gambler's bluff.

"The future of the Harrah's Automobile Museum is in jeopardy after Harrah's announced Wednesday [Oct. 8, 1986] it intends to sell up to two-thirds of the cars originally promised for the collection," wrote the *Nevada State Journal*. The cars the newspaper meant were the 75 (though the two-thirds calculation dated back to the mythical 200) still being withheld because the city and the foundation had not finalized ownership of land or plans to build a museum. "Without them the collection will be a second-rate museum," said Reno Mayor Pete Sferraza.

At this point, in addition to the earmarked 75 cars (plus two antique aircraft) at risk of forfeiture, the foundation still hoped H.I. might donate its remaining holdings.

But 82 cars went in a final $28.8 million private sale on Dec. 31, 1986, to General William Lyon, who that November had gone cash-flush in the sale of Air Cal to American Airlines. Some cars sold to Lyon, including the second, more valuable Bugatti Royale (the Coupe de Ville) and several Duesenbergs (among them the 1929 Murphy dual-cowl Phaeton SJ that starred in the movie *Annie*), were among the ones the foundation believed had been earmarked for the museum. There were 75 cars left, but if the parties ever did agree to a particular 75, Holiday's list no longer agreed with the foundation's.

Predictably, announcement that these particular cars had been sold outraged Reno. Unnoticed in the controversy was a provision— made a condition of the sale to Gen. Lyon—that any one or all of the 27 rarest cars be returned for display in the new museum for 60 days a year for 10 years.

But so far as the city was concerned, and very much according to what Satre intended the city to believe, even the critical 75 were in jeopardy. "It was just unbelievable," says Dasher today. To him those

WILLIAM FISK HARRAH
THE LIFE AND TIMES OF A GAMBLING MAGNATE
BY LEON MANDEL

Cover of the Harrah biography, published by Doubleday, December 1981.

last 75 were make-or-break for the museum. Without them, he was ready to recommend that the city sell the original 100 and use the money "for parks."

The shock was enormous. Hadn't everything been settled long since? State Sen. Randolph Townsend, a former professional racing driver who had given a $250,000 Kremer 935 Porsche to the foundation (one of 50 non-Harrah's cars private parties had donated in support of the museum effort), sued to stop the sale. Although his suit would be settled amicably a short while later, it was a vivid example of how deeply the announcement affected the community.

It was electric shock therapy and it resulted in just exactly what Satre had hoped it might. From the newly combined *Gazette Journal*, Nov. 11, 1986: "The Reno City Council agreed Monday to use up to $10 million from the Redevelopment Agency to buy the remaining downtown land for a permanent Harrah's Automobile Museum."

After almost six years of agony, a Harrah's CEO had finally gotten the city to complete its part of the original bargain.

Exactly one month later, Phil Satre stood before the corporate board of Holiday Inns on 57th Street in New York, and five hours into a tough, down-year budget presentation came to the final item on the agenda: the cars. He recalls the day was dark, the weather nasty as only December in New York can be. Staring up at him from around a U-shaped table were, among others, two school principals (one the superintendent of the Memphis city school system, the other a professor at the Harvard Business School), a banker and a large handful of professional board members and managers, including CEO Mike Rose.

Satre reminded them of the original agreement. He detailed progress in the city's acquisition of the final parcels of land. He revealed that thereafter Dasher had gone to the First Interstate Bank in Reno and gotten a loan on the cars large enough to construct a building. And he said he'd sold those last cars, including the critical 27 with the return-for-display proviso. Then he told the Board it had an obligation to donate the final 75.

Although Satre was holding his breath, there was no discussion; the Holiday Inns board approved. Flying back to Reno, Satre recalls relief at being able to "keep intact a great treasure and benefit our property at the same time." He was particularly happy that everyone's effort succeeded in making sure the museum was in downtown Reno and that it would be housed in a first-class facility. At the same time, Satre knew success for the museum was not ensured.

In fact, as part of Harrah's long-term support, he agreed the company would underwrite over $500,000 worth of admissions during the first year alone. The problems are several. To succeed, the museum must attract downtown support to a facility that—although it is in no way affiliated with Harrah's Hotel—carries the Harrah name. Renoites and their families and friends must pay to go through the turnstiles, but tickets have been priced at $9.50—too high, according to locals. Finally, the long history of conflict has left the community confused about the number and quality of the cars.

In fact, the museum that opened that crisp Sunday morning in early November is splendid. Of the cars Phil Satre, Ben Dasher and Mead Dixon worked so hard to keep, more than the museum's share are world-class stunning: the Sindelfingen coachwork Mercedes-Benz 500K Special Roadster and its latter-day equivalent 300SL; a Type J Hispano-Suiza Berline from 1937; the wonderful New York to Paris-winning Thomas Flyer; that inspiration for everything sinister and wonderful in the automobile world, the Phantom Corsair; a splendid, almost delicate 1930 Franklin called the Averell Special speed car; Al Jolson's marvelous 16-cylinder '33 Cadillac 452C all-weather Phaeton; a dual-cowl Chrysler, one of six, bought in 1941 by the owner of the New York Yankees; a 1927 Judkins-bodied Lincoln Coaching Brougham, perhaps the wittiest car in the collection then and now; and an absolutely glorious pair of early sports cars, graceful enough to break hearts, the 1913 Mercer Raceabout and 1912 Stutz Bearcat.

There are race cars to get the blood flowing in even the most languid of enthusiasts, including a 1950 Ferrari 166 Inter, a wonderful evocation of the decade; from the Can-Am's last glorious year, 1972, a Reynolds-engined M20 McLaren; and Don Prudhomme's 1975 Chevy Monza Funny Car. There are cars of recent memory: a '53 Blue Flame Corvette, a '53 Buick Skylark convertible, a '56 Chrysler 300B.

There are odd-shaped cars: Buckminster Fuller's Dymaxion and Big Daddy Roth's Beatnik Bandit. There is perhaps the noblest collection of horseless carriages on the continent, from the 1892 Philion and 1902 Capitol steam cars to the 1911 Pope-Hartford 7-passenger Touring and the 1913 Stanley Mountain Wagon—and many in between. Wonderful cars, the stuff of a first-rate museum,

Will the city support the William F. Harrah Foundation National Automobile Museum? Business projections show that with a quarter-million admissions a year, the financial requirements of debt service and operating costs can be met. In the most successful year of the old collection, ironically its last, when it seemed to people in Reno that they had one final chance to see the cars Bill Harrah had brought to Northern Nevada, 280,000 persons went through the turnstiles. The town's attitude is summed up in a facetious saying: "Nothing Reno has amounts to much, or it wouldn't be in Reno." And the initial reaction to the new museum seems to underscore this lack of self-respect.

What that means is clear: However excellent the museum, however clever the displays, the battle to build the Heather Fire-mist pink-and-chrome building by the Truckee may have been won; but the *war* to save the collection has just begun.

AutoWeek *publisher Leon Mandel wrote the authorized biography of William Harrah during his decade-long residence in Reno.*

The Man in
the Kosher Corvette

Jan. 19, 1974

THE CAR WAS LIKE THE MEN WHO DROVE IT. It was brutal and direct. It was impatient with grace. It had a hard mouth and a hard record. So did its drivers.

Bill Pollack drove the first one on the West Coast and he set the style. He drove the car as he had driven Tom Carsten's Allard—with a fierce joy that made him seem almost . . . mindless.

Perhaps Pollack intimidated lesser drivers. Perhaps the Corvette did it all alone. Whatever the reason, the early West Coast racers who followed him in Corvettes seemed more committed than their delicate contemporaries in Porsches and Jaguars. For those who saw Andy Porterfield and Bob Bondurant and Davey MacDonald and Dick Guldstrand, they will remain almost uncomfortably insistent images in the memory.

So will Herb Caplan, the last of the fierce West Coast Corvette-men. Now, in the Greenwood era, it is all polish and finesse, all technique. Now even the car itself is refined, and it threatens to become even more so. Then, the car was like the men who drove it. It was brutal and direct. It was impatient with grace. It had a hard mouth and a hard record. So did its drivers.

Andy Porterfield ended in jail. Dave MacDonald died in the fire of the 1965 first-lap Speedway crash that also killed Eddie Sachs. Bob Bondurant turned school teacher. Dick Guldstrand is submerged in that relentless tidal wave of anonymity that sooner or later engulfs all car flakes in Southern California. Skip Hudson tends an orange grove.

But Herb Caplan, the survivor, is chairman of his own $4 million business and the new owner of an M20 McLaren for Scooter Patrick and the 1974 Can-Am.

They were apart from the others even then. Swaggering, boastful, vigorous young men. Guldstrand sits in his office now, with two new Panteras his company is building up for production SCCA racing, and tries to think of the word for how he felt when he was a Corvette driver. The words flow in the manic, zigzag pattern that orchestrates the Southern California argot, filled with images, bright pictures, highly spiced asides, but somehow the best he can do is to call the driving (and his feeling about it) "zestful." Guldstrand laughs about those years as he speaks. He talks of himself and the others as legendary people he almost doesn't recognize anymore.

"It was a foregone conclusion that you'd have to string your ass out a bit to get the job done." He chuckles. (He seems to be shaking his head in wonder and admiration at the other end of the telephone.) "But that wasn't a deterrent. I guess it was zest we're talking about. I got myself upside down three times when I was Corvette driving. But it didn't really bug me too much because lying in the hospital all I could do was figure out how to win the next time."

Up north, in Sonoma County, Calif., Bob Bondurant is cast back into the same frenetic Camelot by his memories. He doesn't know either how to find the word that describes how he felt, what it was that distinguished him as a Corvette man, what distinguished the others.

"Nothing, not even a Can-Am car, gives you the feeling a Corvette did. That real neat hairy feeling."

You can make generalizations: They all wanted to win, they all succeeded as race drivers, they were all as committed as literal madmen. They were arrogant and they were superbly competent so that they got away with their arrogance. Most were products of the California Car Culture. Even if they only seemed to be, they were zealots in the cause of promoting American engineering, and as a result they dripped with contempt for the products of a decadent Europe. They were humiliated at first to be beaten by Ace-Bristols, but the sweet juices of their later victories dripped over the Corvettes drivers' chins and drip, drip dripped their insistent recounting on the Bristol drivers' scrapbooks.

Then came the Cobras, which appeared in 1962 and became, particularly the black ones of the Shelby works team, the Corvette *betes noir*. And it started all over again.

Herb Caplan was not young. He was 37 years old when he began racing a Corvette. But he had the fierce, independent bold ambitions of his predecessors. He was a GM man, had been ever since he sold the '33 Ford three-window coupe (complete with Ardun heads) he owned at Sacramento's McClatchy High School. So, as with the distinguished line that preceded him, his was a religious cause: underdog GM and underdog America against the effete, smirking drawing room hordes from England (Jaguar, Bristol) and Germany (Mercedes 300SL, Porsche).

In line of succession, Pollack, Jerry Austin, Andy Porterfield, Bondurant, Tony Settember, Skip Hudson, MacDonald and Guldstrand had been up to it. Pure western frontiersmen sent into the trenches of the Ardennes! Sergeant York! A cause that's righteous can resist the swarming Boche; repel the savage Hun!

Herb Caplan, the Jewish frontiersman, was up to it too.

There was a stretch when Caplan won 46 of 49 races he entered, and one of the three he lost was because his car broke down. Aging Herb Caplan, who drove his first races in his air-conditioned coupe complete with telephone, had accepted the mantle of Defender of the Faith and was wearing it proudly.

Even competitively. He had a tired but savagely aggressive Red Faris to contend with as Northern California Corvette competition and Sandy Greenblatt. But Caplan had trained in a hothouse of competition.

Caplan's father fired him from the family business. Incompetent. No drive. And then there was the Great Father/Son Sacramento Street Race.

Of course, Caplan bought a Buick; his father owned a Roadmaster. And it happened inevitably that shortly thereafter, they met on a suburban street one Sunday morning. No sooner did they see each other than the two wallowing, stumbling Buicks careened up the street through the unsuspecting Sacramento suburbs in an all-out pre-Woodward Avenue shootout. Somewhere in the middle of it, with the results still undetermined, a florist's delivery truck turned a corner and blocked the Roadmaster's path. Without backing off an inch, Caplan's father took to the manicured lawns on the other side of the curb, hurtled through a driveway sending an elderly early morning walker into a lifetime of horror at the memory, howled back through a double hedge and took up the race just half a car length behind Caplan's Century.

They don't call it the California Car Culture idly.

Herb Caplan has an office in Reno, one in Las Vegas, and his headquarters in Sacramento. His Reno building is sizeable, the back filled with the heavy mining equipment he builds, sells and leases. It's a modern building; Caplan's own office is austere in the IBM restrained school. He sits behind a desk, not too large but not embarrassingly small either, in a white leather MacGregor that is almost a bike jacket, in tooled boots, in maroon polyester knit trousers. His shirt collar is wide open, his chest is hairier than his 21-year-old son's head. Caplan knows it.

"Every man has his own length and width, and he must shape his life to fit. I always wanted to race. I always loved cars. I always drove with emotion. A man who drives without emotion is a man for whom I have little respect: A guy like Walt Hansgen, he could cut out your heart and hand it to you while it was still beating."

Caplan, the heir to MacDonald and Bondurant, Guldstrand and Andy Porterfield, begins to wander in the whitewashed cottages of sportsmanship. "A gentleman," he begins each sentence. A gentleman would; a gentleman would not.

When the senior Rockefeller mellowed and the senior Carnegie and the senior Mellon and the senior Morgan as well, they talked about their philanthropies, forgetting the zestful days of their youth when they were brilliantly productive, happily rapacious.

Caplan remembers himself as a gentleman. And probably he was. But when Bondurant drove a Corvette, he had a fiberglass sponsor and for a very good reason. "I never worried about bodywork," reminisces Bondurant from his little cinderblock schoolhouse at Sears Point. And Caplan was Bondurant's spiritual inheritor.

Has that zest gone forever? Are the Porterfields and the Bondurants dinosaurs, long-fanged curiosities? Probably. No driver today would think of saying to another what Davey MacDonald told Guldstrand about his Indy car a week before his fatal crash. It was an awful car, he said. It scared him. He was sure he was going to have a crash with it, but that didn't make any difference. He was going to drive it anyway.

Guldstrand looks at the club racers today and says, "They show up with their cars on trailers and, if it isn't too inconvenient, they race."

And Caplan? Caplan sits rocking in his ExecuChair talking about what gentlemen will and will not do while around him the walls reflect the raw ambition and strength of a man who built a business from nothing to an imposing weight.

Guldstrand is probably right. There are no more Bondurants. And no more Caplans either. Chevrolet will be glad to take your order for a Corvette; though next year, in addition to a rotary engine, you can probably order a tea cozy as a comfort option.

Immortality

THE MEANING OF GETTING PINNED
HAS CHANGED OVER THE YEARS
Oct. 19, 1987

THIS ONE'S ABOUT IMMORTALITY. All right, maybe not immortality achieved but immortality pursued. Well, immortality fecklessly pursued by almost all of us. Excluding you. But including me and a lot of people I know.

I know people seeking immortality in the shapes of the cars they pen.

People chasing immortality in the words they write. In the families they father. In the careers they rush along at a perverse 200 mph putting the lives they wish to make immortal in immediate and dire danger of instant mortality.

Nobody ever said the pursuit of immortality had to make any sense.

I'm getting too tired to keep looking. At least I thought I was. Then, just when I'd come to that conclusion, immortality played a joke on me. Somebody went to Big Jim Sullivan, the Gutzon Borglum of the cloisonné pin business, and had one run up emblazoned with the logo of this publication on it and beneath that a far-too-flattering image that purported to be my likeness.

It was done in kindness, in commemoration of an eminently forgettable speech I gave before some very nice people at the All British Field Meet [see p. 226] in Portland, Ore. (So they were Sprite and MG and Triumph and Jaguar owners—all that meant was they were weird, not un-nice.)

It was done because this moment's icon of a generation that scorns icons in its rush to the end of the century is the pin, the cloisonné pin, signifying places and people passed along the way.

Once upon a time, there were luggage stickers that said "Hotel Excelsior-Roma" or "Compagnie General Transatlantique," which told the world it was dealing with a traveler in times when travel was expensive and perilous. "Plaza Athenee" turned into "Holiday Inn, The Dells" over the years and its currency so devalued thereby it became a mark of shame not distinction.

When designer things were new and trendy, we took to wearing tiny reptiles on our shirt pockets and names across our buttocks. Those of you who know about these things wouldn't be caught dead, I'm given to understand, with Liz or Ann or Hugo's name anywhere in sight anymore.

Once upon a time there were T-shirts. But then the Russians took to them as did the Swedes and the Sumerians, and now nobody in his right mind wears his persona on his chest any longer.

Every activity of particular interest has its own mark or badge or identifying sign, like the tattoo of the newly enlisted marine.

These days in motoring it's the pin.

A pin from SRE, Big Jim Sullivan's company, marks status and place and length of time in whichever path of motoring endeavor your energies have taken you. (Big Jim may not be quite as large as he used to be, but he is even more charitable, if that's not a non sequitur. It will distress him to read here that his substantial contributions to the charities of auto racing blow his curmudgeonly self-image to smithereens.) He is racing's epigrammatist when it comes to cloisonné commemorations—the man who understands which coinages, quips and truisms are to be emblazoned as pins to mark which passages. So that in addition to making pins for which he is commissioned, he also makes some he feels are simply necessary to memorialize a moment or an event. Thus, against a background of black and white squares, he pointed out the indecisiveness of the CART officials at Sanair a few years back when they threw the checkered flag after lifting a yellow light one turn from the end, in violation of their own rule saying warning had to be given, allowing Pancho Carter to jump John Rutherford for a seeming win, shortly reversed in John's favor: "READY OR NOT WE ARE GOING GREEN," read Big Jim's pin the following race.

His advice to the world (and racing in general) is embodied in pins that read "If you can't beat 'em, cheat 'em" and "Life begins at 200 mph" and two comments that are eternal for racers: "Growing Old Is Mandatory; Growing Up Is Optional" and "It's Never Too Late to Have a Happy Childhood." Mainly, though, Big Jim's company makes pins in Great Racing Drivers' images that people collect and wear on hats. Hats or vests or shirts. It says about the people who wear the pins that they've been there. Wherever there is. That's what it means to have a pin. Let me tell you how it feels to have a pin.

It feels somewhere north of having a baseball card, I guess. We always, my generation at least, collected and coveted and traded baseball cards. Baseball cards were currency. Baseball cards belonged to, well, they belonged to the immortals, and if somebody thought you were worth putting into the kids hall of fame, they put a washed-out picture of you on a piece of almost-cardboard and they made you immortal. Just like that.

So when I walked into the banquet hall at the All British Field Meet dinner and saw this pin, and I picked it up and there on the front of it . . . You can have Mt. Rushmore. You can even have a baseball card. I'm not asking if I deserve it, or even if the people who had it made knew what they were perpetrating, or if Big Jim has as wicked, as downright evil a sense of humor as his making that pin seems to say he does.

I'm plain not asking. There's a pin with my face on it, and that's as close to immortality as I'm going to come. It puts me right up there with Ralph Ligouri and Jigger Sirois. If you don't tell anybody, I won't tell anybody. I'm flattered as hell and disgustingly delighted and I feel like I stole something big time, but you could torture me and I wouldn't confess to feeling anything but that a pin with my face on it is what I justly deserve. Sure.

We may even have one or two lying around for the asking.

I mean if Eddie Gaedel could have a baseball card in his image . . . who knows? In fifty years, when the name at the top of this column is unfamiliar not just to the entire rest of the world but to everybody, some nosy anthropologist/collector/catalogue compiler might just wonder who the odd-looking monkey on the pin might have been and put some outrageous price on it. Stranger things have happened.

Synchronous Idiosyncrasies

Oct. 19, 1987

THERE WILL ALWAYS BE A BRITAIN and there will always be those fiercely independent folks who fixate on British cars.

Somewhere, somehow it has entered legend that Americans became enchanted with foreign cars through an osmotic process involving contact with them during World War II.

In fact, during that war car owners hid their cars to keep them from being confiscated and were deprived of gasoline to drive the ones that weren't hidden. What's more, during those times, passenger car travel on the highway was at the very least perilous.

We fell in love with foreign cars after the war because some entrepreneurial Americans spotted them squirreled away in obscure corners of the European Theatre of Operations and thought they could make a buck by bringing them into the United States during a time (after peace was declared) when you couldn't get a domestic auto for love or money.

We fell in love with them because we were influenced by the earliest manifestation of the genus Yuppie, the first wave of travelers to a European continent where the lights had gone back on and from which anything, even what was then called "L'eau Qui Fait Psssst," later to become known as "Perrier," was saleable in America because it was, well, it was exotic.

It always rains in Portland except when they put on a car event, then it never rains; it wouldn't have dared rain during the All British Field Meet, the most outrageous orgy of sharp edges, piano wire wheels, winged mascots and polished wood since the fleets of the world passed in review for the coronation of Edward #7.

For two days at the end of August, Portland International Raceway was chock-a-block with: Austin-Healey (the honored marque on this 11th annual occasion), AC, Bentley, Dellow, Fairthorpe Electron, Ginetta, Healey Silverstone, Invicta, Jaguar, Lagonda, Morgan, Ogle,

Panther, Rover, Riley, Standard, Triumph, Vauxhall, Westwind and Y Series Tourer. Xebecs and Zebras were busy elsewhere.

They sat shining in the bright Pacific Northwest sun, in rows of one (the Fairthorpe and the AC) and rows of fifty (the MGs). There were north of 500 of them. Think of it. Imagine it. Believe it. More than 500 British cars still running, gathered together, not in some elephant's graveyard, but on the greensward of a municipally owned racetrack, in celebration of our past. Their owners had brought them there to rejoice together in the pleasures and agonies of membership in the band of brothers, in the legions of the S.U. Carburetor.

Postwar owners of British sports cars (the tiny, sad sedans that came over—Austin A30 for example—were all but ignored) and sports sedans banded together for self-protection. And in pride. And to exchange sparse and hard-to-get information about their balky, recalcitrant charges. They formed a nation within a nation. And within each nation, there were tribes.

There were the MGs, tattered, battered warriors who could be distinguished by their pugnacity. There were the Jaguar people. They came complete with Tam o'Shanters, stringback gloves and Norfolk jackets. You could spot them in a room by the way they were forever running their hands over anything made of wood. Morganatics were the easiest of all to identify: They simply could not bring themselves to sit in a chair without first checking to see whether it was fitted with a whoopee cushion. (For those of you spared the Morgan experience, understand that the adjusting mechanism on the seat consisted entirely and wholly of an inflatable cushion.) Less wealthy Austin-Healeyites, that is to say Sprite owners, sported glasses with lenses ground so their eyes bulged for all the world to notice. Rich Healeyites, the ones with the red and black Le Mans model, wore belted shoes (as even their bonnets were leather belted), belted blouses, belted shirts and some of them even had their cheeks louvered. Triumph persons always wore long-sleeved shirts. Their elbows were worn through to the bone from hanging out the cut-down doors of their TR2s and 3s.

The tribes may have been diverse, but the people were as one.

Individualistic, stubborn, wrongheaded, sure of themselves and though independent, also willing to share woes and sorrows as well as pleasures and parts. Indeed it was the best of times.

John and Fern Rollin began all this getting together business in Portland. They were members of the Jaguar Car Club, and they knew in their hearts that if anyone were to be able to organize such a zany gathering as a conclave of the followers of the S.U., it would have to be people used to dealing with that most idiosyncratic of creatures, the Jaguar. Not to mention creature keepers, Jaguar owners. (It had little to do with Anglophilia. Event chairman Kirk Krueger forever endeared himself to Brit-o-phobes by hanging the world's biggest Union Jack upside down in the banquet hall.) They were right. Compared to what they wrought in bringing together the British car owners of the Pacific Northwest, forging a peace agreement in the Middle East would be as easy as getting Orrin Hatch and Pat Robertson to shake hands.

It helps that Portland is the epicenter of a loosely organized collection of car clubs called the International Conference of Northwest Sports Car Clubs and has a couple of SCCA regions that exchange relatively friendly diplomatic missions.

It helps too that what seems to be the hub of parts and information distribution outside Los Angeles is in Portland. Places like Faspec, Vintage Motor Books, Northwest Import Parts, Steve Rollin prop. Steve Rollin? Ah, that would answer some unasked but obvious questions about involvement on the part of the second, perhaps even the third, generation. It's in the blood, some people say. The young are supposed to take a step beyond their elders, no? John Rollin is the successful proprietor of a business selling carpet. He spends what he makes on cars. His son is the successful proprietor of a business selling restored MGs and MG parts. He makes what he earns on cars. The very definition of generational progress.

There was a purity of purpose in the mists of the past. So who paid the piper? It's hard to remember. There were stories of amateur racers who had pawned their fiancées' engagement rings. There were other stories of dark-side activities, and there are records somewhere of antisocial behavior reprehensible enough to have landed the behavers in jail. One of the great venues for the celebration of the car was in the Bahamas during Nassau Speed Weeks, simon-pure. Sure. Talk to Speed Weeks veterans today and they'll tell you about Lola and March distribution deals done on paper stretched so thin it wouldn't bear up under the weight of ink. Yes, indeed.

Cars? Cheater cars? Oh, goodness gracious no. Peter Revson never ever ran a Cougar in the old Trans-Am so feathery light it had to be weighed with a bogus set of tires Bud Moore had filled with concrete. Revson's own backup helmet never had a filling of lead poured into its inside so that he could saunter over to the scales and toss it into the driver's seat. Racing as it was done during the grand old times was pure. Believe it.

At noon on Sunday, the more than 100 Austin-Healeys registered were given a parade. It was to be led by Bill Bolton's car; well, one of Bill Bolton's cars. Bill has seven Austin-Healeys; this one was a particular pride. Bolton is a vice president of computer development for U.S. Natural Resources in Portland. He'd owned MGs and Morgans and then he married a woman who loved—plain loved—Healeys. Theirs must have been a strong, good marriage.

Now in his early 50s, Bill is a widower and he seems to see many of the values and the charms and the cleverness his late wife saw in the sheet metal of the cars she loved.

His car, designated to lead the parade, was just a good ol' Austin-Healey 100-6, a 1960 BN7 Mk 1. Um, er, with some cleverness added, as in the aluminum body panels. And some charm, specifically the magneto ignition and the Ruddspeed intake manifold and triple one-and-a-half-inch S.U.s. Cheater car? Don't you believe it. There wasn't a set of concrete-filled tires in sight. You wouldn't have suspected the car of a breach of manners from its behavior, much less its demeanor. A scrutineer's conundrum indeed.

Inevitably things began to change. Of all activities with the automobile, it was racing more than anything that brought change about. The primitive prescription in the SCCA's General Competition Rules for a borax dip in which to fireproof your balloon loose Dunlop driver's suit gave way to something a little better through the magic of chemistry. Pete Snell's death at Arcata propelled Dr. George Snively to investigate helmet standards and to set new ones according to real world tests.

You may be sure that through it all there was a howl set up that reached the moon on dark mornings in the tech lines. "Put a roll bar in this car? Ruin the looks of my LeMans? Whose head is it anyway?" Ah, my, the arguments. The disputes. The debates. The endless exhausting floor arguments from Westport to Oakland.

The cost of progress is the pursuit of sanity. Sanity and safety. How long has it been since someone has been killed at Indy? The cost of progress is the end of isolation, the end of recalcitrance, the end of fierce independence, the end of tribal government, the end of individualism.

Jerry Cathey has the prettiest Healey of the lot. And there are more nice ones here than Donald Healey saw in a week's oversight of the plant. It's just what it should be: a red and black LeMans. Cathey is a vintage racer, an autocrosser, a British Field Meet participant. He plain loves cars. He is president of University Hardware, a TrueValue marketer, and he is a Roberto Guerrero fan. The field meet, taking place a week before Guerrero's accident at the Speedway, is thus innocent of the shadow of Roberto's crash. Cathey is not yet cast in its gloom. He is in discussion about an upcoming vintage race in Seattle.

Cathey has met Roberto and he likes him. He is unaware Guerrero is a full-bore safety fanatic. Listen to a middle-aged man who has realized his dream in the LeMans on the same subject. "A roll bar? In my LeMans? Well, you know I have a removable one and I use it, but to put in a permanent bar would mean cutting into the rear deck and I won't spoil the car's looks.

"Yes. I know. Yes. I've heard the arguments. But it is my head, isn't it?

"Probably doesn't make much sense. Still. I've wanted this car forever. Isn't it nice?"

Sometimes the early car clubs, they weren't all SCCA regions by a long shot, would stage a strange event called a concours. Originally, the progenitor of the SCCA required that the owner of a car must offer it to another member before selling it on the open market. But that was long discarded practice, and at the concours there was some surreptitious looking and lusting and, well, if you have to know, buying and selling. Not much, mind you. Some. After all, how else were you to get a used sports car? They were available at the stores that sold them new, but it wasn't the same. Buying at a car store just didn't provide a sense of being admitted to cult membership. It wasn't about making friends. You passed money and signatures. Nobody passed signs and secret handshakes.

That's exaggeration, of course, but not much. It was probably more true in the east than on the frontier that since a given social cachet came with the ownership of a sports car, it required a certain social standing to be admitted to the circles in which they were owned. It pretty much followed that if you had to be part of the crowd, there remained a sort of vestigial screening process. To say it kindly, the sports car crowd perpetuated itself in the reflections of its fenders.

On Sunday, the paddock area of PIR became the parking lot for the British Field Meet and in it were parked two lines and then three and then four of cars for sale. A nice Bugeye ($1,795 plus T and L new) was $6,995; you could have an MG TF 1500 ($1,995 West Coast showroom price) for $18,000; even a '61 Mini had climbed to $4,995, three times and then some what you might have paid in Aquarian dollars.

Jim Feldman showed his lovely AC Ace-Bristol, black with red, and not for sale, but he did say it would bring $35,000, almost six times what you had to write the check for if you wanted a new one from Hollywood Sports Cars at the end of the '50s.

Do not ask about Jaguars.

The price of admission has risen. And so what? We are older, we are richer, there are more of us bidding for fewer cars. We want as much to belong as we ever did and the rewards of belonging are as great. If anything, the glorious day in the Portland sunshine showed they are greater.

They were "them" then and we were "us."

We are still "us" now, but so are they.

Chapter Five

Personalities

" You can take the asphalt bullrings out of the boy, but the tar macadam clods of Willow Springs and Paramount Ranch stick to the ear cavities and between the toes through the Gasometer and the Carousel no matter how hard you try to swab them out. "

Leon sat me down early in 1986 to tell me something he thought I needed to hear if I was going to write for him at AutoWeek. *"The cars are just objects, they come and they go," he said. "Events that seem momentous in the news cycle turn out to be ephemeral. For any real writer, the topic is always people—who they are, what motivates them, how they got that way." True to his word, Leon wrote most about people. Whether they were the big names in the headlines or the workers on assembly lines and racing circuits, they were interesting—often he didn't like what they were doing and wasn't shy about saying so in print. Sometimes he found them admirable and made friends. And frequently, the same people stirred both admonition and admiration, because if you can't be honest with your friends, what does friendship mean?*

Salute to the Captain

May 28, 1990

IN MAY, THE INDIANAPOLIS MOTOR SPEEDWAY is Page One sports of every newspaper in the land. TV evening news pounces on the local angle to justify leading with Indy crashes and hyperspeed.

When newsies talk about Indy, they talk most often about the Legend of Roger. It's Horatio Alger. It's General George Patton.

Trouble is, encomiums to Penske the Tactical Genius and Penske the Money Maestro miss the point. They overlook the Man's real achievement, which is this: He brought auto racing out from behind the Red Neck Kerchief.

Sit these days in a new grandstand seat just up from turn four at the Speedway, enjoying its perspective on the long front chute, and you can profit from an equivalent perspective on the Penske contribution. When he arrived at the Grand Old Track, it had a wonderful tradition; it also had hidebound rules, old-fashioned garages, primitive facilities, provincial teams and a world outlook that went about as far as Brown County, Indiana.

It was a true reflection of the place of racing in sports. Now some mourn the passing of racing's charm—its sweat and its down-home manners. Understandable. For those who lived inside the magic bullring, that sweat was the mark of good work in a better cause. Those manners, however rough-hewn, evinced the simple decency of artisans who respected each other's achievements. But neither manners nor sweat offered much promise for the future of Indy car racing.

When Roger Penske arrived at the Speedway in 1969, he came with ambition and vision. He also came with a few crates of car wax and a box of brooms. "How You Look Is What You Are" was a Penske motto. "Effort Equals Results" was another. They were to be the hallmarks of the most successful invasion since Attila dropped in on the Roman Empire.

As you might expect, the Penske arrival engendered considerable resentment. There is no society so insular, so exclusionary, so uninterested

235

in receiving new people—much less new ideas—as racing. Bright, clean Penske race cars were an object of derision. Right up until they began blowing the doors off everything on the track. Suddenly shininess was next to winningness, and clean cars became the foundation of a new religion, at least a new superstition. But clean cars were only a superficial manifestation of the Penske racing revolution. Along with the likes of Pat Patrick, Carl Haas and Teddy Mayer, Penske brought contemporary business values into the arena in which he competed. It is no exaggeration to say that Penske's vision, his ability to find and attract talent and his broad view changed the fact and the image of American racing. Championship Auto Racing Teams is the first and best example of the Penske world view where racing is concerned. His absolute belief in the worthiness of the business perspective is reflected in the structure of the organization, an association of men with a common purpose. With Pat Patrick, he led team owners away from USAC when that organization became self-absorbed and uncaring about the interests of its constituents. In effect, Penske reconstituted racing when he led CART onto the high ground.

Vision is indispensable to progress, but the high ground is never gained without remarkable people. Without exception, Penske watchers remark on his ability to attract and keep men of great talent, beginning with a new variety of racer. From Mark Donohue to Rick Mears, drivers of the true Penske stripe are thoughtful, analytical and marketable.

To see how Penske graduates populate successful race teams, you need look no further than Porsche's Derrick Walker, who still admires the Master even though they've parted ways. Mario Ilien and Paul Morgan, former Cosworth engineers who are the soul of Ilmor engineering, are people Penske identified as strong enough to become the foundation of a major program, and he not only backed them but convinced Chevrolet to do likewise.

The scope of Indianapolis racing today, in contrast to even 10 years ago, is very much a projection of Penske horizons. Its major TV audience, the involvement of 95 team sponsors, its $150 million in revenues are indicators of great economic health. That's not to say

Interviewing Rick Mears in the Penske garage at Indianapolis' Gasoline Alley.
AutoWeek Archives

the sport is without problems, but its vision is at least appropriate to its aspirations, a lot more than could have been said of the backyard efforts of the late '60s.

Not much of this would be worthwhile, no matter how profitable, without at least a hint of commensurate decency—an area in which many insist Penske is deficient. The Rahal radial case says otherwise. It involved both a Penske benefactor, Goodyear, and a Penske fiefdom, Michigan International Raceway. It also involved live television of a Penske 500 Mile Race. Bobby Rahal, early out in the first official practice session with the newly developed radials, smacked the turn two wall at nearly 215 mph. Examination of the wreck was inconclusive but did not rule out the possibility that the tire was at fault; there were no old-fashioned bias-plies available. That was enough for Penske. Despite pressure from the network to go ahead with the telecast, he postponed his own race and sent the crowd home.

Penske's reputation for coldness in pursuit of business was firmly established when it was (accurately) reported he hired his first great driver, Mark Donohue, at the funeral of racer Walt Hansgen. Penske confirms he talked to Donohue at the time. But there is a closer funeral story, and it is mine. Peter Revson, one of the great drivers of his time, a Penske friend and Mark Donohue's archcompetitor, was given a burial service at which Penske and I were pallbearers. I had just finished collaboration on a book with Revson, who seemed then and still seems now one of the greatest gentlemen I have ever known. As I rose to deliver a eulogy, I found myself unexpectedly in tears. At which point I felt a hand on my knee, keeping me in my seat, and a voice in my ear whispering that I should take a minute to myself, nobody would notice. It was a moment I desperately needed, and my very human advisor was, of course, Penske—the cold, unfeeling businessman.

Next month sometime, having won the most races (60) and the most poles (80) of any entrant in Indy car history, Roger Penske will submit his 500th entry to a race promoter. Happy 500th, Roger, and all the best. You've earned it.

Taking Care of Business

ROGER PENSKE'S IRREPRESSIBLE APPROACH
IS REFLECTED IN HIS 25TH TRIP TO INDY
May 17, 1993

WHEN A 34-YEAR-OLD ROGER PENSKE finally decided in 1969 he was ready for Indianapolis Motor Speedway, his hair was shorter and darker than it is today, and his company was not yet on the radar screens of the people who compiled lists of the top 400 in America, but other than that, he was very much the Penske of the ninth decade of the 20th century. The same could not be said for Indianapolis.

The cars were very different, the facilities were very different, most of all the money was very different.

For example, each of the 84 cars for the 1969 race cost its owner $1,000 to enter—which, considering it bestowed full access and owner's credentials, was the cheapest ticket in town. It was such a good deal, some of the entries didn't even exist.

Although the great tire company wars had subsided, a good many of the cars that did exist and did run were actually owned by Firestone or Goodyear.

There were 13 different chassis in the '69 event; of the top 12 finishers, nine were different makes. "Designers" as such were an unknown breed. Crew chiefs welded up chassis based on their own inspiration or somebody else's design. (Three years later, Grant King was said to have used a picture of the '71 McLaren from a Goodyear calendar as the pattern for chalk marks on the floor. He laid tubing over the marks and called the resulting chassis a "Kingfish.")

Most of the cars arrived in enclosed goose neck haulers or on open trailers. Parking lots were gravel. There was no such thing as a hospitality motor home; the accessory companies might have had offices under the grandstands on the main straight, but the extent of their catering consisted of shrink-wrapped packages of ham, bologna or cheese, nestled next to a couple of loaves of bread and, as the month wore on, an increasingly crust-laden jar of mustard. The first VIP suites—outside turn two—would not open for four years. Just 10 years earlier, only the center lane of the garage areas was paved. Rodger Ward's winning car, which was housed on the south side of Gasoline Alley, had to be pushed back and forth to the track over cinders. Only eight years before Penske's first appearance, the main straight had still been bricks. Two years before that, his driver could have practiced in a T-shirt.

Lap speeds in 1969 were right at 170 mph; tellingly, top speed for the Turbo Fords was just about what a Cosworth will turn today. But there was considerable slowing for turns. Spins often avoided the wall; the technique when losing the rear end was to crank the wheel to the left and spin down onto the grass.

Most interestingly, considering the talents and predilections of the man who was about to make such an extraordinary impression on Indy, as of '69 it was typical for 8 or 10 cars to qualify without a main sponsor. Owners and crew chiefs would then cast around for a sponsor whose car hadn't made the show. Knowledgeable local companies would wait until qualifying was over and try to hook up with the best unsponsored car in the race.

(One insider tells the story of a car owner who approached him with a main sponsorship availability for $2,500. The deal never went together because the man he sent over to the owner tried to bargain the price down to $2,000.)

In 1969, Penske's driver, Mark Donohue, qualified the team's 4wd Lola Turbo Offy fourth and got up to third before a magneto problem forced a long pit stop. The team's four-year victory plan would only take three, but Roger's influence would extend far beyond even the immense consequence of his on-track success. Some of the brighter people inside the fences understood, in 1969, that the Penske Era had begun at the Speedway. It wouldn't take long for almost everyone there to become aware that the place was changing irrevocably.

To those who watched approvingly, Penske was the Man Who Could Make Miracles. Others, far more critical of what they saw as the transformation of a Grand Old Institution into just another slickly packaged sports promotion and who identified Penske as the self-centered automaton responsible, cast him as the Machine That Changed the World.

By 8:31 on April 17, 1993, at Long Beach, on the morning the King verdict was announced, Roger Penske had not only been awake for two hours and 36 minutes, but he had completed his morning run around the track, showered, dressed, worked the phones in the real world and finished breakfast at the Marlboro compound to the ocean side of the paddock.

It was 35 years and three days after he drove—and failed to finish—his first race, in a Corvette.

Thirty-two years since he had been named Driver of the Year by *Sports Illustrated.*

Thirty years since he entered, and won, his first NASCAR Grand National, beating Joe Weatherly and Darel Dieringer in the Riverside 250.

Twenty-nine years since he came to the conclusion that while there was no future in being a racing driver, there might be a significant future in being an owner and entrant.

Twenty-seven years since he formed Penske Racing with Mark Donohue as his driver.

And approximately 31 hours and 11 minutes before his newest protégé, mini nova Paul Tracy, would win his first Indy car race and the 72nd of the Penske Era, including eight Indy 500s and an equal number of Indy car national championships.

Eight thirty-one is uncharacteristically late for Penske to be arriving at the office, but today he has had to deal with a special problem. After the last verdict, all hell broke loose; there was massive disorder, a condition that is the very incarnation of all that he despises. You cannot control verdicts, and unfortunately you cannot even control reactions to them, but you can damn well control how you deal with those reactions, and all morning he has been going over the disaster plan at Longo Toyota, America's largest retail dealership. The

A chat with Danny Sullivan during the latter's time with Penske Racing. Leon would interview Danny after every race to create the "Editor at Speed" column that appeared under Danny's byline in *AutoWeek*. *AutoWeek Archives*

cars will be stored in the massive parking lots beneath the building. Employees will be sent home "because we don't want any of our people at risk." Penske is comfortable that his plans will be carried out. The man on the scene is the person it is said Roger Penske most trusts in the entire world: his number two son Greg—the second coming of Roger himself.

Now, good fortune has followed good planning, exactly as it did at the Speedway during the first of the Penske four-year plans, and the verdict has rendered everything moot. That's the good news. The bad news is that Roger must now resign himself to one of the most difficult tasks that confronts him anywhere, anytime: He must bend his time to fit somebody else's schedule; untimed practice begins at 9:00.

Here in the paddock, his office is inside one of the two great black Marlboro Penske transporters, all chrome and air-flowed wheels that look like they are auditioning for *Blade Runner II*.

At 8:32, just as he prepares to mount the stairs for a meeting inside, his sponsor-hospitality chief begs an audience to resolve "some problems at Indy only you can solve." She has invoked two magic phrases, the first beginning with "Sponsor," the second with "Only you." Potential problems entertaining sponsors at Indy are high on the Penske list; for all intents and purposes, Roger is the inventor of the modern sponsor contract. He has certainly shaped the current sponsor relationship. Very early in his racing career, when almost everyone was an amateur and the racing world was free of commercial contamination, Penske noticed a company name painted on a competitor's car at Nassau. It stuck with him, and later, he mentioned the fact to an acquaintance in Philadelphia. "Call these people," said the man, a magazine space salesman, who turned out to know the executives at DuPont who would be handling the marketing of their Telar and Zerex antifreezes. Instead, Penske wrote a five-page proposal and got the Telar—and later and famously—the Zerex sponsorships. Today, Penske's Marlboro deal is said to be in the neighborhood of $20 million a year. It is certain Marlboro not only values the relationship but values Penske. He sits on the parent company's board of directors.

It's 8:36: Inside the transporter, Paul Tracy is perched on the built-in, full-length wooden storage cabinet that lines the far wall, talking to his race engineer. When Penske climbs the metal stairs to join them, the engineer pauses, Tracy falls silent. Both turn to Roger, now standing in a characteristic pose: arms crossed in front of him, head cocked to the side. He wears the invisible cloak of great generals and world statesmen, and so despite the uniformed egalitarianism of a race team, there is no mistaking the power center. It is one of the fundamental secrets of the Penske success, always has been, always will be, that wherever he goes, people listen. Somebody once said Penske's speech was like "a verbal ticker tape punched with robotically mechanical syllables." With only the slightest nod to civility—"You all right?"—Penske gets straight to the point. "I thought you were going to softer rear springs like on Emmo's car?" Very early in his career, Roger gave an interview in which he laid down the principal precept of Penske car preparation: "I want the car to be perfect before we start." He saw to it then, he has seen to it since, he sees to it now.

Tracy, whose on-track behavior in the last race has brought into question his willingness to adhere to the Code of Roger, seems all deference. "Should we go softer?"

Like an automatic weapon firing in bursts, Penske addresses the minutiae of car set-up. If somehow the world could eavesdrop, it would not be surprised. Penske is said to be a master of detail, and if ever there were confirmation of his uncanny understanding of the gynecology of a race car, it could be found in this exchange. By now it's been broadened to include the car's designer, one of the two of its engine architects, the team manager and a former owner of one of the great Formula One teams, now a senior racing counselor to Penske.

It's 8:44: "What do you think?" Good thing for the Penske legend the question is asked in the privacy of the transporter. If conventional wisdom practitioners eavesdropping on Roger's oversight of the race car would be reassured by his encyclopedic knowledge, they would be shocked by the vision of Roger Penske asking for advice, Penske asking for agreement, Penske seeking consensus. Yet that is exactly where the mythologists are most in peril of veering widely off the mark, missing perhaps the greatest of the Penske attributes: the ability to create ownership in an idea—to invest the people he needs to rely on with a sense that what they are doing is pursuing a goal of their very own.

It's 8:46: "Paul." This is not Paul-the-race-car-driver but Paul-the-engine-architect. With what seems for all the world like a mischievous smile, he says to him: "We're doing a V-12. How long does it take your guys to do a pattern for a block?" Sometimes it's really hard to keep up. Roger has just taken a sharp right, and driven into a whole different country. He is in the land of Great Diesel Engines, back in Detroit at the company whose minority partner is General Motors and whose principal owner and chairman is Roger Penske, and he is asking his other engine company partner for a little perspective.

"You do it in 12 weeks? We take two years and two million just to decide what we're going to do." It may be or it may not be that Penske is serious; what is certain is that his mission in life is to get things done, and if having a pattern for a 1,350-horsepower marine diesel made by somebody who creates race engines is the best way to do it, he will not hesitate.

Come to think of it, Penske did the very same thing when it became clear that using somebody else's racing engine relegated him to everybody else's field of play. At that point, he ferreted out two Cosworth employees burning with the entrepreneurial spirit, and set them up in business, as Ilmor Engineering, with Chevy as a 25 percent partner—and Roger with an equal share. That goes very far, by the way, in explaining why Paul-the-engine-architect and Roger are having this conversation in the first place. Yet another reason why when Roger speaks, whole legions of people in sponsor-logo'd shirts listen.

It's 8:45: It's time to go out to the line. The car is there, the driver has left a minute ago—R.P. walks down the stairs at the side of the transporter, through the open flaps of the immaculate M*A*S*H tent that serves the team as the Long Beach operating room, and out into . . . chaos.

Would the L.A. Raiders open their dressing room to spectators? Would the Lakers walk through the stands on their way to the floor? At Long Beach, beneath the leering Southern California sun, $15 buys owners' rights to climb into the uniform pockets of the teams, and at those prices there is a biblical swarm of half T's, tank tops, tattoos and sweats; torn knees, patched knees, naked knees and lycra; big hair, red hair and no hair; fat arms, bony arms; Michelin thighs and sleek thighs pulling and shoving for equal access. By mid-morning it's only the suntan lotion lavished on all those limbs that makes it possible for anybody to move at all.

Into this sea of lubricity steps Roger Penske, who at Long Beach, as at Indianapolis, as almost everywhere he goes, is the Biggest Draw of All, bigger than Craig T. Nelson here to drive in the celebrity race, bigger than Jim Nabors, who will sing "Back Home Again in Indiana" at the Speedway, big almost as Michael Jackson if he were here, which, thank God he is not, because the seething, tumbling, demanding swirl around Roger is bad enough.

Signing hats to the right, programs to the left, he parts the waters breasting nubility and suet alike until at last he is through the swarm, past the credential gate and out onto the pits, where it is only a little better. Because he has at least as many people who have to talk to him, who need him to talk to them, who insist on being seen with him even if it's only for a second, as on the outside. And now, with one foot inside his own racing pit, he's stopped one last time. It is H.L. Galles, patriarch of the Galles clan, father of the man who runs Little Al Unser and Danny Sullivan and one of those wonderfully gracious westerners who has taken a second of Roger's time to say "how proud he was of that boy of yours." He means Roger's son Mark, 16, who, as a participant of his prep school outward bound travel group, had been feared lost in a widely publicized national scare earlier in the year and who had, as one of the heroes of the group, helped the others to safety.

To which Roger, who is widely seen as a man who bleeds ice, answered, "That showed him what he could do, which is terrific. The boy is sometimes too hard on himself."

Something Roger Penske should be able to recognize when he sees it.

Thirty-seven days before his newest race winner would have a shot at the record books as the sixth Penske driver to win the Indy 500, Roger Penske arrived at his office at Detroit Diesel Corporation in Redford Township at the more customary hour of 7:45.

It was 29 years since he gave up racing to buy McKean Chevrolet in Philadelphia.

Twenty-four years since the formation of Penske Corporation.

Twenty years since he bought Michigan International Speedway, which with Nazareth Raceway (bought seven years ago) became the principal piece of Penske Automotive Performance Group. Eleven years since he formed the joint venture with Hertz Corporation that became Hertz Penske Truck Leasing, which today, 100 percent owned by Penske, rents and leases 57,000 vehicles.

Eight years since he bought Longo Toyota, the centerpiece of a retail automobile division that sells 40,000 vehicles a year.

Five years since he formed a partnership with GM that is now an 80 percent ownership in DDC.

And approximately 72 hours before he will make his next blockbuster announcement, which is that he and Mercedes-Benz have joined forces to produce and distribute a commercial diesel engine in North America to be badged Mercedes in Europe and DDC on this side of the ocean.

There doesn't seem to be any question that the new venture will boost Penske Corporation even beyond its $2.8 billion revenues and therefore higher than its present *Forbes* standing of 37th-largest private corporation in the country right behind Hallmark Cards. Nor will the new partnership dim the Penske reputation for entering into remarkable joint ventures, including the one with General Electric Capital that helps him fund Hertz Penske Leasing. Not to mention, of course, the GM partnership and certainly including the partnership that is represented by the very existence of Penske Performance Group, a company Roger started to service his sponsors, er, partners. A whole

247

company, please note, that exists to help cement the relationships that have built Roger into the Most Successful Racer on the North American Continent while serving coincidentally as a pattern for everybody who would follow in his tire tracks.

But none of that is on his mind now, 45 minutes after arrival at Detroit Diesel Corporation on this particular Friday.

He is sitting in his windowless office—the one with the wall-sized map and the rose tweed carpet, the wind tunnel model of his '91 Indy winner and the huge photos of Ilmor Chevrolet and DD Series 60 engines—that looks forever like an admiral's stateroom on a nuclear submarine. He is in his shirtsleeves with his glasses slipped down on his nose and he is huddling with his chief of administration, deciding how to tell his employees.

Most of them are hourly workers who belong to Local 163 of the UAW. Five years after he bought the company, with market penetration increased from 3.3 percent to more than 26 percent, with the ledgers turned from red $600 million in the seven years before Penske bought it to strong profitability from $1.4 billion in sales forecast for this year, the people out on the floor are believers; and what they believe in is Roger.

At least that's what Jim Brown—now half stretched out in a chair in front of Penske's desk, looking like an unpretentious anesthesiologist relaxing in the doctors' lounge—would like us to accept. Brown is the chairman of the local, and he almost can't wait to summon his very favorite statistics to make his point. When Penske bought it, Detroit Diesel had 1,500 hourly employees. There were 2,700 open grievances on the table with General Motors. Now, with the hourly work force increased by about 250, the grievances total 14.

It all has to do with communication, he says, making the people who work on the floor feel a part of things. "The average employee in this plant probably knows as much about the business as the average executive in any other company." Ownership, signing people onto ideas, getting them to believe it's as much theirs as it is his. Roger and his president Lud Koci hold update meetings three or four times a year in which they meet with small groups of employees and Open the Books. Tell Them Everything. Answer All Questions. Make Them Owners.

Which explains why Chairman Brown, like Roger, is concerned that nobody find out about the Mercedes-Benz deal from anybody else but Roger Penske. In a few minutes, Penske will excuse himself to make a telephone call to the No. 2 man at GM—the very same man who has been quoted as saying, "GM has learned incredible lessons from what's being done here"—with the final details of the announcement, but between now and then, Penske will go over his daily business reports. They take up two lined sheets, and they sit on his beautifully clean glass-topped desk next to the multicolored folders containing his monthly business reports. Both encapsulate everything worth knowing about the arithmetic of the Penske Empire so that wherever Roger is and whatever he is doing he can find out what's happening up to the second.

And that is exactly, precisely what scares a lot of people when they think of the $2.8 billion company named for the man who can't be replaced. "Things would never be the same," says Penske Corp's Mr. Inside, Walter Czarnecki. "But we are a conservative company that has benefited from traditional means of financing precisely because we've been able to convince banks we have a stable structure and a sound business strategy."

The phrases linger in the air long enough for the mind to travel south from Detroit to central Indiana. Nobody would dispute that stable structure and sound business strategy are in place at the Speedway, largely attributable to the bright new management there. Still, the fact that life itself would continue to change at IMS at almost exactly the dizzying rate it has been changing for the last quarter of a century is as much the result of the influence of Penske as anything else. And that has a life and a momentum of its own.

"We are smack dab in the middle of the Penske Era (which could easily last into the next century), and when it is over, the residue of it all will linger for decades," says racing historian Carl Hungness. And it is true. And it is visible. And when the legions of sponsors and ranks of luxury suites and miles of new paving and carloads of new plumbing and inventories of new hotel rooms and reels of new telecommunications and banquet halls of new caterers and runways of new fashionable people—and most of all, open-mind-fuls of new attitudes are contrasted to the simple, homely racetrack of the '70s, the differences are stunning.

"The business of running an Indianapolis 500 car is now about as businesslike as it gets, and the state of the sport is due in no small part to Roger Penske."

Which must mean that somehow, in some way he influenced not only by example, but by . . . what? Worthiness? A knack for innovation? Or could it be—of all astonishing things—a willingness to invest in and rely on other people?

"Roger Penske did more than simply play the game," says Mr. Inside. "He stayed within the foul lines. He didn't try to become bigger than Indy, he respected its traditions, and he deferred to its heroes."

Which is the way change really works, of course, giving credit where it's due and shifting landscapes for everyone's benefit, not just your own. It's the way change works in racing, and at great institutions like the Indianapolis Motor Speedway, and maybe at places that have seemed as immovable as, yes, even General Motors.

Racing data compiled by Steve Schuler, Auto Racing Analysis.

Voice of the 500

HAPPY ANNIVERSARY, SID COLLINS.
HAPPY ANNIVERSARY, MIDDLE AMERICA.
June 10, 1972

FOR 25 YEARS THIS WEEK, SID COLLINS, the voice of the 500, has been oozing out of 100 million radios carrying the message that the 500 is the "greatest spectacle in racing" ("I invented that") and by now the country is beginning to believe. From humble beginnings to the Voice of Motorsports, the story of Sid Collins is the story of the spectacular growth in popularity of that curious ritual in central Indiana that means auto racing to America as no other race in the country. Indianapolis is racing; Sid Collins is Indianapolis.

When Sid Collins began it all 25 years ago, the broadcast of the race featured a local sports announcer—it was all that Indianapolis had. He did a 15-minute warmup, ran down the starting lineup, called the start of the race, came back for a couple of five-minute progress reports, did a quick interview in victory lane and went off the air. The program was carried by 26 stations and went to maybe a million listeners.

Today, Collins heads a team of 11 announcers and a staff of 35 who are otherwise involved in the production. It lasts over four hours and it is carried by 1,200 stations in this country alone. Whatever it used to cost for a 30-second spot, it costs that no longer. ("I don't really want to say exactly what the figure is; I wouldn't want to step on anyone's toes.") It is estimated that the broadcast of the Indy 500 is the most profitable sports venture on radio since *Fibber McGee and Molly*.

Collins is a young-looking if slightly jowly 49. A graduate of Indiana University, he came back from the Great War wounded to become a recruiting officer whose burning ambition was to get into broadcasting. He tried the big time—Chicago. They wanted no part of him. He was willing to settle for Indianapolis—they were no more

251

cordial there. So Collins, who had come back with high hopes, "was anxious to go to New York as soon as possible and be a national M.C. type like Bert Parks," found himself, aged 23, in a little station in a remote town in Indiana doing just about everything and anything.

But talent will come out, not even rural Indiana can hide it, and almost before anyone knew it Collins was in Indianapolis. From there it was a small step to the broadcast of the 500—on the south turn where he could see both turns one and two. "In 1950, Bill Slater was ill, and they looked for a replacement for him as chief announcer for the Mutual Network. They chose me."

Collins, visions of Bert Parks-like fame dancing in his head, was unsatisfied with the brief coverage of the race. "I suggested [along with Gil Berry] that we go on for four and a half hours, from start to finish. Do the whole race. Gil would sell it and I would find announcers and produce it and plan the four-hour coverage. It had never been done before. The first year it was tried was '52. We took a wild chance and I was allowed to hire five announcers. The reaction was less than enthusiastic—even Wilbur Shaw said, 'What are you going to talk about? It'll be boring as hell.' Well, we must have done something right because we're still using the same basic format we used then."

There was one little problem: Mutual wouldn't clear four and a half hours of time. In one of the great business decisions in the history of radio, they turned the program down. Undaunted, Collins, who had by then incorporated with the Speedway to form IMSN, International Motor Speedway Network, spurred the building of the Speedway's own competitive network of stations, including all four in Indianapolis. It worked; the rest is history.

There have been great moments in the 25 years of Collins' tenure with IMS, and there have been godawful ones. One of the worst was the 1964 crash and fire which took the lives of Eddie Sachs and Dave McDonald. The race was red flagged at 11:06 a.m. and did not restart until a few minutes before 1 p.m. Collins is proud of the eulogy he delivered for Sachs (there was very little mention of McDonald; he was a newcomer and worse than that, a sports car driver), "all off the cuff."

He also volunteers that he was ready for anything. "I always prepare a suitcase with material in there for thought starters." Not even a double fatality could catch Sid Collins napping.

But it was the discovery of a young Englishman, Donald Davidson, that marks Collins' career as innovative. Davidson, whose near eidetic memory allows him to rattle off fact, figure and anecdote about every driver who ever ran at the Speedway, was a projectionist in a London newsreel theater when he wrote Collins asking for his fare to Indianapolis. "Thinking this was rather presumptuous," Collins recalls, "I wrote him one of those 'don't call us we'll call you' things." Davidson, not a man to be put off by niceties of etiquette, promptly came over on his own, looked up Collins and proposed he go on the broadcast. Collins, nonplussed but polite to the end, chose to challenge Davidson's claim that he could tell him anything and everything about any driver Collins cared to name. Collins mentioned something about Spider Webb, certain that Davidson had never heard of him. Davidson gave him chapter and verse "without taking a breath. I had to get out a book to see if he was right and he was. So I hired him." Davidson almost immediately became one of the most popular additions to the 500 broadcast. Collins paid him $75.

The questions crowd one upon the other; there is so much that Collins has seen and so much he must know. Have things changed so much in 25 years? Who is the greatest driver of them all? What does it mean to him, looking back on all those years?

It is Collins' virtue and at the same time his great weakness that he cannot offend anyone. He has so many friends; they are all his friends, everyone he has come to know, everyone he has ever talked about. It would be indecent to suggest anything critical about them. Still, "if you have to choose one driver, one outstanding driver, I would have to say it would be A.J. Foyt." But things have changed so much, "how can you compare Foyt with, say, Vukovich? It would be like comparing Cassius Clay [sic] with John L. Sullivan." Today, the tight little world of championship racing is no longer that series of friendly provincial outings that it used to be. Collins says with some awe about the drivers,

"Why, you see them at a banquet or something and they are wearing ties and jackets. They're businessmen."

It must be very strange for a simple Indiana sports broadcaster to meet and deal with this confusing, tumbling, seething multimedia world. Collins is just a little puzzled and hurt that television has not discovered him and that he is not Jim McKay. After all, he was first, and after all, he is the voice of the 500. But still, Sid Collins cannot bring himself to be really critical. "I think motorsports must be as difficult or more difficult than any other sport to broadcast. You know, I haven't just done racing. I've broadcast over 1,000 basketball games and, before I quit that, over 300 football games. I've done all kinds of sports." Pressed, Collins will admit reluctantly that he is disappointed in the job TV is doing on motor racing. "I'm not sure what they can do," he says wistfully. "But I don't think they're doing the best job possible." But he hastens to add that he's not putting the knock on anyone in particular. Especially not Jim McKay.

The Indianapolis 500 is a Midwestern phenomenon. It is loud and hokey and basic and archaic. It appeals to the simplest emotions; it does not pretend to do anything else. The race rewards Midwestern virtues: persistence, courage and willingness to come to grips with the basic elements of survival and conquer them. In this electronic age, there is nothing slick and nothing sophisticated about Indianapolis. Perhaps that is why it has such enormous appeal in the heartland.

Perhaps that is why Sid Collins is its ideal spokesman.

Being Teddy

IT IS NOT EASY BEARING THE MANTLE OF
AMERICAN RACING'S SENIOR STATESMAN.
PARTICULARLY WHEN ALMOST EVERYONE BUT
YOUR EQUALLY BATTLE-SCARRED OPPONENT
HAS FORGOTTEN YOU. AND HE LIES IN WAIT.
June 18, 1984

EDWARD EVERETT MAYER wouldn't even begin to be Teddy without enigma. Herewith the enigma of Teddy:

• He is an American aristo (a characterization with which he agrees) who has no business getting his hands dirty with March cars and Tom Sneva but does better at it than anyone in this galaxy or the next. Substitute McLaren cars and James Hunt if it makes you feel any better. Teddy wouldn't care.

• He is a baby-skinned, white-haired man who was almost certainly a baby-skinned, white-haired adolescent and a baby-skinned, white-haired college kid. He does business as though he were chairman of all the barracudas. He is 48 years old and has always been. He enjoys helicopter skiing in Canada almost as much as he likes going home after his team wins a race and having a tuna fish sandwich. By himself, by the way.

• He flies home to Esher, England, after every race in the steerage section of the airplane because the flight is billed to Mayer Motor Racing. He flies first class when he's writing a personal check for the trip.

• He is the other giant—with Roger Penske, his longtime antagonist—in American racing who would rather not be. In American racing. E.E. Mayer is an internationalist.

· · ·

Teddy Mayer doesn't know why everybody called his younger brother "Timmy." He was referred to as "Tim" by his proper Scranton family. Scranton, by the way, with a serious capital "S." Capital "S" because *its* name was Scranton up to and including his mother's brother, William, who became a Republican governor of Pennsylvania much admired for his humanity by everyone, except maybe Teddy who still considers Uncle Bill leftish. Anyway, "Tim" it was, and Tim turned out to be a race driver of vast talent while Teddy became a racing entrepreneur of equal if more enduring stature. Brother Worthington (Tony) turned out to be a Time, Inc., corporado and then an executive recruiter, but there was curious fate in store for both of Teddy's brothers: Each died in a car accident. Tony's was four years ago on the highway; Tim's was 20 years ago on a racetrack.

Teddy practiced to be his brother's mentor by staying away from him. He went to school in Arizona to get rid of his asthma, and then he prepped (when the word still meant something) at Pomfret in Connecticut on his way to Yale and Cornell Law School. In the summer between, Teddy dropped down to Chile (this is the summer of '58 for those keeping track) to teach skiing. To teach skiing? "As long as I have an opportunity to do something that isn't totally insane, I do it." Exactly.

That is a key to the Mayer personality and it shows early. In the first place, the Mayer family could afford to have its offspring engaging in those pursuits considered fashionable at the time. This has always been the way of transatlantic aristocracy, something we tend to forget in this egalitarian age. We also tend to forget it didn't used to be necessary for the wealthy to sully their white gloves with labor. Teddy trained for the law because lawyering was something gentlemanly and something many members of his family did. But it was not Teddy's *metier*.

"Racing was a world that fascinated both Mayers. . . . In a way that was a shame, because the result was that Teddy never practiced law, and he might have become a brilliant lawyer. If Teddy had practiced, he would have been the kind of lawyer who would have been in a Washington law office, unknown to any but his colleagues but respected enormously by them. His conservatism would have served him well and his thoroughness, too."

The biographer of one of Teddy's drivers wrote that; in retrospect it is not entirely true, for Teddy never wanted the law, which would have made him a lousy lawyer. But he did want racing.

As an undergraduate at Yale, Teddy (Tim joined him later) owned a Chevy wagon he used to go skiing and shared an Austin-Healey 100-6 with his brother. He had dialed over to Thompson Raceway when he was at prep school, which was his introduction to the likes of Lister-Jaguars, Allard J2Xs, D-Type Jaguars and Testa Rossa Ferraris. He remembers the cars. He does not remember who drove them. "I was not particularly fussed by the drivers" is the way he puts it in the argot of a man who has lived in England for a long while and speaks in tongues. "I wasn't even aware that you needed a good driver to make a car go." This view has been modified over the years, but not much. In a way, it may all go back to what happened to Tim, although Teddy would likely be violently upset by any such analysis.

When Teddy realized his brother had considerable talent as a club racer, and after he was frustrated by the military (which seized Tim by the scruff of the neck and set him to the defense of Puerto Rico), in his crusade to make Tim the national Formula Junior champion he arranged a drive for Tim with Ken Tyrrell in the works Cooper Junior team at the very moment Tim was released from the service.

Teddy has never been accused of a failure of planning, and he had lined up an F1 seat for Tim during 1964, but over the winter the two went from Tyrrell and England to Australasia and Bruce McLaren for what was then a booming Tasman Series. They made a deal with Bruce to build two Cooper-based Tasman cars to be driven by Tim and McLaren. One of Bruce's biographers, Jeanne Beeching, picks up the story: "As the series moved to Longford in Tasmania for the last race [Bruce McLaren had already won the championship, Tim had clinched third; their main competition was the Brabham team with Jack Brabham and Denis Hulme] . . . tragedy erased all elation. Timmy's Cooper became airborne in practice, smashed sideways into a tree, and Timmy was killed instantly."

Tim's death would lead Bruce McLaren to craft the most poignant epitaph ever written for a racer: "Who is to say that he had not seen more, done more and learned more in his 26 years than many people do in a lifetime? To do something well is so worthwhile that to die trying to do it better cannot be foolhardy. It would be a waste of life to do nothing with one's ability, for I feel that life is measured in achievement, not in years alone."

Who knows how his brother's racing death affected Teddy Mayer?

What we do know is that he decided that racing was his life's theme and, with Bruce McLaren, he returned to England and became a partner in McLaren, which after Bruce's death in testing in 1970 he took over. McLaren Racing was a power in F1, it dominated the Can-Am, it won Indianapolis (it won both Indy and the F1 title in '74) until—with the arrival of the factories again with their turbomotors and military budgets—Teddy took in partners who bought him out in 1982. Last summer Teddy Mayer came home to work, if not to live. It is not likely that CART racing is going to be the same until he decides to leave again. If ever.

If he is rich (made more so by the sale of McLaren: "I don't know if it was my partners' ambitiousness or their eagerness to get rid of me, but they really did offer a deal that was too good to turn down"), subdued, successful, lawyerly and mid-Atlantic conservative, why does Teddy still race? Particularly, why does he race in the successor series to lunchbox USAC's dirt-track roundelays? Simple. Because he is very, very good at racing and we enjoy doing what we do well.

Teddy Mayer is good at racing because he follows the rules. His rules. Here are some of Edward Everett Mayer's racing rules:

• Organize people to do things. Get the right people. Get them to do the right things.

• Do everything else yourself.

• Enjoy what you're doing because when the end comes it's final.

• If you want to do well in racing, do it as a business.

When Teddy talks about organization, he really means being on time. Being on time is racing's most important mandate, and about being on time, Teddy is succinct: "You had better have your car ready to go on Sunday afternoon at 2 p.m. Even if you have to shoot the customs officer and rent the Concorde."

You wouldn't want to forget designer John Baldwin (Lotus to Parnelli Jones to McLaren to Spirit to Mayer Motor Racing) or Kiwi chief mechanic Phil Sharp, but when Teddy says "right people," he means "right person," whose name is Tyler Alexander. Tyler was Tim's mechanic in the Tasman. He is from Massachusetts, although it is almost certain he was not picked up as a gofer straight from the Gloucester docks where he was testing a very early version of the now ubiquitous topsiders. Tyler doesn't talk very much, particularly to people he doesn't know, and it is likely his remarkable racing instincts come close to making him able to do what the superstitious Buffalo people of northern Nevada suggest when they call such a person a "Man Who Sees through Mountains." About him, Teddy says: "Tyler is probably the most practical racing engineer you'll ever find. He is very hard-working. He never forgets anything that ever went wrong. Anywhere, anytime. He is reasonably difficult for a designer to work with because he never, never lets up on what he knows to be important."

The Mayer/Alexander relationship is "very much of a partnership," according to Teddy, and according to Teddy it could be more so if Tyler only appreciated himself: "He's much more capable than he gives himself credit for being."

As for everybody else at Mayer Motor Racing, easy. "Some teams competing simply don't know where to go to get the people or the expertise." Teddy does. Most of both came from McLaren.

Furthermore, Teddy is right. One of the key people and a large part of the expertise are Teddy's. He doesn't do everything else himself, but he does some of the key things. Contemplate this from the same racing biography earlier invoked:

"Teddy Mayer making a formal protest is one of racing's truly imposing sights. Teddy is a lawyer and litigious by nature anyway. I have seen him spend an hour drafting a protest just in case he might have reason to file one. He uses long, yellow legal pads, isolates himself somewhere, twists his face into awe-inspiring grimaces and laboriously writes his briefs."

. . .

That is part of making racing a business. There is more. Teddy talks about Bernie Ecclestone as though he were invoking a deity: "Bernie dragged F1 out of amateurism and into the 20th century. On his own. Without a lot of help and probably some hindrance from Ferrari." (Listen to Mayer for very long and you soon realize that he absolutely hates Ferrari. In the James Hunt championship year, Ferrari did everything it could to frustrate Teddy's pleasure and success by protesting in order: car width, fuel, and wing height. Teddy does not forget such things.)

Back to Bernie, about whom he will finally say, "I'm too much like Ken Tyrrell and too little like Bernie for my own good." Teddy worked with Bernie as a consultant to FOCA after he sold McLaren, and he believes that if Bernie says something he will do it. Absolutely. Without question. Teddy calls Bernie "The Ultimate Gunslinger" and says he loves "seeing him in action. He's just magic."

Well, what's action?

"Bernie's technique is to throw a hand grenade into a room and come in afterward and clean up."

Some deity.

. . .

Anyway, Teddy came home last summer and found Roger Penske waiting for him. No surprise. What was a surprise was that during the time that Teddy and McLaren had been gone from the Speedway and the Can-Am, Roger seemed to have grown to approximately Godzilla-size. Roger this and Roger that; it must have driven Teddy crazy. For what a whole generation does not remember is that it was Teddy who dominated the Can-Am and it was Teddy who built and sold Roger the car he used to win his first race at Indianapolis. What's more, it was Teddy who moved up and out, into F1 where he won world constructor championships, a task at which Roger was a conspicuous failure.

It must have been like coming back to the little old hometown bully who should have been respectful, even welcoming. That's the way it certainly must have seemed this year at Phoenix, where Teddy was first and second and Roger was nowhere.

"We knew Roger's car wasn't going to work. We knew it going in. I'm not going to say why. Roger is a good businessman who runs a good team. But because his business is not motor racing . . ." And then he leaves the rest unsaid.

Except, a funny thing happened to Teddy on his way from Phoenix to Milwaukee.

Indianapolis.

[*Rick Mears had just won the 1984 Indy 500 for Penske after early leader Tom Sneva, Mayer's lead driver, fell out with a broken CV joint.*]

"One of these days, Roger for sure will get it right." For sure. Just on the wrong day.

What's more, it wasn't the first time. In 1972 Roger ran Teddy out of town. Well, Roger and Porsche. McLaren had owned the Can-Am. Owned it. Made it into a joke. The Bruce and Denny Show first, then the Denny and Peter Show.

Until Roger cheated and got a car that was so fast and so strong it simply crushed the McLarens, squashed them like mangos.

Maybe Teddy forgot.

Probably he didn't. Probably he was ready to be beaten at Indy; probably E.E. Mayer is ready for whatever motor racing hands him. Lord knows he almost always has been.

We should hope so. As long as Teddy wants to run Roger on his home turf, American open-wheel racing is going to be a sumo show, a fencing match, a chess game.

Seats available wherever fine tickets are sold.

[*Teddy Mayer died on Jan. 30, 2009.*]

This Is Tyler

THAT'LL BE TYLER ALEXANDER FRONTING UP AT THE PAY WINDOW TO COLLECT FOR TEAM MCLAREN'S WINS AT INDIANAPOLIS AND MILWAUKEE
June 22, 1974

IT'S BEEN A WHILE. Tyler remembers the Can-Am when promoters at every track in the country smiled their sickly smiles, called him "Ty" and tried to borrow five bucks to hold them until bingo night at the Elks Club.

He remembers also that last year, when McLaren was winning in Formula 1, not only was he in this country running the USAC team, but he wasn't even sharing in the F1 purses—much less getting any credit for them.

In fact, he was sitting in Livonia, Mich., with Gary Knudsen on the receiving end of some of the nastiest telexes since Attila cabled the Roman Senate he was on his way. McLaren managing director Teddy Mayer may be an organizational genius, but he isn't particularly benign.

Well, maybe he isn't an organizational genius either. Certainly he isn't the organizational genius who put the McLaren USAC team on the right track. That's Tyler Alexander, who has stood in the shadows too long.

Not to take away from John Rutherford's great moments in the Midwest, it would be a mistake to underestimate Tyler Alexander's contributions. They are immense. But interestingly, they are no more immense than those of the other American racing shadow dwellers. Around the Speedway, George Bignotti's is a revered name. Howard Cosell has never heard of him. Everybody knows Mark Donohue because he was a driver, but who has ever heard of Don Cox? Do they write about Lujie Lesovsky's contributions in the *Los Angeles Times*?

This is not in favor of singing the unsung. Rather it is to suggest that we might all be missing a great deal by ignoring the Tyler Alexanders.

They're incredibly busy, they're impatient, and they do not wear high recognition orange name badges. But why are they anonymous to the knowledgeable?

I have been around racing for 22 years. I have learned more from Tyler Alexander in the past 18 months than I had from anyone or anything in the previous 20.

Not, certainly, about suspension pieces (that's a hopeless exercise for me), nor about late-night engine changes. But it has been in the understanding of dedication for dedication's sake, in the acceptance of motor racing as a dignified and even noble enterprise, that I have newly discovered the stunning value of the unknown professional.

Tyler Alexander is a young man and mostly he looks like one. But in the bright sunlight of Ontario or Phoenix, you can see the wrinkles around his eyes. Those wrinkles came from countless late nights in makeshift garages all over the world. They also came from the sad and pensive moments of introspection at the funerals of a great many friends. Tyler started as Timmy Mayer's mechanic. He was in awe and enormously fond of his employer, Bruce McLaren. He was as close to Peter Revson as any man alive.

All the dead young men, all the despair. How do the Tyler Alexanders cope with that? I asked Tyler at the Revson funeral in the spring how he managed to persevere even during such moments as these.

"You do it," he said simply in as quiet and impressive a presentation of his code as I have ever heard from him.

There was a particularly difficult moment when the Revson coffin arrived. "How you doing," I whispered thinking naively that Tyler might be as confused and unhappy as I was at the sight. He probably was, but his pride (much like Revson's) and his dedication and his perseverance wouldn't let him show it. "Eight on a scale of 10," he answered. For a moment I thought that a particularly callous thing to say. Unpleasantly cocky, filled with machismo.

But then I understood it wasn't any of those things at all. The Tyler Alexanders (and George Bignottis and Don Coxes and Lujie Lesovskys) are the ones upon whom we must count for continuity in motor sport. They are the bitter-end professionals who must endure while the rest of us indulge ourselves in vacillation and dramatics. They are the ultimately committed and ultimately courageous. They must take their private feelings into their own private corners; for of everyone in the sport, they can afford least to despair. So it is the Tyler Alexanders who are the distillation of all that is admirable in racing.

Why then, particularly among us, are they unknown?

Richter = Riverside

July 11, 1983

Les Richter, a NASCAR vice president, officer of ISC and head of California Speedway, was inducted into the Motorsports Hall of Fame in 2009. Long before that, he was inducted into the College Football Hall of Fame for his achievements as a guard and linebacker at UCLA, which was followed by a standout pro career with the L. A. Rams. Leon makes reference to the man's size but not his football prowess in this column occasioned by Richter's decision to sell Riverside International Raceway—five years later, it was closed and the site became a shopping mall.

THE OTHER DAY THE SUNSHINE SUPERMAN QUIT. Riverside is never going to be the same. Not for me, not for anybody else.

Les Richter and Riverside are the same thing so far as I'm concerned. And Riverside is the place I cut my teeth. In 19 and 58 I crewed at the USAC-sanctioned Times Grand Prix, the track's opening professional event. It was for Fred Knoop and the car was a Huffaker Special. It was pitted next to Max and Ina Balchowsky.

Loss of virginity.

Ina was the first woman I ever heard cuss like a proper crew chief.

That weekend I was introduced to manners USAC style when Lance Reventlow stormed up to Babe Stapp at the start/finish line to whine about a ruling; and that ancient, diminutive short-track veteran set him smack on his ass with a crisp right to the jaw. Rules were rules then, and officials enforced them on the spot.

NASCAR came to Riverside, I don't know how many years later. Richter was responsible for that. Mario Andretti was driving, so was Little Joe Weatherly who crashed in a turn and died. So did Billy Foster, Mario's friend. It was agony for the future world champion—a moment in his life during which he made up his mind to keep his distance from other competitors, the better to avoid the pain of loss.

I only remember Foster's death, I'm ashamed to say, because when he went into the turn nine wall I was lying underneath a dagger of glass with my head halfway through a pressroom plate glass door through which I had fallen. It wasn't so extraordinary that during a moment of high tragedy I was preoccupied with my own pratfalls. I pratfell a lot at Riverside, and every time I did, Richter was there to pick me up.

He picked up Charlie Fox, too, when Charlie was in the Gray Bar Hotel after charging through town in a J.E.B. Stuart raid on the Mission Inn.

When the Can-Am came to Riverside, somebody decided it would be really slick to film the start from a helicopter hovering right over the start/finish line. When that helicopter got itself tied up in some P.A. wires and dropped right on the grid, who do you think was there to clean up the mess?

Les Richter grew as Riverside grew and as racing grew. He was large to begin with; his presence loomed huge on racing's landscape in SCCA promoters' meetings and in his ties with The Tall Man, Bill France Sr. Nobody ever told me, much less Richter, but I don't think there would be a Winston West today without him. And I don't think the Can-Am would ever have reached its stature in the late '60s without his intimidating influence over the sporty car club's delicate deciders.

Richter is a warm man, but he doesn't extend his respect to all that many people. Richter's imprimatur was his calling somebody "coach," which was a great honor, but one for which the recipient paid heavily. When Richter calls you "coach," he puts his elephant-leg arm around your shoulders and crushes every bone in your upper body.

One year at Daytona, I went drinking with Les—and that was during his drinking days—and watched him inhale a sea of industrial strength homemade. A drunken Richter was an awesome sight, tacking and weaving through traffic (human and vehicular) like a torpedoed battleship that just wouldn't go down.

After that he called me "coach." When I got home, I looked up an orthopedic surgeon. "Figure you're going to spend a few weeks every summer in traction or don't go down and see your friend," he told me. The traction—however painful—was a small price to pay.

So Les quit the other day, and I don't think I'll go back to Riverside. The first Tom Wolfe said it best. For some reason that parched track in the smoggiest county in the nation, 500 miles from where I lived up north was always my home track. It was my home track because Les made it my home track and not only for me. For a whole generation of racers and writers.

When he left last week, I called to tell him I thought his departure marked a continental divide in the postwar landscape of racing.

I wondered why he was leaving.

"Peace," he said. And "solace."

He's earned them both, but I don't expect to see him in an easy chair for a century or two. He'll be back at Riverside from time to time. He'll be making his presence felt elsewhere, although where, I can't imagine.

It always was a big presence. Given Les, it always will be.

The Prince of Cruel Sport

THE TRUTH ABOUT CARL HAAS
Aug. 22, 1983

NOBODY LIKES A VILLAIN.

Naturally, I'm the exception.

The object of my high regard is Carl Haas. Carl is to racers what Spiro Agnew was to newspapermen during the depths of the ex-VP's power. You remember. It wasn't that Agnew was a thief, nor that his boss was a crook. The real problem lay with the press, which was irresponsible enough to report all that bad stuff. You can imagine how newsmen loved that.

Carl is as much the object of rage as Agnew ever was.

Trouble is, unlike Agnew, Carl is successful. He makes money at racing. Unforgivable.

I'm sure he does. I'm sure he charges top dollar for every part and piece he sells. Not only that, it's a matter of record that he's sold so-called customer cars to competitors while retaining the unfair advantage of racing the house piece himself.

Carl keeps to himself, which is also unforgivable.

Worse still, he takes racing—his living, after all—seriously. That means winning. Not liking villains is lightweight stuff compared to attitudes about constant winners.

Carl is so serious about winning he hires drivers who have talent. Patrick Tambay. Brian Redman. Mario Andretti. This clearly is cheating.

Carl also has what is loosely termed an "association" with Eric Broadley whose Lolas do what Broadley wants them to do—at least most of the time. That means they do what Carl wants them to do as well, which is also reprehensible.

So it's probably a combination of racers not being able to beat Carl and his drivers, and Carl's charging them a lot of money for the privilege of losing, that sends them off crazed.

It is a totally reasonable reaction on their part. It is also, most likely, a source of considerable satisfaction to Carl.

Maybe because I don't have to deal across a desk from Carl, I find him one of the world's delightful men. He is deliberately enigmatic. He works hard at it. I appreciate anyone who puts real effort into such a bizarre hobby.

One morning at Laguna Seca, Carl spotted me over at another team's motor home and began striding in my direction in that Westward, Ho! determined fashion he has when he's up to something.

He came close enough that his cigar (unlit as usual) was almost in one of my nostrils. "Racing is a very cruel sport," said Carl, turning on his heel and walking away without ever explaining a thing. He hasn't to this day, and he knows he drove me absolutely wild with that one line. Something had to be behind what Carl said to me that morning, I concluded. Well, nothing was. Nothing but mischief.

So Carl is mischievous, and I like that.

In 1981 at Las Vegas, Carl spotted my pale green wristband at dinner, the one granting me access to the pits during both the Can-Am and the Grand Prix. He offered me $500 on the spot. He whined about not being able to go where he wanted to go and do what he wanted to do. He made me feel even more self-important than I normally do. I had something Carl didn't.

On Saturday, which was F1 race day, he showed up with a red wristband, which allowed him to sit in a race car if he wanted.

Carl, as the Brits would say, was having me on at dinner. What's more, he set me up using his own weakness, his own avarice, to convince me he meant what he said.

So Carl makes fun of himself, which I like a lot too.

The other day, at Michigan International Speedway, Carl approached crabwise and whispered in my ear, "I can cause rain, I can really do that." Carl knows that I know he is desperately superstitious. Carl knows that I know that before each race he goes through a sort of Aztec ritual of prayer and laying on of hands. Carl knows as I know that I'll tell this story to racers who don't know him, thus giving them even more Spiro Agnew ammunition.

Carl knows there is a part of him that is pure snake oil salesman, utter fraud, and he's not ashamed to admit it. He glories in it, in fact. That, too, I find admirable.

I will not tell you I think Carl is as honest as the day is long. Although I believe it absolutely, I don't expect you to.

Nor will I say it is my conviction Carl is a genuine sportsman since he is perceived as the exemplar of the barbarian. But I know he is because I ferreted out the fact that he put up a purse for his competitors in one shaky Can-Am when the organizers couldn't come up with it. Put it up out of his own pocket. And threatened the life of anyone who said anything about it.

The other day when Carl swore he could cause rain, I answered him with the ultimate threat. Someday, I said to him, I would tell the world he was a genuinely decent, funny man. Carl paled at the thought. For a moment there, I thought he actually shook in apprehension.

But I meant it and I've done it.

Take *that*, Carl.

The Last Days of Peter Porsche

Dec. 28, 1987

AT 2:30 P.M. GERMAN TIME, Dec. 16, Peter Schutz, the American chairman of Porsche AG, whose seven-year career at one of the world's most sacred sports car companies went downhill with the worth of the dollar, was released from his contract.

While the German press was implying Schutz was fired and such prestigious American newspapers as the *New York Times* and the *Wall Street Journal* were using phrases like "being replaced" and "resigned unexpectedly . . . leaving behind dwindling profits and deep structural problems," *AutoWeek* has learned the action was not so clear cut.

Sources close to Schutz revealed that as early as September the Porsche CEO had discussed with them his frustration with the failure of the Porsche and Piëch families, who control the voting stock of the company, to understand his proposed strategies. Schutz went on to say he hoped he could leave early and "under amicable circumstances," said one source.

In an exclusive interview with *AutoWeek* a month before Porsche's supervisory board and Schutz "mutually agreed that Mr. Schutz will resign his position," he had said, "In a corporate culture filled with firefighters, I am the arsonist."

Thirty days later, Schutz's fires went out. The shock waves that went through the American and German press were the result of the timing, not the fact, of Schutz's departure. Knowledgeable observers had for some time agreed the American CEO of Porsche was headed for trouble. He had counted too heavily on the American market, they said privately. He had taken Porsche into the aircraft business, where results could not possibly bring profits for a decade or more, they said. He had spent hugely on plants and equipment rather than product, they said.

They said the result of all this was Porsche's trouble with lost

271

revenues due to the dollar/D-mark imbalance. They said Porsche's model lineup, particularly in four-cylinder cars, was obsolete and vulnerable to the heavy attack being mounted by the Japanese. The Porsche and Piëch families were split violently on the aircraft strategy, they said. They were right about all the things they said, they were even right about what would happen to Schutz in consequence. They were just wrong about when it would happen.

As late as the night before the end came, at the elaborate year-end award banquet celebrating the European and American Porsche Cup presentations, there was only a hint of the drama taking place behind the scenes.

To the canny Porsche-watchers among the 1,000 sequined and glittering guests, Schutz's absence on the awards podium seemed ominous. Nor were they reassured by the presence of the man who would soon be named his successor, Heinz Branitzki, a 22-year Porsche veteran, as well as that of board members Hans Halbach, Rudi Noppen and Helmuth Bott, who was on the presentation stand where Schutz had stood in years past along with Prof. Porsche. Ironically, the evening's entertainment was a magician specializing in making objects disappear, a fact commented on in context not of the Schutz decision but of speculation in the German press of the possible vanishing of Porsche itself into the maw of Daimler-Benz.

D-B vice chairman Werner Neifer had been quoted only days previous saying his company would "step in before allowing Porsche to fall into American or Japanese hands." The openness of this speculation had so unnerved the Porsche and Piëch families that Ferry Porsche issued a statement immediately denying that the families would sell. Schutz himself had addressed the subject in his *AutoWeek* November interview. Could a company of Porsche's size (50,000 units a year) survive in an era of mergers to meet the cruelties of an increasingly merciless marketplace?

"No one ever has," replied Schutz. "But is that our objective? Yes. And I think if we do the right things, and do those things right, Porsche can survive."

To Schutz survival was predicated on increasing the portion of outside engineering the company engaged in. "If there's one strategic element [that's it], by far it's the fastest growing part of our business."

Clearly, Schutz's view of the importance of engineering, added to his emphasis on the worth of the aircraft business, was not shared by his board. Even as *Auto Motor und Sport*, the most distinguished motoring magazine in Europe, was delivering its mid-December issue to the newsstands containing an article saying all was well at Porsche and Schutz's position was secure, the press department at Zuffenhausen was preparing the statement to be read the next day.

"Mr. Peter W. Schutz and Porsche AG have mutually agreed that Mr. Schutz will resign from his position as Chairman of the Board of Management effective Dec. 31, 1987."

The starkness of that statement could not help but fuel speculation that Schutz's contract was cut short of its expiration date because of his emphasis on the American market. It did him no good that October sales had plummeted and that November's were even worse. Although signs had begun to appear a year ago when the dollar's fall became precipitous, and were writ larger and larger on the wall last spring when Porsche announced its cutback of the four-cylinder program (it had expanded the number of different models and production volumes of four-cylinder cars the previous summer, with near-disastrous consequences), it wasn't until after the stock market crash that a sense of panic seemed to seep into the Porsche mindset. Sixty-one percent of sales in North America with a dollar halved in value prompted them to look for a reason. The reason was named Schutz. When the American refused to back away from his emphasis of the American market over all others, his fate, as far as the Porsche board was concerned, was sealed.

Nevertheless, at least one expert, Steven Reitman of Phillips and Drew in London, challenged conventional rumor. He said of the reason given for Schutz's replacement: "The U.S. dependency issue was a red herring because it was the right decision [when it was made]."

Others were quick to agree. Bob Snodgrass, president of several Southeast Brumos Porsche dealerships, commented:

"I think that probably what we have is a situation where we have a number of individuals in the Porsche family, as they age, realizing they have to plant their feet in the company in one form or another.

"There's an anticipation and realization that Prof. Porsche cannot live forever, and when Prof. Porsche dies there will be a huge power struggle within Porsche to see who's going to take real power.

"With sales down, and the American market not responding at all, this would seem to be the ideal time to move against Peter Schutz."

Snodgrass' comments were echoed by West Coast Porsche dealer Alan Johnson:

"I think none of this [Porsche's sales downturn] has to do with his leaving. I think it has to do with, perhaps, disagreements within the family. He's a very astute man. He understands what's been going on within the family, and he wasn't going to stay around for it."

Schutz had had a hard, fast, spectacular run during his tenure. He came to Porsche in January of 1981 from the diesel and turbine division of Klöckner-Humboldt-Deutz.

But if diesels and turbines seemed an unlikely background for a chairman of a major sports car concern, Schutz would soon reward the selection by building Porsche volumes and profits to record heights. In 1980, the year before he took over, Porsche had sold barely 10,100 cars in the United States. By 1986, it was selling 30,000 cars here and a record number of cars worldwide

U.S. enthusiasts rejoiced when Schutz decided early that Porsche should treat America as its primary market. For a number of years Porsche had sold only its weaker models in the United States and even then, it introduced them here well after they had gone on sale in Europe. Under Schutz's leadership, that all changed.

Schutz also earned points from enthusiasts for backing the company away from an unpopular phase-out of the 911 series. He also spearheaded the effort to create cabrio versions of the 944 (yet to be introduced) and a new Speedster version of the 911 (*AutoWeek*,

Nov. 23). If those were Schutz's accomplishments, in addition to his plans for expansion of the role of the R&D department at Weissach and outside engineering contract work, he also had brought the first of a series of new cars to market. The 959 supercar was only a precursor of production vehicles to come, Schutz told *AutoWeek* in November:

"There is no product [of ours] now on the market that will not be extensively changed over the next three years."

Schutz was concerned about the increasing competition by the Japanese, but he concluded that his investment in plant and equipment would allow his company to catch up. His feelings were echoed by board member for marketing Hans Halbach two days before Porsche severed its ties with Schutz. "Our four-cylinder cars go to a [segment] most embattled worldwide. Competition [is fiercest] from Japan—in terms of sporty cars, and it's the 'y' that counts in that word, including the Mazda RX-7 as well as limousines made to perform like sports cars." Halbach confirmed that included in the present de-emphasis of the four-cylinder market is a program of "rationalization."

Porsche's plans under Schutz included not only new products, but high capital investment in manufacturing and engineering. This spring, for example, the 911 and 928 facility at Zuffenhausen will have a brand-new body building capability that will finally do away with much of the hand assembly that is so cherished by Porsche die-hards within and without the company but is expensive and less efficient than its robot-equipped competitors'. These and other investments in production and manufacturing facilities will mean that Porsche, finally, will be able to build its total production itself. (Currently, all four-cylinder models are assembled under contract by Audi.)

Beyond future production car plans and plant and facility improvement, Schutz must also be given either credit or blame for the direction Porsche racing has taken. In a company whose street products and whose entire image are so dependent on its achievements on the racetrack, racing decisions carry great consequences, and it was

Schutz who reversed the company's intended reduction of involvement in the early '80s.

He was also responsible for the woefully unsuccessful (so far) Indy car program. . . .

Schutz not merely understood the magnitude of the failure of the Indy car program to date, he seemed to revel in it. In his November interview he said: "One of the things that delighted me about the [failure of the] Indy project was how absolutely it demonstrated our vulnerability. I miss no opportunity to remind our people of that."

The final prong in Schutz's grand marketing strategy was his concentration on the turbo flat-six Porsche aircraft engine. Schutz told *AutoWeek*, "Porsche cannot survive [solely] in the sports car business. We must identify a worldwide clientele and satisfy its need to have pleasure in its choice of transportation."

So in '82, the aircraft engine was conceived and on Nov. 11, it was introduced as a production part by Mooney aircraft in Texas. Schutz again:

"We are certainly not selling cars as transportation. What we are selling is a means of motion. That could mean a sports car or motorboat or sports airplane. We are closer to being in the entertainment business than the car business."

New cars, new plant, expanded engineering, entertainment in motion business, which at the moment meant aircraft. So what went wrong?

Many things, beginning with an effort that if it did not intend to bypass the dealer body in the United States, appeared to American dealers to go in that direction and left with them a lasting resentment: the Great Distribution Debacle.

When Schutz took over, Porsches were sold in the United States through Audi dealers. In early 1984, Schutz moved to abolish that association and make Porsche stand alone—the only way he felt it could grow to the degree he envisioned.

He over-reached. He tried to institute a wholly new system in which the dealers would be reduced to order-takers, with distribution centers prepping and servicing the cars under a new marketing umbrella, Porsche Cars North America Inc.

Predictably, dealers rebelled. And won.

But Schutz won, too. Porsche Cars North America survived the scrap between Porsche and its dealers and in so doing severed a link with Audi. That separation, in hindsight, seemed inspired.

In the words of one prominent Porsche dealer: "Where would Porsche be today if they were still teamed with Audi? Audi is basically a tanker in the Straits of Hormuz with no engines."

American dealers were soon on his side, and if PCNA is not yet the fully grown, fully professional distribution arm of a German auto company, it is an independent entity. The U.S. dealers we spoke to for this article, impressed by Schutz's marketing acumen and accomplishments, were universally disappointed in his dismissal.

Nobody can make a judgment on the worth of the Schutz-inspired investment in plant and equipment except to say that it seems to have delayed introduction of badly needed new product by diverting development money. The verdict will not be in on the wisdom of that choice until the efficiencies and savings can be calculated on production of the new cars. On the other hand, there is much disagreement on the worth of Schutz's investment in the aircraft program. A First Boston financial report dated last spring said, "Aircraft engines represent a very small opportunity for diversification. The current status of the industry is best described as a *Jammertal*—the German word for 'valley of grief.'"

Finally, there is an almost unspoken criticism of the Schutz stewardship that speaks to his own admission of being a difficult man to get along with. Most particularly that manifests itself in Porsche's recommitment to doing things its own way. The "Not Invented Here" syndrome, in the words of one longtime Porsche observer, "is not confined to Detroit."

Where then does Porsche go in the post-Schutz era? First of all the company must regain its equilibrium. That is ensured under Branitzki, an old Porsche hand and a finance man whose economies are already coming on stream.

There are some who see Branitzki's appointment as a temporary one, although his contract runs through 1990. Some observers feel that a pattern is forming, that just as Schutz, a marketing expert, was an expedient choice in the early '80s when Porsche desperately needed marketing savvy, Branitzki is an expedient choice at a time when money woes are the company's primary concern. When the current financial crisis is over, they theorize, Porsche will begin looking for a successor.

In the meantime, Branitzki, who is not a "car guy," is expected to delegate all responsibility for products to Helmuth Bott, the widely respected Porsche Research & Development chief.

The car programs that are under way will be continued. In terms of product, there is not much disagreement about their worth. The strategy of aiming at the high end, however, is certainly subject to review. Clearly the same can be said of emphasis on the American market. "In a perfect world," Hans Halbach told *AutoWeek*, "the split would have up to 50 percent of our sales in the U.S., 25 percent in Germany and 25 elsewhere in Europe and in Japan. This would give us a ratio to minimize our exposure and contain our risk."

At the same time, Halbach concedes, "There is a difference between what you want to do and what the market will allow you to do."

As for continuation of the aircraft plan, Halbach seems to be a proponent, but there are many more questions than answers. Moreover, there are more immediate solutions to more immediate problems that have to be arrived at, and in any case nothing was expected, even under the Schutz regime, until the mid-'90s.

Rumors and reality about a Daimler-Benz buyout/merger will, as the expert from Phillips and Drew in London suggested, persist. How soon they will be put to rest depends on imponderables over which Porsche has no control. A small sports car company in Zuffenhausen has little influence over the dollar/D-mark relationship, and until that balance is redressed or until Porsche can derive a larger proportion of its profits from sales in countries with harder currencies, the rumors of Porsche's precarious slate will hang over the company. (The value of Porsche stock has plummeted with the company's recent woes; although some family members are said to be interested in selling off their shares, they almost certainly will not do so until the stock rebounds from its current depressed levels.)

However, some who have been close to the company over the years feel a sale is inevitable—and that the owners are in a race against time. Witness this analysis offered by one longtime U.S. Porsche insider:

"The brains, the enthusiasm, the genius that created these cars up until the last few years is no longer there. And it's no longer there because these people have retired or they're dead. Ferry Porsche, my God, he's pushing 80. This guy Bott is the last of that breed, and although he's wonderful, he's near the end of his rope."

His prediction: Porsche will be bought out, probably by D-B, within two years.

Expansion of Porsche's engineering business is already a reality. One highly knowledgeable source, who asked that his name not be used, quoted chapter and verse on the esteem in which General Motors holds Weissach's R&D work. "GM thinks these are the best engine and powertrain people in the world," he said. This from a man whose company competes for some of the same contracts being awarded to Porsche by American auto manufacturers.

So Peter Schutz, the American who led Porsche for seven years and who was responsible for much of what the company accomplished not only in product but in racing during that time, is almost certain to come home to America. While Schutz told *AutoWeek* he had been "in conversation with Roger Penske," who has just become a majority owner of GM's diesel manufacturing and distributing facilities, Detroit Diesel, he added, "there is nothing under current discussion."

Porsche's CART program will go on without Schutz, and there is every reason to expect eventual success. Porsche lovers will surely have a series of brilliant cars upon which to lavish their affection. Schutz's departure does nothing to threaten that. And while it might be distressing to encounter a refusal by Porsche to *AutoWeek*'s request that some statement beyond the bare announcement of Schutz's replacement be made attesting to the company's recognition of his contribution, that refusal would not surprise Peter Schutz. Schutz himself, when asked to comment on his separation from Porsche shortly after it occurred, replied: "If I do, I would be violating a contractual agreement. I would be jeopardizing my pension."

In his final interview as Porsche CEO with *AutoWeek*, Schutz admitted many of his goals were not reflective of the views of the Porsche/Piëch family. But he seemed resigned to whatever might happen. His genuine fondness for Porsche automobiles emerged almost wistfully when he smiled and offered what turns out to be his own Porsche epitaph: "Whoever said 'money can't buy happiness' never met a Porsche owner."

Peter Schutz may be gone, but that is a philosophy his successors surely understand.

George Levy, Dutch Mandel, John McCormick, Kevin Wilson, Cynthia Clues and Richard Johnson contributed to this report.

The Planet's Most Influential Car Designer

Aug. 2, 1999

TURNING A PAGE TO SEE A PROFILE OF J MAYS in *The New Yorker* is a little disorienting—like encountering your mother having dinner with Wolfgang Puck.

No knock on your mother. No knock on Wolfgang Puck. Simply that we have been trying to fix them up with each other for a decade or more. For all that time, we have been hoping simultaneously that homespun American cooking could seep its way into the native cuisine, while haute preparation could bestow its ambitions on red beans and rice.

There is no better voice to America these days than *The New Yorker*. Its previous impresario, Tina Brown, was so captivated by the elaborate trills of the celebrated that the magazine's voice was just that little bit off-key. But if you subscribe to the notion that a popular magazine's job is to tell its audience who they are, *The New Yorker* is doing a superb job of exactly that.

The audience, said *TNY* in its piece on J Mays, was being powerfully represented by American automotive design at the end of this century. In choosing automotive design—about time—*The New Yorker* aimed straight at a nerve center. In choosing J Mays—and his *oeuvre*—as representative of American auto design, the magazine showed how astute its editors are and clearly how onto their subject.

When he was at Art Center in Pasadena, for instance, Mays used to tell his friend and associate Marta Solas-Porras Hinson that it wouldn't be all that hard to overwhelm the auto design establishment because all there were along the way were bars of soap.

He was distinguished enough that Audi offered him a job. On his design journey at Audi, he was much influenced by Martin Smith, who had overseen the development of the Quattro, and thus taken up in the complex and conflicting tides of that tumultuous time.

But through it all, Mays reminded his audience at Pasadena there remained a magnetic north.

"Reach into your pocket and look at your keys. . . .

"You will probably find a nasty piece of black plastic with a piece of metal sticking out of it." Not fashionable, he needlessly reminds us, but "an opportunity for the maker to create an umbilical connection to the consumer." Like an analogous message to the owner of a luxury car, a key to a device that is unmistakably a passport—an invitation to climb aboard and enjoy the ride—or a passport-like device, carmakers could create tiny pieces of foldout sculpture: brand identity.

"I believe people purchase products for emotional reasons, not rational ones," Mays said. "The moment they reach into their pocket and pull out their wallet—it's an emotional decision, it's about the ability of the product to meet their aspirations."

Haute magazine readers are supposed to be far more interested in fashion, architecture or food than auto design; perhaps they are. In any case during the decades that *Vogue*, *Harper's Bazaar* and *Gourmet* have held their subjects up to the light and examined every last kink and corner, auto design has gone all but unseen.

Where it has been noticed, it has been written about as a jukebox phenomenon—not calculated, just loud. In fact, since the beginning of design in Detroit, the aesthetic of the car has reflected national tastes and in turn influenced them. Yet in common with other powerful influences we have been pretending that auto design belongs in the back closet.

But now here comes *The New Yorker* making damn sure we notice that Mom and Wolfgang Puck are over there in the corner having lunch together. Eating red beans and rice.

Confession
of Failure

May 28, 1984

I'M TRYING AS HARD AS I KNOW HOW to dislike Jim Trueman and I can't. Everything I know to be right and true says I should hate the man. Can't be done.

Indulge me while I talk a little loathsome.

Trueman is a happy, healthy, fit man who is rich and doesn't give a damn about it but enjoys every second of his life. Disgusting. He is a hugely successful businessman, having started Red Roof Inns because he was a contractor who specialized in apartments, and there weren't any apartment contracts to be had. What the hell, we'll build some motels, he said. And went forth and did so—120 motels' worth, all of which he owns. Privately. And manages. Profitably.

He is a hell of a race driver. Has been since the late '60s when he drove under an assumed name (a matter of being underage). Was an amateur national champion. Was a semi-works driver (Bobsy). Drives now because it provides a lot of fun. Well, why not? We have fun at what we do well, and Trueman does racing very well indeed. This does not sit well with an ante-diluvian editor who gave up racing two decades ago, if "racing" it could be called (only the charitable . . .). It particularly does not sit well because Trueman is of an age, 48, where he has absolutely no right to be as competitive as he is.

Age and competition. More annoyances.

Trueman wears his 48 years like Joan Collins displays her half-century, well, perhaps not so prominently. In his Hamlin, Ohio, headquarters he has full Nautilus equipment for employees and families; tennis, racquetball and indoor track facilities; aerobics classes and a fishing lake. The people who work for him are "encouraged" to use these things on Red Roof Inns punched-in-on-the-clock time. "Encouraged" is set off because Trueman hates out-of-shape people.

He himself is going to the Speedway even as we speak, and he will do a special fitness program for the month. Endurance is important for a car owner as well as a driver, he thinks.

That is a very competitive attitude. Which is what makes Trueman as successful as he is. He downright relishes competition. It is intimidating how much he looks forward to it.

His language is spiced with the words of combat.

The executive committee of Red Roofs is called by the in-house name: War Council.

Speak with Trueman for any time at all and you hear "keeping score," "competition" and "war" repeated and repeated. As in, "It used to be in CART that only the top 10 percent or so of the field was competitive. This year, oh, maybe 50 percent could win. CART racing this year is the closest thing to a war you'll ever see."

As an entrant for Bobby Rahal, he has a driver with the same competitive missionary zeal the entrant has. His crew chief, Steve Horne, is a single-minded winner. God help the man who tries to make idle conversation with Horne when things aren't going right. Horne has a delightfully light side, but damn few people ever see it. He is a glacial competitor. Suits Trueman to a T.

A former Trueman employee remembers about seven years ago when Jim sat down with a map of the Hailstone and Sarsparilla belt and tried to find the perfect place to build a racetrack according to market mandates and commuting ease for competitors. It probably never occurred to him Mid-Ohio would come up for sale. Mid-Ohio is in the perfect place. Mid-Ohio now belongs to Trueman.

When he got it, the place was a swamp. Oh, it was a pretty swamp, but it was a place for primitive animals, which is how drivers and spectators alike were treated. Trueman has made of Mid-Ohio what is certainly the premier road circuit this side of Laguna Seca. And while Laguna has been made civilized by the county of Monterey as a park, Trueman has done Mid-Ohio as a road racing venue.

Laguna has wonderful plumbing. Nice campgrounds. A lake. What every family wants. Mid-Ohio has gloriously thought-out

Mid-Ohio, Jim Trueman's "perfect place," Labor Day weekend, 1984.
AutoWeek Archives

garages (transporters can back right up to them and unload, for example). Viewer mounds in the infield. A timing/scoring and press tower. Race facilities. Soon, though, it will have what Laguna has: stuff to coddle families with. And then it will likely be Eden for the racer and his family.

All this is Trueman's doing. He is a bloody perfectionist, accused by some of being enormously difficult to work for because of his standards. To which he replies he gives his people the resources they need and the room to achieve without interference and expects results. Well?

"There are a lot of people who don't understand Jim Trueman," says Trueman. "I can't help that."

I'm not sure I don't belong among those people.

But I do know some things about him.

I know that when I traveled as part of the Can-Am, he tried as an unselfish member of a group including the likes of Carl Haas,

Paul Newman, Garvin Brown and Al Holbert to help keep the series afloat. Noble company, if you please.

I know he has sponsored dozens of his competitors.

I know he has provided and continues to provide dollars for amateur competitors.

I know you never even need to shake his hand to be able to count on what he says.

So, back to where we started. Despite everything Jim Trueman is and has, I find myself admiring, even liking, the man. It disgusts me.

I promise you to continue to make every effort to generate genuine dislike. I am not sanguine about the outcome.

Edgework

Oct. 1, 2001

HE CRACKLED WITH ENERGY, so when he died early last month it barely seemed possible that Jack Flaherty was really gone. Everything he did he did faster and harder and more completely than anyone else. But mainly faster. Also outrageously.

By and large he was a terrific businessman, which he got to be because he was such a wonderful racer. He didn't exactly cheat, but he didn't exactly not cheat either. Dashiell Hammett called it edgework, but we're getting pretty far ahead of ourselves.

When Jack got out of the navy, he started racing roadsters and then he bought some brand-new tools, which he swapped for some used tools so people wouldn't think he was a novice. The roadsters of course were the fastest ones around. So Jack moved up to midgets and sprint cars. And before you knew it, he was the western states sprint car champion. By then he had put those used tools to work in Kjell Qvale's Burlingame British Cars' body shop, which made him a natural candidate for a factory MG ride at Sebring. You expected a West Coast sprint car champion to come in second? Of course not. From there Jack went on to drive some monsters in Kjell's stable, including a brutal Lister-Jag. Perfect. But also by then he had become more and more adept at managing and had moved into a front office at Burlingame.

Which is where, having observed him from a calculated distance, I really met him. Get this picture: Jack was a tough, dirt-track guy who had earned what he'd gotten. I was a smart-ass college kid who hadn't gotten his hands dirty in the last decade. That changed in a hurry. I was one of three salesmen who worked for Jack and not the best of them by far. Got so I dreaded going in when the store opened. I was upside-down on my draw more often than not. For some reason Jack didn't fire me, but he stood there while I made phone call after phone call and wrote letter after letter. Gradually, gradually . . .

I knew things had changed forever between Jack and me one Christmas Eve when Kjell came into the store, stayed only a moment and began to walk out when Jack took his arm and held it out to me. "Say Merry Christmas, Kjell," he said. Typically impertinent. I was thunderstruck. Jack and Kjell laughed. It occurred to me in that odd way that Jack had become my mentor. It happened later that Jack became my lifelong friend.

He went on to own Monterey British Motors and then he got into the restoration business, where, like most of us, he was badly burned. Nobody would like that, Jack hated it; he saw himself as particularly immune to scamsters and car scamsters most of all.

What he did like—what he flat loved—were airplanes. He was a commercial pilot. He raced P-51s in the Reno air races.

But what more than anything and everything encapsulates Jack's life is his air force deal. He bought one. El Salvador's. All 10 of its fighter planes. And then he went down there with some pals and flew them back. Without insurance.

Edgework.

The Bull

GEORGE FOLLMER'S FI FOLLIES
July 21, 1973

This piece takes Follmer to task, but in the very next issue after this scolding appeared, Follmer had won a Can-Am race and Mandel referred to him in the resulting story as "a consummate professional."

BERTIE McCORMICK, THE LATE PUBLISHER of the *Chicago Tribune*, was absolutely right: There's something dreadfully corrupting about the effete swirl of European air and culture, not to mention actual contact with the natives. Take George Follmer, unsullied American, who has spent the last six months in the swamps and cesspools of London, Stuttgart and Rome.

For a man with an abnormally short fuse, Follmer's pan has taken an unconscionably long time to flash. But flash it has. There were hot spots and sizzles during his USRRC career, and they lit the sky with increasing frequency during his adventures in the Trans-Am. But only last year as a double Trans-Am/Can-Am champion did the whole seething, volatile mixture go nova. George Follmer—the double champion, idol of Stuttgart and Sindelfingen, the great rough-hewn cowboy of Grand Prix Shadow racing—threw open his sinister Shadow cape and finally exposed himself to the world.

It has been a dreadful mistake and we may never see George again. Fearsome Follmer, convinced his ultimate revelation would stun the opposition, showed himself to be a mere middle-aged, xenophobic, undistinguished mortal. Less formidably equipped than his effete European competitors, it was apparent that he was mainly composed of bluster and not, greatest shock of all, Superman in any of his incarnations.

His early GP points came from the killing pace of the real articles in front of him who retired one by one to leave him, astonished, well within the top six finishers. At the time, this was hailed as the greatest moral victory since Bataan. But his competitors were being quoted as less than enthusiastic about his driving style. "He will have to learn to behave here," said one veteran. "George does things that are simply not tolerated at this level."

You can take the asphalt bullrings out of the boy, but the tar macadam clods of Willow Springs and Paramount Ranch stick to the ear cavities and between the toes through the Gasometer and the Carousel no matter how hard you try to swab them out.

More damaging still has been Follmer's belief in his own press clippings. If George is to be labeled "truculent," truculent George will be. If he is said to be curt and snappish, George will hone and cultivate curtness and snappishness until they become verbal nukes in his social arsenal.

George is now the newly successful star of pit and paddock. And he has waited so long to get there, he is determined to make the most of it. Unhappily that means someone has convinced him he is above his team, his sponsor, his fans and even his own opinion of himself, an almost impossible accomplishment. Thus he insists on the right to say publicly that the Rinzler Motor Racing Team, which fields his Can-Am Porsche, is made of a "bunch of bungling amateurs." He barely condescended to make an appearance at a cocktail party given by sponsor RC Cola to honor its drivers as well as the executive vice president of the firm, up to see his first Can-Am and find out where that almost 1 million is going. He announces publicly that if the Rinzler team doesn't get its act together before race day he is flying home. He cannot be bothered carrying UPI news film of the first Can-Am with him on his flight to London, thus saving UPI some 12 critical hours in delivery.

Jackie Stewart and Peter Revson and even the unapproachable Denny Hulme would have long second thoughts about this kind of public petulance. And George Follmer, no matter how far he thinks he's come, is not yet in the Stewart/Revson/Hulme league.

It is a great pity. Follmer has worked long and hard to become an overnight success. But now that he is there, his chief asset—a kind of cheerful, earthy Alexander Woolcott cynicism—has degenerated into a Gloria Swanson bitchiness, which is the mark of the second rate.

The result is that he is in jeopardy of losing his Can-Am ride, maybe even his Formula 1 ride. He is making excuses because his car is not right, instead of admitting he is off his game. He is blaming his team instead of himself. He is bad mouthing his sponsor rather than admitting his own deficiencies . . . one of which is all but abdicating all testing responsibilities on the Porsche in favor of Charlie Kemp. And it was Teddy Mayer himself who said that testing is at least as important as driving in a race.

And he is doing all this publicly.

There was a time of promise for Follmer. He seemed to be a zephyr in the stagnant air of gentlemen's racing. Instead he seems to have blown himself out and is content to swirl languidly, aimlessly in a fetid and suffocating corner.

It could be that this is the fate of all fresh and ambitious breezes. If so, George Follmer has gone to terrible waste. He appeared with everyone's best wishes; he promised much. He was Pershing at Ardennes, Eisenhower in Normandy, Patton at the Remagen Bridge.

None of those grand expectations has materialized. Follmer is not being Follmer. Follmer is not even being Yossarian.

Chapter Six

An Automotive Life

❝ **My son,** from the moment he discovered his first country stream and flopped down on his five-year-old belly to stare and discover its infinite mysteries, was captivated by fish. I have ordered smoked salmon on the *Ile de France* and enjoyed it, but a trip through the Fulton Fish Market on my way to somewhere else was a desperate and unexpected plunge into a hostile land. I was dragooned into accompanying a sixth grade field trip to an aquarium and all I could think was that the walls of the fish tanks that stood between me and the octopus were made of glass only. Had it been my choice, they would have been of three-inch chrome-moly steel with iron bars. ❞

In this chapter we find Leon at home, though almost never literally so, and on the road with some of the special cars he owned, his wife, Olivia, and family and friends. "We do not write about ourselves," eh? Just for kicks, let's start with the story that puts our "car guy" both figuratively and, quite literally, at sea.

Absalom and the Wily Salmon

A RELUCTANT FATHER AND HIS BLOSSOMING SON AT SEA, STALKING THE SALMON: A RECOLLECTION OF LOVE AND THE MANHOOD RITUAL

American Boating

October 1972

In the early 1970s, after he returned to Competition Press *from* Car and Driver, *Leon's duties were as editorial director for all the company's publications, which included the monthly* American Boating, The Journal of Western Waterways. *It was a natural enough inclusion for a publisher headquartered in San Francisco, and though Leon would be the first to tell you he was no sort of outdoorsman or much of a boater, he knew how to tell a story. This one is a prime example.*

AMONG THE TAROS PEOPLE, it is still the custom for a young warrior to undergo an initiation rite to become accepted as an adult member of the tribe. He must walk into the bush alone, and with only the most primitive weapon he must kill a lion. Until he does, he is still a child, indulged by his elders. What would be a deadly insult among equals is passed over as a mere indiscretion of youth; his voice is not yet heard in the councils of the men. First he must kill his lion.

We are infinitely more civilized than that. We nourish our children's growth to adulthood with the pabulum of Montessori, the austere (but ever-so-indulgent) chipped beef of prep school, the Brie of college. They are insulated from the chill winds of the world by the pages of Dr. Spock; they are swathed in cotton turtlenecks and double-knit jeans to shield them from the shock of adolescence. Not for them the brutal initiation into the cruel necessities, the clawing for a livelihood they will soon discover when adulthood bursts upon them. We have learned far better than the Taros. They are aboriginal, and it would be a betrayal of our struggle to become civilized if we were to revert to their brutal methods. Unthinkable. Out of the question.

Why, then, have generations of American fathers taken generations of American sons to the North Woods for their first hunting trip? And why is that hunting trip a moment the father has thought about, planned for, dreamed of since his boy was squalling in the crib? Why the long evening sessions in the warmth of the living room—protected from the cold of winter outside—initiating the son into the mysteries of the rifle, into its care, its cleaning, its importance as a family institution, its exclusivity as the property of the head of the family—the *male* head of the family? Why the intricate legends of fly tying? The promises that some day, that young boy, too, will become a part of the annual, all male, reaffirmation trip to the mountain trout stream with the ritual of the camp, the rising before dawn. The elaborate waders, the exquisite rod and reel, the flies so lovingly tied that will become a part of his life, too—and from then on, from that week forward, he and his father will be equals.

My son is 14. A great hulk of a boy with that curious combination of awkwardness and grace a boy who is a good athlete seems able to project simultaneously at that age. In my family, he is the atavist. From the moment he took his first step, he longed to explore the woods; I was brought up on the melting summer asphalt of Chicago and New York and oak trees fill me with anxiety—oak trees in battalion strength induce terror. My son, from the moment he discovered his first country stream and flopped down on his five-year-old belly to stare and discover its infinite mysteries, was captivated by fish. I have ordered smoked salmon on the *Ile de France* and enjoyed it, but a trip through the Fulton Fish Market on my way to somewhere else was a desperate and unexpected plunge into a hostile land. I was dragooned into accompanying a sixth grade field trip to an aquarium and all I could think was that the walls of the fish tanks that stood between me and the octopus were made of glass only. Had it been my choice, they would have been of three-inch chrome-moly steel with iron bars.

And so, as my son grew older he joined the National Rifle Assn. on his own and went in his own lonely way to the rifle range and learned from his instructor there—who had a hundred other boys to teach—of the beauties of the rifle, of its power and of the enduring truths about the relationships between people you could comprehend if only you first learned how to group five rounds within half an inch at 50 feet. He watched his friends go off with their fathers hunting (for all he knew) wolverine and Siberian tiger. The weekends would come and his schoolmates would disappear into the backwoods with their fathers and their older brothers—and my son would wander off wistfully on his own to do whatever boys do when they're hurt and disappointed and know something is wrong but don't know what to do about it.

He began to fish on his own in the little streams that defined our property in rural Westchester County, New York. Sunnies and perch. One smaller than the next but all great trophies—significant of enormous accomplishment. He would bring them home brimming with pride, but he knew better than to bring them to me. Once, when he was younger, his dog, a Scottie, had dug up a mole, and with the intense terrier pride of the conquering hunter, strutted into the house with it in that peculiar, seafarer's gait that Scotties have and deposited the filthy thing at my feet. It had no eyes, it was mangled beyond belief, and it was barely out of puberty. My son had seen the whole thing, and he watched in fascinated horror what happened next. From that moment on, he knew better than to expose me to an animal of any sort: alive or dead.

Still, things did get better. A father is, after all, not the only tribal elder in a boy's village. There is the father's father and the father of the boy's mother. In my son's case, both were great fishermen—especially his mother's father. Both, sadly, lived in Florida. But once a year there was a pilgrimage to Florida and then the days were filled with joy as each grandparent took turns, introducing him to the pleasures of deep sea fishing, teaching him, leading him, instructing him as his own father never had. For the grandfathers, it was an emotional elixir; they shed 20 years on those days in the bright blue Gulf Stream. For the boy it was fulfillment. But not, he began to think, the fulfillment of his contemporaries. A grandfather is not a father after all, and although he would never say anything, never dream of mentioning it, there was reproach and some sadness when the day on the water was over and he came home with his report and his catch.

It happened then that we moved to California—the frontier. Mountains filled with streams filled with fish, marshes whose skies were black with ducks, redwood forests in which bears and catamounts roamed. Surely now, I must respond. Certainly I could no longer keep to my bed and my typewriter—my obligation was magnified 10-fold; in the midst of this paradise, I would become transformed.

I knew he expected it to happen, I knew he longed to have it happen. I tried to make it happen, but I just couldn't. I could not bring myself to slay a ptarmigan, bring down a gazelle at 1,000 yards; my air-conditioned den beckoned and there were all those books in my library unread and reproachful.

But . . . but, I did have a friend. And my friend had a ranch and he hunted and fished and on the ranch, he said, game of every description abounded. It was the Serengeti plains transplanted to Petaluma, Calif., he said. If my son would now have to do without his enchanted grandfathers, he would at least have my friend—and my friend, who had no son of his own and clearly longed for one—was delighted with the whole arrangement. The two went off one weekend for their first expedition to slay great beasts, my son's heart beating, his eyes bright with expectation. Three hours later he came back, emotionally destroyed. The ranch was no Kenya game preserve; it was a working chicken spread. They had gone out behind the coops, set up some pumpkins and an old radio and blasted away at them with a .45 handgun from 15 feet. Admittedly, the pumpkins had made a very satisfactory splash all over the landscape when the .45 bullets had hit them square, and the old Emerson was definitely dead, its tubes and its dial shattered and twisted and dangling at crazy angles from the splintered cabinet. But how do you bring home a dead radio on the fender of your bicycle? How do you mount an exploded pumpkin above the fireplace? Worst of all, he thought I would laugh at him and tell him he had been foolish all along. "Forget about it all," I would be able to say. "You see how silly it all is; this hunting and fishing, this 20th century charade, this echo of a day 5,000 years ago when a man really had to go out and find food for his family."

Instead, I almost cried, and while I was not sure why, I was sure the time had finally come for me to act the role of the father. I would go out with my son. I would take him fishing.

We went on a Friday, cheerfully accepted members of an *American Boating* expedition led by the editor and part of a group that included the publisher and the publisher's father, the associate editor and the graphics director. Heady company. Veterans all, salts, seafarers, fishermen. My son was almost bursting with pleasure in anticipation, and he was up at 4:30 a.m. rejoicing in the pure pleasure of the need to rip himself from sleep, delighted at the chance for this ritual sacrifice knowing what it all meant, what it was in favor of, what it would lead to. He had never been on the bay before; he had never been on the Pacific—by itself that was stunning enough to reduce him to monosyllables. When he did speak, he (very uncharacteristically) called everyone "sir." He was clearly making sure nothing he would do would jeopardize his being a part of this magic trip; it had taken so long for this to happen, it seemed so impossible the moment was finally here, the threads of reality were so thin, so fine, so tenuous that he was in agony that something might destroy it all. That he would say something or do something terribly wrong and the awesome and the all-powerful and totally arbitrary adults (most especially his father) would suddenly bring the entire magical trip to a halt, demand to turn around and go back, shatter the dream forever. No, it would be best for him to say as little as possible.

Going out through the Golden Gate, the city behind was shrouded in early morning fog; we had started later than the commercial boats and party boats and we were almost alone except for the *Mary D.*, a 50-foot commercial trawler, one of a kind you might see anywhere in the world, rusty, weary and resigned on her way out to bottom fish. A small yellow runabout materialized, bouncing on the minuscule seas, very brave and very intent on getting where she was going in a great hurry. The gulls soared, the mist was lifting, the Pacific was very gray. It was a scene so ordinary to a veteran salmon fisherman that he would barely have noticed his surroundings. It so filled my son with joy that he could not sit still. More than that he *had* to say something, and so he took me aside and whispered as if terrified to break the spell. "Look at the birds," he said. "Look at them, Dad. You don't see birds like that in the Atlantic. They're pelicans." He wanted me to know that the birds were fun to watch, that they were astonishing birds, strange and extraordinary birds, but he was 14 years old and he couldn't say to me "the birds are fun to watch," so he kept insisting that I watch the birds. If I were perceptive enough, he was saying to me, I would understand what the birds meant to him. That kind of thing goes unspoken between father and son—and is the enhanced fidelity of the unspoken communication that is nurtured by such a trip as this.

He said he felt at home on the Atlantic, he missed the color of the Gulf Stream; he said the Pacific was more pacific than the Atlantic and he didn't expect that. But he said that the smell of the diesel exhaust mixed with the salt air was so sweet and so familiar that it was almost enough, even if we caught no fish.

Four miles out we came to the first buoy, killed one engine and took the other out of gear. The editor took my son aside to show him how to bait the hook. The shaman and the initiate. There was kindness in the instruction, but it was not patronizing; it was clear that a one-time run-through was all my son would get and then he was on his own. If he wanted to fish, he'd better learn this, learn it now and then get about his business. The editor had his own affairs to attend to.

All his fishing life, his grandfathers had baited his hooks for him but that is the way you treat a child. The editor approached him in the manner in which you approach a near-adult. It could not have been done better, and my son flushed with pleasure that he was being so treated. He backed under an overhang on the cabin where he might not be so easily seen to bait his own hook for the first time. He put the anchovy on upside down. It made no difference to him, he was elated. It was the first critical moment in the initiation ritual, his passport into manhood, and now he could enter the sporting camaraderie of the expedition on a man-to-man basis. He wiped the bait stink and blood off his hands and onto his shirt—professionally, disdainfully, seemingly as preoccupied with more important matters as a charter boat mate in Bimini. His line went into the water.

The publisher's father got a strike: a salmon, hooked, netted and boated. Too small, and back it went. He got another. Again too small. And another. The same. My son's face grew longer, his frown more desperate. The publisher got a fish. Too small. The editor. Too small. Then finally, the editor got a fish worthy of his eminence: a fine silver, 28 inches long and maybe 18 pounds. My son's expression was appropriate to a funeral, his depression near terminal. Originally, he rejoiced in the editor's accomplishment, in his good luck, that it was the editor who caught the first fish we could keep. But it was not, after all, *his* fish and he was disconsolate. But then he began to realize it could have been someone else's—the publisher's father, for example, and *he* had already caught six—too small, of course, but still six, and my son had caught none. It was a thought that was immensely comforting and with the emotional adaptability of adolescence, he cheered up instantly.

And then he caught his first fish. As he brought in his line, the council of elders dropped their rods and moved over to surround him and watch his triumph. Closer and closer, farther and farther toward the boat it came, and then the hook broke the water and the fish was revealed before everyone's eyes. It was a bullhead. A three-inch bottom fish that had somehow strayed four miles out into the ocean from the silt and muck of the bay. It would have been shameful enough to catch a bullhead with a line dangling from a dock at Hunter's Point. At sea, it was a humiliation almost too great to bear. He did not know what to say. He would not look anyone in the eye, but gradually, as he was clapped on the back, as he heard the warm and good-natured laughter, he realized that the company of men can have its gentle and understanding side. It was the second stage in his initiation and not the least important.

Throughout the morning, 16 silver salmon were hooked and caught—all but two of them too small to keep. My son caught four, all too small, and one, the smallest of them all. "Bummer," he said. "That's all right, you've got the record," said the publisher.

The morning was ending, the trip drawing to its close. And my son had, at last, gone fishing with his father. If it never happened again, that would be all right, too; the need had been fulfilled, the ritual satisfied. If he was too preoccupied or not sophisticated enough to notice what the future might hold for him, it was just as well. As he reacted to the pleasure of being a son to his father, if he did not see the odd, contrapuntal role reversal between the publisher and the publisher's father, in which the son was acting as teacher and elder to the father, if he could not foresee that this is what age holds in store for all fathers and all sons, the time would come for that. There are years enough for those truths to gently intrude themselves between a man and his son, and to change them both, to make a man of the younger and a child of the elder. Time enough to find those things out.

It was finally done. It was at last all right. He had caught his fish, caught his fish with his father in the company of men. My son had slain his lion. So, in a manner of speaking, had I.

Cars That Control Your Life

Feb. 6, 1984

An SVO Mustang drove into my life the other day. One moment it was just another car to evaluate, but somewhere this side of Flint it wedged itself on the far side of my family, but on the near side of most everything else important that happens to me.

It started when the leather-covered wheel suddenly began directing me back to where I always end up when I'm in a car that has that magic. Where I always end up is driving aimlessly just to drive, just to feel the car and the road, just to punch the throttle and get a little loose and irresponsible again.

I.

You haven't driven the SVO yet? You know about its parts and pieces, the lovely five-speed, turbo 2.3, Baron von Richthofen rear wings, but it's time you found out about the whole. When you do, you'll meet Christine—one of the real Christines who insinuate themselves into everyday routine and take over.

The SVO's spiritual predecessor, the GT350, did that to a lot of people I know. Best example I can give you about how it drove its owners right in and out of marriages, away from some jobs and into others, apart from old friends and into the arms of new ones, is William Jeanes. William was flat run over by his first Shelby Mustang. There he was, a nicely educated young Mississippi striver, all ready to take up the harness of the family diesel distributing business, when he became Mustang-struck. Instead of a William Jeanes living in Jackson, Miss., with a Mrs. William Jeanes and a flock of toddling Jeaneses, William, in order:

Threw himself into a feckless racing team called Bolus and Snopes (if you're old enough, you'll remember Bolus and Snopes, which was "Good and Nice," and which fielded a serious racing team but didn't have much, ah, truck with the rest of the sober-sided world).

Went north to indenture himself to *Car and Driver*.

Slid into the ad business where he became point man for the Citicorp Services multiyear sponsorship of the Can-Am.

Lives in Detroit these days and is the general manager of the ad group—the performance ad group—that represents, of course, SVO among other clients.

Somewhere along the line, you can be sure there was a conversation in the Jeanes household between Jeanes' mother and father in which one turned to the other and asked the classic parental question usually brought up in the households of hookers and thieves.

But the answer is that William Jeanes did not go wrong. He went at the moment and the place where he and that GT350 met up to a career that makes his life a joy. Driven there by a car that controlled his destiny.

The same tug came as a non-delete option in the steering wheel of the SVO Mustang. It was a nice reminder that cars like that still exist. Although, Lord knows, I certainly didn't need one myself. Probably.

II.

The sociologists love to talk about the moment of getting a driver's license as a "rite of passage." It means freedom, they say. No longer is the adolescent a house slave, perhaps even a family slave. There's something to that, naturally. If it's obvious enough for a sociologist to notice, it's a broad-brush phenomenon.

Certainly there's a great middle-level class of youth for which "freedom" is the right word. For a smaller group, "avocation" is a better one. And a smaller one still, "vocation." You can think of it either as real freedom or enslavement. Perhaps it depends on the First Car Owned.

Let us be clear. First Car Owned does not have to be First Car Driven-without-adult-by-your-side. More likely, in fact, it means First Car Owned by Choice.

III.

Inskip Motors did not want to take my '50 Studebaker convertible in trade. There wasn't a wholesaler in all of New York State who wanted it on his lot. Well, one, $500 worth. It was not yet two years old, and it didn't have but 20,000 miles on the odo. Coming and going Studebakers are legend now, Raymond Loewy design and all; Studebaker Clubs are worshipful of them, articles pop up like turnips in hardcover quarterlies about the things. "Landmark" is a word a lot of people these days use about that car. "Junker" was what most people called it when it trundled the streets of '50s America. So I took the $500 mainly because I had watched the black/red MG-TC slide right out the front door of Inskip, right out from under my $50 deposit, and into the arms of another. You know the Breck shampoo (or whatever it is) beach commercial with the two lovers running in slo-mo toward each other? I saw it first, before it was even made. And with it one of those carefree passionate people—the lissome, heartbreakingly beautiful blonde—I had thought was betrothed to me. Never again, goddamn it, I said to myself.

Well, I did what it took, and I won't tell you what it was. You've got your own story or your own memory or your own payment stub book somewhere in the basement or attic or conscience anyway.

Except by the time I got my weirdness together, the TC had gone away altogether to be replaced by the TD on Inskip's showroom floor.

These days, I still wince at my presumption in suggesting I was there early in sports cars. How could anyone who didn't own a TC claim that? Nobody asks anymore, but I know.

Today's wince doesn't count. What counts is how I felt then. Does any one of you out there think you know what black paint looks like? Black paint on a car with a red leather interior? You don't. I'm not sure I do, either. It was long ago and all that's left is this memory of an ache in my heart when I saw it. Black paint on a new TD smells. Crackly frost mornings smell. Big, beautiful, savage warships smell. Sierra Nevada sunsets smell. That's the best I can do.

Yeah, I know about leather. That too. And new cars. All of that. This was something absolutely, totally different.

And getting in. Well, there aren't many of us who don't remember about that one. All our lives we slid around inside some kind of cavern that said Ford or Chevy or Studebaker on its outside. TDs won't have a part of any of that. You put the things on like underwear. They touch your skin and I swear, they reach right inside too, even standing still. For damn sure driving, when you begin hearing bad things from your kidneys.

You see how easy it is to slip into facile derogation of 30 years later? All right, maybe there was a little boniness in the immediate neighborhood of where later, you'd discover, soft worked better. It didn't matter. What mattered was that stubby shifter, the windshield that folded flat so you could catch flies in your mouth at 60 mph, the doors that took an elbow in their own crook and allowed you to pose with a Cary Grant casualness; allowed, hell, you didn't have any choice.

Lord, the steering wheel. You could ignore that big, four-spoke (do I remember right?) wheel like you could ignore your own chest. So with your left arm crooked outside the door (the top was down, the

The Mandel family. Daughter Olivia (far left), wife Olivia (sitting on hood) and Lewis and Clark College student Dutch, in the late 1970s. Leon is leaning on the test car. *Mandel Family Archive*

side curtains off—who did you think we were—featherbed salesmen?) and your right running that little shifter up and down 'til its life was in danger, off into the world like *Road & Track* taught us to, we went. Look out! The wheel turned the car. In direct ratio. Not until 10 years later, in a formula Junior, would that feeling come again when a sideways glance into the apex pointed the car's nose violently in the direction of the gaze. Unconsciously and attended by terror and an atavistic memory. My hands had moved a tenth of an inch, the car a dozen feet in the wrong direction.

Well, that was what it felt like, but that's not quite enough to say, because there was something else that had never happened before. Everybody stared.

You're some nobody punk kid, and it feels like New York City has stopped whatever it's been doing and turns its head to take a look at you.

You mean to tell me *that's* not going to affect your life?

IV.

Maybe a quarter of a century later, I gave a speech to the national convention of the Sports Car Club of America. You want the truth, I didn't have much of an idea what I was going to say even when I climbed up the stairs to the podium. So I took a little water, as much of a grip on myself as I could, and started. What I didn't know, or at least realize when I was sipping that water, was that unconsciously I was paying a lot of attention to who was in the room.

There were a lot of people out there I knew. And they made me think of a lot of other people I knew, and many of those weren't around anymore. So I began to talk about—actually I began to talk to—my friends who had just wiped the machine-made SAE90 banquet gravy from their mouths. There was a man I'd stewarded with over in Japan when they ran the Can-Am at Fuji. Maybe it was my night to be sentimental, but it suddenly hit me that I learned a lot about big-stakes business poker from him; the foreign service would call it "negotiation techniques." Somebody else, a lumbering New Yorker in middle age who had devoted a lot of his life to making racing work, showed me over and over again at places like Lime Rock and Road America what it meant to be fair, even at the risk of losing friends.

There was somebody who would have been there if he hadn't been betrayed by a faulty upright in testing at Kyalami; who was there for me nonetheless; who, in fact, is almost always there in almost everything I do. If I know anything at all about honor, if there are moments I can bring myself to behave gracefully, it's because of his example. I said a lot of this, and one more thing I'll talk about if you'll only be a little more patient with me, and afterward somebody asked me for a copy of my speech and I said I didn't have one. Copy or speech. He didn't believe me and I suppose he still doesn't, so I'll ask him if he's reading this to remember his own life with the car and decide which one drove him to where he's sitting right now and what he learned along the way.

V.

When Holiday Inns bought Harrah's and discovered to its corporate surprise that the casinos and hotels brought a 1,400-car collection with them, it sent a platoon of tape recorder-carrying eavesdroppers around behind the people who were walking through the collection. Surprise. After a month of study, found out that Americans mark the passages of their lives by the cars they owned. What they listened to over and over again as they played a month's worth of tapes was recital after recital of births, marriages, deaths. "I courted your mother in a car just like that." Or, "When you were three, you got a terrible case of pneumonia and I drove you to the doctor in one of those."

As a matter of fact, Bill Harrah remembered his grandfather's funeral in Venice, Calif., only by the fact that it was his first ride in a Marmon.

Your neighbor isn't a car guy, but 8-1 he's got a dozen car stories he wants to tell you. Sorry, though, he doesn't have time to listen to yours.

Probably he wouldn't understand anyway. Maybe you wouldn't be all that inclined to share them in the first place.

I don't know if he'll forgive me for telling you, but Danny Sullivan's career probably started because he was a different kind of kid in school and not one who was much liked by his classmates. He lived in Louisville, which can be very social and very superficial, and he wouldn't have any part of that. For Danny, as for a lot of us, he didn't find freedom in the car as much as he found escape. And, if you must know, rebellion. Bonnie and Clyde were law-abiding compared to Sullivan even before he was old enough to get his license, which he probably never would have been given if his violations had been recorded with DMV instead of the juvenile overseers.

Just so he doesn't think I'm betraying him alone, somewhere in the archives of the police in a small Westchester town lives the criminal automotive record of one of the great adolescent highway felons of the 20th century. Peter Revson.

You can talk to our man on the Left Coast about Mark Donohue, who was his boyhood friend, his partner and his frequently indicted co-conspirator.

Cars. Control. Lives.

Don't talk to me about Christine.

Anyway, I was standing on the platform at that sports car convention talking about people in the car world who had made a profound difference—almost all of them for the better—in my life, when I looked down toward the front and saw this woman.

I expect some people in the audience wondered why I stood there like an ass and laughed out loud and then didn't tell them why.

So I'll tell you instead.

Once I got a call from a local fire department about this woman. She kept driving a C-Type Jaguar with a full-on dry sump D motor and 45DCE0 Webers—big mothers—to the grocery store. Every time she climbed back aboard, bananas and Grape Nuts in arm, she'd crank that beauty up and pump the throttle. Guaranteed carburetor fire. Happened every time. Seems the fire department was getting weary of responding. As the little town's visible sports car person, I figured to them as the logical person to turn to for a solution. Not exactly.

It was this same woman who took me to my first motor race, Watkins Glen, 1953, and signed me up to sit on a corner and wear a headset because she did.

Told me to buy that Morgan or else.

Came over to say hello in the first place because she liked black/ red MGs.

She got that look in her eye again the other day when she saw the SVO.

Remembering the TD

March 6, 2000

SOMETIME SOON THE MG T REGISTER will hold its annual meeting in Charlotte. My friend Tom Cotter, the only man I know under 50 who is as besotted with British cars as I am, wonders if I'll address its members. I did my time in TDs and TFs of vintages '50, '54 and '55, and I have a lot of seriously ambivalent things to say about them.

I met my first MG-TD at the New York dealer, J.S. Inskip. Well, I met my affianced; I had flirted with others well before. Built and imported from 1949 until 1953, the TD—meant to gather in American dollars—was squarer, squatter-seeming, softer-riding and easier-steering than the prewar-based TC, which, because of its tall, narrow spindly wheels, was a nightmare to steer straight. I wanted a TC, but it took me a while to save the money, and by that time TCs had been replaced by a car more suited to colonial tastes.

Anyway, there it was, black with a red interior and wholly, completely intoxicating. The automotive surroundings in the early years of the '50s were populated by dull, six-cylinder Chevys, envelope-bodied Fords, monster Buicks, weird-looking Studebakers and turtelian Hudsons. To drive a TD at a time when consumer conformity was inundating America in the shape of Muntz stereos and Sears freezers was to stand out like a wallaby at the Westminster Dog Show.

Which was exactly why so many people chose to do it. It was the very same contrarian instinct that made VW so popular in years to come with a larger and only slightly less daring constituency.

What did the TD buyer get for his delivered $1,795 price? In strict mechanical terms, an ancient, obsolete, outdated cluster of parts, including a 1248-cc engine, independent front suspension from the Y-type sedan and rack-and-pinion steering.

Which is about like saying what you get when you go out with a supermodel is arms and legs and a highly styled hairdo. It was the experience that counted: sitting deep in the leather seat with your

Getting ready to race his MG, somewhere in Northern California or Nevada, in the mid-1950s. *Mandel Family Archive*

elbow braced on the cut-down door and convinced you were driving the automotive equivalent of a Spad. The big, plastic steering wheel was close (it was adjustable by a kind of sleeve that required a wrench when it was new and didn't work at all when it was older and rusted). If you were wise, you kept a cocked eye on the double-arc flat fascia that housed two large instruments, speedo and tach, which in the early cars worked chronometrically—that is to say, in jerky increments. There was a fuel gauge, an oil pressure gauge (very important) and a temp gauge. The wipers worked off an electric motor mounted atop the windshield, which could fold flat. Weather protection was courtesy of side curtains and manual canvas top, the common technology of the time.

The TD had a stump puller rear end and a four-speed gearbox with no synchro on first. Brakes were drums and almost adequate. You could accelerate with slow traffic and hold a steady 70 on the highway.

Some people, including me, actually raced them. They were terrifying on a racetrack: not very fast and desperately tippy. Even so, when a shoal of TDs got out together in the Sports Car Club of America G production class, they provided wonderful fun—and even began some spectacular careers.

As a car, the TD was not much; as an experience, it was glorious. In the context of today's cars, TDs are terribly primitive and only fun to drive on brilliantly sunny days in the summer. Unless, of course, you can think of yourself driving along in 1950, head high, scarf flying, ready at a moment's notice to wave to an oncoming fellow MG driver—a chosen member of a wonderful clan, an adventurer.

So Now There's
a New Morgan

April 17, 2000

IT'S CALLED THE AERO 8 AND IT IS MORE OR LESS. It has an aluminum chassis but don't worry, the coachwork is constructed over an ash hardwood frame. It is powered by the 4.4-liter BMW 32-valve V-8, and since the car only weighs 2,200 pounds and the engine makes 286 hp, you can bet it goes like the hounds of hell.

I don't know what current Morgan owners will think. Dennis Simanaitis, *Road & Track*'s engineering editor, is one, and an unrepentant one at that. You might assume that as someone who still celebrates steam, he would hate the car. And you would be right. I think I know what Lew Spencer might say. He terrorized SCCA class E racing in the '50s in a Morgan SS, aluminum body, Weber carburetors. He called the car "Baby Doll," and these days there are almost as many "Baby Dolls" in vintage racing as there were Morgans of any kind in the first place. Or as Denny Hulme used to say about McLarens at old timers' events: 68 of the original 11 were entered.

Anyway, the new car will come into the United States in a while, which is about as definite as Morgan gets about anything. It won't have the sliding-pillar front suspension, probably just as well since it was a nightmare. And it won't have the old Moss non-synchro-on-first gearbox; it gets a Getrag six-speed instead. It will also have, get this, 30,000 exterior paint choices and 40 interior combinations. It's priced at 50,000 pounds sterling, Porsche Turbo country, which means you'll have to be a true Morgan fanatic even to think about it. Of course, you always had to be.

In the dim distant past when British cars were respectable, it seemed to me that in descending order of purity came the harsh, spindly and primitive MG-TC, the harsher, spindlier and even more primitive Morgan and the masochistically harsh, incredibly spindly

Leon wearing "plus fours" to test-drive a Morgan Plus Four. *AutoWeek Archives*

and unimaginably primitive HRG. (Somewhere on the coddly, cosseting end of the scale were the rack and the iron maiden.) But the point is that they were pure. At least that's what we told ourselves when we bought them, trying to rationalize their pathetic performance and evil handling.

The Morgan that lured me into its clutches dwelt in the basement of British Motors in San Francisco, where were kept the legacies of the

315

trade-in world—the mistakes of the sales managers. In retrospect, it's where the car belonged and I was lucky to get it, given that for a trade I had a Rover 75, a sedan known as the Poor Man's Rolls-Royce and was actually, at least in terms of performance, the poor man's Humber Hawk.

The Morgan was as irresistible-looking as it was absolutely svelte in comparison to the Rover—which is to say it looked very much like the Aero 8. It had the TR2 engine, recently upgraded from the Vanguard and the dreaded Moss gearbox. It also had stout English ash at its heart, and just to emphasize it would have no truck with contemporary technology, the seat adjustments consisted entirely of blow-up bladders. I loved it, my only regret being the company had dropped the dual rear spares the year before. If I was enchanted, my wife was bewitched. She became a familiar sight dashing around the San Francisco peninsula in that red '54 Paleozoic device with our Airedale sitting at attention, forelegs locked and braced, at her side. An old sprint car mechanic, Slim Sumner, who held forth in the back end of British Cars of Burlingame, consented to tend to the Morgan, which needed more than its share of tending to. The image of the Mog careening around the corner with my wife, sporting her Sherlock Holmes fore 'n' after with the dog properly braced riding right seat, remains vivid to this day.

The Aero 8 has big shoes to fill.

Sometimes It's Best
Not to Remember

Dec. 28, 1998

NEW YORK MAGAZINE, MY SOURCE for all things pretentious, delighted me the other day by referring to a model as having "Fetchingly Imperfect Posture." It gave me cause to think.

How would I characterize cars that I had driven, or tested, or owned in comparable terms?

Charmingly Inadequate. The Subaru 360, a disgraceful little egg, made its appearance when I was editor at *Car and Driver*. The entire staff, practical jokers all, insisted that my car insight was incomplete unless I drive a 360 home one night. The magazine's garage was a few blocks from the headquarters at 32nd Street on the east side of Manhattan.

My house was not far from Ossining in Westchester County, perhaps 30 miles away. But 30 Lesotho-like miles. Don't ask me how I survived the rush hour up the East Side Drive; don't ask me how I survived Bruckner Boulevard in the Bronx; don't ask me. The memories are too painful.

Marvelously Hopeless. Caught in the turmoil of the changing of the editorial guard at *Car and Driver*, the Opel Kadett was judged by the outgoing editorial mandarins to be as loathsome a device as they had ever driven. I insisted on my own evaluation, counseled by the incoming technical editor, the incomparable Patrick J. Bedard. We were unanimous. The Kadett was disgusting. As the savage test was being written, the then-art director, legendary Gene Butera, decided to make a visual statement. He posed the car on top of a stack of crushed cars in a junkyard. By now famous as the Opel-in-the-Junkyard piece, its photo galvanized all five divisions of GM to cancel their advertising. The fact I had been editor for about a week probably saved me. Bill Ziff, proprietor of Ziff-Davis, the magazine's publisher and an immensely civilized man, summoned me to his office. Why? he asked. On behalf of the readers, I answered. But didn't I understand there was a middle ground that would satisfy the editorial obligation to the readers without sacrificing $1 million in advertising? Four hours later I left, still bewildered. It's been 30 years, and I don't have a whole lot more understanding.

Elegantly Disastrous. Just before Christmas in 1954, I drove my MG-TD down from Ithaca, N.Y., with my fiancée. Mainly, it turned out, to stand by while she bought things. She was so adept that a TD didn't begin to suffice as a goods carriage. It was only right that as she bought, I drank—an acceptable activity in New York in the '50s. Came time to go back to Ithaca and it was manifest that the TD would not serve, so I drove to Inskip, the selling dealer, and asked for a luggage rack. "Won't be good enough," the salesman said. "All right," I said filled with good cheer, "give me a Riley." Now whatever else a Riley was, it was gorgeous. Inskip had a used four-place drophead available, and it took my heart. It also took every last item my love had acquired and we set off on our journey. Oh, perfidious Riley! It took us the full distance without a murmur. But when it got there, and for a month thereafter, it suffered every ailment that could afflict a car.

It was a beautiful woman with a heart of tar. Finally I was determined to require Inskip to resolve my agony and drove it back to New York. It was January and snowing. Inskip's service department was gotten to only by driving down a ramp and turning sharp right to avoid a brick wall. The service manager got snow on his shoes. The Riley did not pass the crash test. Neither did the service manager. I got my TD back. These days I read that Bernd Pischetsrieder, chairman of BMW and therefore head of Rover, which owns the Riley name, wants to revive the marque. I'd advise him as strongly as I could to beware a pretty face.

The C-Type Problem

Nov. 4, 1972

WHEN I BOUGHT MY C-TYPE JAGUAR in the spring of 1962 (give or take a couple of years), I was neither rich nor fond of Jaguars. Certainly I hadn't the faintest intimation that I was buying a classic: to me the C-Type was an old, tired race car and about the best I could afford.

When I sold it a year later, an era in my life had clearly come to an end; I was still no fonder of Jaguars as a species, but I had come to have affection and admiration for the C-Type. It had done me no good on turns, I had won nothing with it on the race course, and if I was not rich when I bought it, I was downright broke when I traded it for a '54 MG-TF 1250 and $800. But I had learned what it meant to own a thoroughbred—how it felt to have a moment of history sitting in my own garage—and that peculiar British tradition that insists a race car be capable of being driven on the street as well as at Le Mans had finally been made clear to me. From those moments on, when I watched the Astons or the Lotus GTs wherever they were I had instant respect and affection for them, too.

I never knew the history of my C-Type, but it came to me from Jack Woodard, who, like me, has fallen on evil times and is now a motorsports journalist in Sacramento. Before him, the car was owned by a man named Simpson who ran it at Bonneville, ran it as fast as 172 mph as a matter of fact, but in order to accomplish that, he had had to replace the Alfin drums with cast iron ones, and the car, which was never good at stopping anyway, would, after that, come to a halt for no one.

I will not bore you with the details of how vivid my life in a California tract community became the moment the C-Type took residence in my garage, snarling and spitting every evening as its enthusiastic but amateur crew chief tried to understand its foibles. But I do think you should know that it was driven almost daily on the street by my wife and that the suburban California police were amused and tolerant of that strange spectacle. Not so the local fire department.

Ken Dallison illustration of Jaguar C-Type leading a Porsche 550 Spyder in a race. *Mandel Family Archive*

I am baffled by carburetors, and the more complicated they are, the more baffled I become. I only know that my car was fitted with triple Webers and that they were forever belching and throwing out great gouts of flame. Each time they did, and mostly it happened in front of the Lee Brothers supermarket, some well-meaning bagger or some terrified apartment-dweller-shopper would rush to the telephone and call the fire department. They always came and came promptly, but as the phenomenon occurred with greater and greater frequency, it turned from adventure to bore to chore to downright annoyance and soon they would round the corner by the supermarket on two wheels in their great red truck, take one look at my wife and the green C-Type with the chrome roll bar and make an almost perfect bootlegger's turn in mid-stride on their way back to the firehouse.

It never won much when I had it; it was, after all, a very old car. But there was one glorious day at Laguna Seca when Bob O'Brien (now the spiritual and administrative leader of BAP-Geon—a very lofty position) drove it to a third in class and a seventh overall ahead of a couple of Porsche RS60s and that was victory enough for me—and for him too. He came in after the race white-faced and drawn. No brakes again. It was the last time the car ever raced. The next time it was entered (again for Laguna) it was blown sky-high on the dyno the night before it was to be towed to Monterey; nothing was left of the engine at all, not even the carburetors. Had they known about it, the Belmont fire department would have had a small celebration.

The man with the TF and the $800 thought he was getting a great deal, no greater than the one I thought I was getting, but he soon sold the car to a collector named Chuck Davies who restored it to a glittering perfection and won every concours he entered. Evidently that was a bore, because a year or two later he traded it even up to an elegant lady named Maidi Riedel for a new E-Type coupe. Of course he regretted what he had done the moment the deal had been made, and six months later he bought the car back. It is still somewhere, still perfect, but no one has seen it for years.

It was not until some time later that I realized I had been an unwitting member of a cult, the lovers of the C-Type. Maybe I didn't know much about my car, but the others sure did. One who knew almost all there was to know was Jeff Scott (by coincidence, an *AutoWeek* staffer), who has owned and loved his for 15 years.

"The cars," says Scott, "were introduced here in 1952 at the amazing price of $5,800. Jaguar's founder, Sir William Lyons, and his chief engineer, William Heynes, had gone to Le Mans in 1950 and were impressed with the amount of world attention focused on the race. They decided on the spot that Jaguar would sponsor a factory team, using a modified version of the XK120, and that is exactly what they did.

"The car that was to evolve obviously had to be a great deal lighter than the production version, so a space frame was used—although the tubing wasn't all the same thickness It varied in diameter according to the load it was to carry. A very streamlined aluminum body was designed to fit over the frame, with minimum drag characteristics the highest priority.

"The suspension was largely made up of stock XK stuff, especially the front, but the rear suspension was a little more original with a solid axle sprung by a single transverse torsion bar. The bar was anchored in the center and had a trailing link running from each end to the axle. The idea was that, when one wheel began to lift under acceleration, the torsion bar would counteract the lift. It worked fine.

"Harry Weslake was set to work on the engine. He ported the heads and added bigger valves and had the cam redesigned for more lift. Larger SU carbs were fitted, and then, in 1953, triple Webers were substituted on the works cars.

"By the way, the consumer became the beneficiary of all this when the XK120MC was offered for sale in 1951 incorporating the C heads, a lightweight flywheel, high-compression pistons and so forth.

"Anyway John Fitch drove a C-Type at the Glen in '52 and won the Queen Catherine cup; Phil Hill had another one and won Madera with it in the same year. Masten Gregory raced a C with great success and very likely was responsible for the story, which is surely apocryphal, about totalling his own C-Type at Roosevelt Field, walking over to a competitor and offering to write him a check for his C-Type on the spot. Since then, the story has been told about almost every prominent driver with a checkbook, but if it ever did happen, it was probably Masten who did it.

"It was the coming of the Ferraris which really did the C-Type in. They were quicker and they handled better and the Jags were no match for them. Of course, they did cost three times as much.

"The C-Type was built to generate prestige for the standard line of cars and it did that admirably. About 50 were built and probably a high number, somewhere in the 30s, survive. There may be as many as a dozen in this country. Mine is a '53 and the 32nd of the 50 made. The C was succeeded as a factory race car by the D, which is much more famous, and probably an infinitely better car. But for those reasons and because it was an all-out race car, it just doesn't have the appeal the C-Type had.

"Stirling Moss and I were almost going to enter my car at Sebring in 1963 on the 10th anniversary of the car. It would have been hopeless of course (though Moss claimed I would finish in the top 10 because even though it was far from the quickest it would very likely be the most reliable); that was just the kind of grand gesture the C-Type deserved."

Scott, like any devoted C-Type owner, was perfectly willing to go on endlessly about the car, but there was this hillclimb in Pennsylvania coming up, and he had to see about some new tires for the Jag.

Phil Hill, too, remembers the car with both affection and respect: "I drove one of the first ones that came over, one of them that arrived in 1952. I drove the first one at Elkhart Lake and then again at Watkins Glen. It was a very exceptional race car—very advanced and faster than almost any of its contemporaries. But they were a little tricky to drive.

"They were good to drive, but they didn't have the brute power that maybe the Cadillac or Chrysler-powered Allards had, but their road holding was very good. Still . . . they could bite you if you got too carried away with them. I drove a C-Type in the last race that the Glen circuit went through the town. I was in third place at the time—it was just after the start—and one of the cars ahead of me was forced over onto the sidewalk, hit some spectators and killed a little boy. And that was the end of that."

I'm sure there are better, purer, more classic cars than the C-Type somewhere. But not for me. It was so willing, so forgiving, so patient a car that one even tolerated ownership by a man who paraded around to the races for years on the East Coast in a tam o'shanter and kilts. My ownership of the C-Type allowed me to understand what "classic" was supposed to mean: enduring excellence, willingness to be used on street or track, an era sculpted in aluminum and frozen in time—a car of intense individuality and intense appeal.

These days you could lure me with an AC Bristol (even more with an Aceca) or with an HRG, but tell me where a C-Type is and I'll track it to the ends of the earth.

Sadly, there are only too few left to track. But I console myself with the thought that those that are still around, like Jeff Scott's, are tricked-out in deep green paint and roll bar and doing absurd things like driving to the market and climbing hills in Pennsylvania.

And somewhere, in some suburb much like Belmont, one is driving the fire department straight out of its smoke-filled mind.

No. 017 Is Reunited
with Old Friends

June 12, 1995

THE C-TYPE JAGUAR, A CAR PHIL HILL says taught him precision and finesse, came to life blessed by its moment in history. England, gasping in exhaustion after barely winning the second world war and desperate for export dollars, was prepared to allocate rare strategic metals only to companies able to sell overseas. Jaguar was one of the most successful, having debuted its gloriously felicitous XK120 in 1948 and establishing its credentials by an audacious 132.596-mph two-way mile run at Jabbeke (near Ghent) in Belgium. If that weren't enough, and if somehow the 120's combination of voluptuous lines, blinding performance and modest price weren't enough either, there was always racing. First came a remarkable 12th place overall with a stock 120 at Le Mans in 1950. But that was mere prelude; waiting in the wings was the first of a splendid line of pure sports/racers, the C-Type. There were just six weeks left before the '51 race when Jaguar chieftain Sir William Lyons committed to a purpose-built racer based on 120 mechanicals, but with a sleek aero body covering a space frame.

Forty-four years later, Terry Larson, keeper of the C-Type (and D-Type) Register, would write: "Not only did the C-Type of Peter Whitehead and Peter Walker win [the '51 race], they also came in 77 miles ahead of the second-place car." The C-Type would win again in '53, and then be superseded by the D-Type, a car Jaguar enthusiasts admire not only for its successes but as the precursor of their all-time favorite Jaguar, the E-Type.

Today, most Jaguar enthusiasts favor the D and the E. But C-Type adherents—the classicists—remain; among them is the late Tony Hogg, who seized upon C-Type No. 017 to use in a January 1967 *Road & Track* salon. Its marvelous restoration was an extraordinary achievement, Hogg thought, since the car "had been raced to exhaustion."

Little did he know. In fact *R&T's* salon car had been to the seamy underside of amateur American racing, 1950s style. No. 017 came to the United States as a customer car imported by Charles Hornburg in Los Angeles. It was sold to a Northern California aristo named Sterling Edwards, who would go on to create the Sterling, much in the style of Cunningham. At some point in its early career, this particular Jag's birch gray exterior got badly rumpled when one of Edwards' mechanics shoved it into a hay bale; not much later it was sold to Lou Brero.

Brero is a fascinating figure in early Northern California racing. This was an era of pure amateurism. Very much a time for Sterling Edwards, a skillful racer of gentlemanly aspect. Not so good for Brero, a charger and a man who raced for the joy of combat. He was splendidly—if not popularly—successful with the C; its golden moment in his hands was a first overall in a six-hour endurance race at Torrey Pines near San Diego. After two years of local wins, Brero sold the car to a Reno businessman called Ray Seher.

At the time Seher bought the car, racing may have gradually been getting democratic, but winning remained very much the province of the rich. Then, as now, successful cars were cars fresh from the competition departments of European companies building their reputations on the road circuits of the world: Ferrari, Porsche, Jaguar, Maserati. No sooner would one model from one factory come to dominate than another would eclipse it. By the time C-Type No. 017 got to Reno, its racing lifespan was almost over, which fazed Seher not in the least. Ray raced the car 14 times at places like Santa Rosa, Stockton and Cotati. He and it were waiting at Salinas in 1955 to compete against a Porsche Spyder that, famously, never got beyond Cholame on its drive along Highway 46 from Southern California.

Seher won far more often than he had a right to, which may be the reason he said he had more fun in the C-Type than in any other car he ever raced. A good thing too. A photo survives of the car tilted at a

90-degree angle atop a hay bale at the Sacramento Fairgrounds circuit. Seher is holding his arm straight out as though he thinks he would be able to hold both physics and the road at bay. Happily for Seher, the car teetered on the hay bale and remained upright.

By then, C-Type No. 017 had indeed been raced to exhaustion. Perversely, that was a good thing for me. All I could afford in those days was somebody else's discard, and No. 017 came to me for bottom dollar. Even so, I had to finance it at the Crocker Anglo bank, handing the loan officer the California white slip that identified it as a "Jagar [sic], SRDXK120" (some idea of what the state thought the car was worth is reflected in the registration fee: $4).

I owned it with a partner, Bob O'Brien, with whom I shared not only the C-Type but a Stanguellini Formula Junior. Mostly I drove the Stang, because the Jag, even though old and tattered, was far too fierce for me. Worse still, while it went like the absolute hammers of six-cylinder, Weber-carbureted hell, it wouldn't stop since the disc brakes that would appear on later Cs were only approximated by the Alfin drums of the No. 017. The person in our family who drove it most was my wife. When you're young and too poor to afford a race car and a regular car besides, the race car must serve many purposes. So the C-Type went to the supermarket, and in the evenings, it became the soothing cradle for a three-year-old whose croup denied him the sleep that only a rumbling ride in the Jag could finally bring. No. 017 also became a night prowler. Nearby lived a Lister Jaguar and an RS60 Porsche, and in those days it was still possible to use the light of the moon and the public road for an occasional encounter with destiny. The memory of those evenings remains vivid—most of all, how the car felt. Nowadays, driving is a coincidental occupation. Then, paying attention was a life and death matter. Particularly in a race car, most particularly in the C-Type. Driving it was a full-time job. It was the Jag that taught me the meaning of Bump Steer. Hill remembers much the same: "The car would not take any heavy-handedness," he says. "You had to guide it. When driven at its limits, it required you to take a breath and do a precise job."

Even so, or maybe because of its demands, C-Type No. 017 became very much a member of the family. At least until that moment it blew sky-high on the dyno and had to be sold; the cost of a replacement engine was way beyond reality.

Time passes. Things happen. One thing that happened is that two months ago I came into reasonable control of the leukemia my doctors had diagnosed the previous winter, and my son persuaded me to go to Arizona for the Copperstate. He had arranged, he told me, for our friend Harley Cluxton to lend us a 427 Cobra for the event. In fact, as I was about to discover, he and Harley had conspired far more intricately. As I stood in the cool Phoenix evening at the initial Copperstate drivers' meeting, wondering how on earth I would ever forgive myself if I stuffed Harley's 427 into a cactus, I began to hear, building louder and louder, the sound of an unmuffled exhaust. Suddenly, the crowd to my left parted. I looked over my shoulder and there, almost touching me, was the broad, sensuous bonnet of an exquisite black car. In the minute or so it took me to understand what I was seeing, the car's owner climbed out and came over to me, key in hand. "I want you to drive an old friend," said Terry Larson, who had spent all day every day for the previous two months bringing the C-Type back to life from its temporary existence in boxes at his shop.

I can't tell you why someone offers a perfect stranger a precious car from his own collection for a four-day wild drive over crowned roads in back country Arizona. I can only tell you that my son and I were blessed over the best part of a week with lovely memories, learning all the while to cherish more and more a noisy, bouncy, primitive, hot, inconsiderate, obsolete, roaring, leaping antiquity of a car: C-Type Jaguar No. 017. From our perspective at least, perhaps the most glorious automobile ever made.

Escape Road indeed.

Poltergeists

Feb. 21, 1994

POLTERGEISTS ARE NOTORIOUSLY ILL-MANNERED. When ours knocked over a box in the basement, spilling life documents across the floor, I realized just how ill-mannered they can be.

The sales agreement for the Rover is dated Sept. 9, 1954. Total price is listed as $1,981, a lot of money in days when $10,000 would buy a house. The good news, at least according to the faded paper, was that the dealership gave exactly $1,981 for the trade. The bad news was that the trade was a 1953 Porsche America coupe in lovely condition. Now the Rover—a 75—was a solid, beautifully built British car with aspirations to Rolls-Roycehood. Everything you could ever ask of a sensible, conservative sedan. Everything, that is, except exciting. Which is one thing you could never accuse the Porsche of.

It had just carried me—accompanied by a new wife and an Airedale—across the country and it had provided a thrill a mile. In those days Porsche had exclusivity. And Porsche had (relatively) good performance. And Porsche had cachet—at least among the three people between the coasts who knew what it was. It also had unpredictable handling. And what a Porsche fully loaded with passenger, Airedale and family possessions plus a luggage rack on its top had was viciously unpredictable handling.

Within 11 minutes of our arrival in Northern California, I was shopping for relief. Something dull. I found the Rover. Given the nature of the deal (it seems to me today with whatever perspective I now have), the salesman had seen me coming all the way from western New York State. However faithful, however conservative and solid, the Rover had no future with me. Too dull. Too conservative. Too (believe it or don't) reliable.

The second sales agreement that the poltergeist confronted me with was substantially less embarrassing. Written on May 4, 1955, it is a bill of redemption, recording the trade of a 1954 Rover 75 (valued at $1,400) on a new MG TF 1500. I thought then, I think now, that the TF 1500 is the best of the Midgets. Lovely lines. Decent-sized engine. And it only cost me an additional $750.75 paid over the next year at $67.83 a month. Wasn't life innocent?

But the TF couldn't last, and didn't. Car-buying frenzy seized me again. The poltergeist's third sales agreement reads March 1956. It says I got $1,559.46 for the TF in trade on a used Morgan Plus Four the dealership had helped to celebrate a birthday during its stay there. They charged me $1,786.75 for it and rejoiced at the deal. So did I. I rarely remember a car I liked so much. My wife loved it, too. She bought a Sherlock Holmes fore 'n' after [*a.k.a. a deerstalker*] and drove around the San Francisco Bay Area with the Airedale sitting up at her side, becoming a familiar and charming sight.

I have absolutely no idea where any of those cars are today. Broken and discarded, most likely. At the very least old, rusted and mighty creaky. In other words, much like me. As old Sebring chief steward Bill "Don't Do the Same Thing Once" Smythe likes to say: "It's not that I'm so old, it's just that I'm built cheaply."

Goodbye to a Good Man

July 5, 1999

WHEN JOE ESKRIDGE DIED LAST WEEK AT 96, he took a little bit of the best of Detroit with him. Given how much of his life he devoted to the auto industry, how much he saw, how much he was a part of, it would have been hard to find anybody else who represented it more faithfully.

Trouble was that while Joe's memory was acute to the end, he felt that talking about what people had confided in him, or what mistakes his companies had made, was treacherous. He plain wouldn't do it.

And he'd seen a lot and done a lot.

He negotiated to buy BMW on behalf of American Motors.

He was the auto industry's man in Washington for a good part of World War II.

When Hudson decided to enter the subcompact market with the Jet, Joe's voice was the only one to dissent.

In all the time I spent wandering the earth identifying myself as Joe Eskridge's son-in-law, I heard nothing but good words. It's hard for me to imagine that here was a man who devoted himself to the factory floor and to the drawing board and to behind-the-door negotiations, and yet seemed not to have made a single enemy. That was his style and his manner; every man deserved a minimum of courtesy. It was only right.

Joe had begun as a kind of itinerant draftsman, taking work where he could find it, and he found it most often at Franklin Car Co. Life was neither easy nor pleasant, and Joe's hardscrabble memories only hinted at what it took to put together a living. He came from the Deep South and from no particular advantage of any kind, except a mother whose rigid religiosity sustained him.

As we view the history of the American auto industry from this end of the telescope, much of what happened seems inevitable. Nothing could have been further from the truth. It was a tumultuous time, filled with coincidence and chance, with treachery and rascality, in which the pioneers surfaced suddenly and disappeared equally quickly.

Joe could not have been less of that ilk; by the time he got to Hudson, he apprenticed himself to a pioneer Belgian body engineer and learned a new and exacting discipline. It led to his being posted to the coachbuilding firm of Biddle and Smart, whose work for Hudson was astonishingly sophisticated. From that moment on, Joe distinguished what he did from the work of the stylists (of whom there were mighty few at the time), for whom this gentle man had a certain contempt.

As the war years made greater and greater demands on everyone in the auto industry, and Joe devoted incredibly long hours to his role in manufacturing parts for aircraft, his patience was strained almost to breaking. It would have been easy for him to slight his two teenaged daughters, but he never did. The elder told me once how he took her hunting up north in Michigan and to calm her fear of snakes found one, picked it up and showed her how little there was to be afraid of. She only found out later that her father was petrified of snakes.

It must have strained his charitable nature, not to mention his love for his daughter, when she brought me home in my MG. Joe had seen the industry grow up, he had been a part of the development of some of the most extraordinary cars we made in America, and here was this pompous post-adolescent in his toy Britmobile lecturing on truth in design.

He'd learned patience from dealing with the UAW, and I was the beneficiary.

Patience came once again to Joe's aid when he was able to coax a contract from the Marine Corps for the Mighty Mite at a time when survival of the company depended on it.

Joe was there for it all, but gentlemen don't open other gentlemen's mail. And if Joe was anything, he was a gentleman. Good for him. Pity for us.

Of Fathers and Their Cars

Sept. 13, 1999

SOMEBODY TOLD ME MY LATE FATHER's beautifully restored former Mk V Jag went up for auction the other day; somebody else told me it brought $110,000. Never mind that I didn't have the money, I wouldn't have wanted the car anyway. When I said that to the man who first let me know it had been over the block, he seemed astonished.

Mk Vs were never my favorites. They were not as elegantly handsome as their predecessor Mk IVs. They were soft and indistinct. I always thought that if they were dogs they would be Salukis. If they were an actress, they would be someone like Louise Rainer, whom I always hated. And an after-dinner drink? Something perfectly dreadful like Galliano.

They were also slow. It's perfectly all right to be slow if you're stately; it's fine to be slow if you're so dazzlingly beautiful people are grateful for the time you spend passing in front of their eyes. (Catherine Deneuve in her later years comes to mind.)

I don't know how well Mk Vs sold in this country. I didn't get into the Jag business until the Mk VII came along (was there a Mk VI? I don't think so), and however bad the Mk V might have been, the Mk VII was worse. As they used to say about the Lotus 40, successor to the shabby Lotus 30, "It's a Lotus 30 with 10 more things wrong with it."

Never mind the commission, I used to absolutely hate delivering a Mk VII because I knew, just knew, that within almost minutes the phone at the dealership would ring with an erupting volcano at the other end demanding the dispatch of a tow truck.

Anyway, fathers and Mk Vs. The colonel (an earned honorific; operating in India, he was key in the logistical supply line over the hump during World War II) fancied himself an accomplished car guy. It was not within my character or the limit of my bravery to tell him otherwise. Somewhat after the Mk V debacle, he insisted on driving my MG-TD. He was a large man, no, he was a very large man, and either he did not fit the MG or the MG did not fit him. At any rate it was an uneasy drive, and he and I never ever mentioned the incident again.

The TD incident to the contrary notwithstanding my father was a remarkable fellow. He was so accomplished at so many things the

Leon and his pal Leo Bourke pushing a Lotus 11 near San Francisco.
AutoWeek Archives

very idea of his achievements awed me. He was a six-goal polo player; he was a world-class bridge player. He was captain of the Olympic skeet shooting team. He was a prominent member of the Confrérie des Chevaliers du Tastevin. He had a huge circle of friends, many of whom assured me nobody, but nobody was as entertaining as he was. It was nice to hear especially when he turned his charm on me and me alone: It always made me feel very special.

But like others you and I know, achievement in one or another area does not ensure understanding or sophistication in the car world. My father was tone deaf to cars. If they were expensive and looked it, he thought they were wonderful. And so he bought the Mk V. I wasn't at home when he did and I doubt he would have asked my opinion if I had been, but there it was and there he was and the two of them would have to live with each other.

It wasn't the first car mistake he made and it wasn't the last; he would go on to buy a Bentley and a Rolls and then ask the dealer, after some consideration, to put a Rolls grille on the Bentley.

I thought it was an exercise in absolutely vile taste.

But not as bad as the Mk V.

Run, Rabbit, Run

Jan. 14, 1985

IN ALL THE ANNOUNCEMENT of the onslaught of the new VW Golf and GTI, there came not a word of solace to Rabbit lovers about the passing of the breed.

Nary a catch in VW's throat to betray corporate sadness.

That is not as many of us would have wanted it to happen.

For nine years we have lived with Rabbit and Rabbit legend. A lot of us, particularly all-around *AutoWeek* reader Larry Tebo, whose letter in these pages obliquely addressed the omission only days ago, resented the cavalier dismissal of Rabbitry as though it didn't even exist.

Nine years of our lives, not to mention VWs, were dealt with as though they had never existed. That's revisionist stuff. The kind of thing you expect from Soviet historians after the deposing of yet another turnip collective commissar.

To us, the Rabbit was a landmark car. No, it wasn't the pattern for its ilk. That distinction belonged (at least in the modern era) to the Mini and afterward to the Fiat 127. But it surely was the most popular of its genre and the most significant. In its two-box design, Giorgetto Giugiaro created the package the world recognized as its car—the World Car so many had predicted would flood the Earth.

The Rabbit never did that, more's the pity. But it brought awareness to a whole generation of people that small cars didn't need to be dumb to accommodate a family with luggage. In fact, they could be agile and fun to drive. That was the Rabbit's real message, and hold the cards and letters telling me the Beetle did it first and better. Sure it did it first. But not better. And not to the great middle class. The Beetle was outre, odd, bizarre; it became a cult car—albeit a huge cult. But it never turned into the mainstream car the Rabbit became.

Good thing for the Beetle, bad thing for the Rabbit. For inherent in the notion of "mainstream" is the understanding that mass tastes will dictate popularity—or its lack. And they did. And the verdict was

336

a cruel one for VW. That's the trouble with mainstream tastes; they prevail a lot.

But for us, for those of us who are a part of this journal as readers or contributors, the Rabbit always meant a great deal more than the World Car That Made World Cars Acceptable to the Proles. In and of itself, the Rabbit was one of those cars. The MG was one of those cars, too. So was the Sprite. So is the Morgan. Not to mention the Mini and its wonderful variant, the Cooper S. Those cars are cars that presume to have verve. Intelligence is implicit in their design. They possess a longevity in terms of how long the eye can linger over their shape. Most of all, there are legends that came out of their exploits on the highway or the racetrack.

Rabbits were second cars in Porsche garages, or they were first cars for Porsche aspirants. Rabbits were race cars for those who longed for Marches but knew they could never have them. Rabbits were basic sculptures straight from the factory to which the ingenious or the compulsive added flares and bulges and air dams and wings and wheels and tires so wide they wouldn't pass through the Panama Canal.

I owned a Rabbit like that. It came from Al Holbert's race shop, and it was the first car I had bought in 30 years in the wonderful, ritualistic fashion in which I acquired both my first sports car and my unspoken, unwritten membership in the society of the car-lost. It was the third Rabbit in a string. The first lives in Los Angeles and is called, deservedly, "Beater Rabbit." The second is in Portland, Ore., where it keeps a young woman I am very fond of mobile and safe to roam.

This third, this Al Holbert autograph model, is reserved for me and for my wife—a woman who has done time behind the wheels of a Lotus Cortina, an Aston Martin DB3S, a '54 Morgan, a C-Type Jaguar w/dry sump "D" motor and the like. No wimp she, and she and the Rabbit are nearly inseparable.

That says a lot to me about what the Rabbit was and meant—never a car to be scorned, always a car with a strong and willing heart, forever a car that endeared itself to its owners. And this in a cloak as common and ordinary as an accountant's. That seems to me tribute indeed to what was meant to be just another econocar.

Seems that way to me; could seem that way to a lot of you; didn't seem to seem that way to VW, at least to listen to the deafening silence when it put the Rabbit to death.

Lord knows, nobody ever held British Leyland up as a company with a soul much less a company with blood circulating through it; but when B-L killed the MG and then the Triumph two-seater, it had the grace to mourn their passing.

Perhaps it's better VW leave the grieving to us.

Any company that cannot stop to note the closing of a chapter so significant to its history as that written by the Rabbit for VW is a company without grace. Without grace an obituary is a sodden thing. Let those of us who rejoiced in the Rabbit bid it farewell.

Pace.

Twilight of the C-Class

March 20, 2000

THIS WEEK THEY HAVE ME IN A NEW C-CLASS MERCEDES. Others on staff will drive it and make notes; I'm saying goodbye. This fall the car will be replaced by a better, more wonderful, sleeker, cleaner C-Class, which I'm not going to like at all. Won't have anything to do with its shining virtues. Will have everything to do with my history with the current one.

The current iteration of the C-Class and I met at its short-lead intro in D.C., where I drove it harder than I should have, particularly since my passenger was Dieter Zetsche, then the R&D guy, now the board member for marketing. He was, and still is, one of the youngest, most energetic senior execs in the world auto industry, so I must have felt he wouldn't be at all stuffy about riding right seat while I bent the car into corners at high velocity. He and I still speak, so if nothing else, he's at least forgiven me.

Anyway, I drove a lipstick-red Merc back to Detroit and when I got home, I told my wife she needed one. Now Mercedes' long suit has always been safety, and given that she was carrying on an enduring love affair with her Passat, I knew that only by appealing to her sensible side could I woo her away from it.

How right I was; to her, a new (emphasis on the new) Mercedes was pretentious, too expensive and not her kind of thing. Of course that didn't apply to her long-cherished 300D, nicknamed Dr. Diesel since its *Car and Driver* test days. It sat pristine in the garage, almost never used but kept for sentiment's sake.

Anyway, her conversion took long months, which was a good thing since the new car had not yet come into the country. But gradually she came around, and by that time the green C-Class that I ordered for her had arrived at the dealer. From that moment until she died, the C-Class was a much-beloved companion.

Are you getting the feeling that cars with her were something more than useful tools?

Olivia in her kitchen. *Mandel Family Archive*

Driving the new C-Class this week has been more than just another long test drive. It was coming home, particularly since I so liked my wife's car that I bought a C36. Now as much as I approved of the standard-issue car, the C36 was an entirely different caldron of horsepower.

I don't know about you, but to me there are very few cars whose responses seem directly patched into my neuro-network. Many Porsches, most Ferraris, C-type and E-type Jaguars and the C36. Evidently others felt the same way because a remarkable number of my friends owned one, including Tim Lombardi, team manager for Penske, Raul Boesel and that manic collector, David Mohlman. When I got my car, AMG was still a separate company from Mercedes, so the enabling PR person in Germany suggested that I have the car returned to the factory to be put precisely in spec. Also, he said, I should specify that the interior trim be carbon fiber.

I had known, when I got into this week's tester, that faux fiber had crept into the C-Class sport and it irritated me mildly that the unenlightened would be confusing this with the real stuff. But there it was confronting me, and seeing it irritated me more than mildly. Made the car seem like a poseur.

Anyway, I have spent the week revisiting my life with Mercedes. Inevitably, I have had bittersweet memories of the green car and of my wife. Inevitably, now that I know we are near replacement, I have thought about how much better the new car will be and how hard it will have to work to ingratiate itself with me.

We mark our lives by the cars we own, and the current C-Class lives vividly in my mind. For the likes of us, isn't that what cars are all about?

Made No Difference When; It Still Came Too Soon

July 31, 1995

Olivia, the wife who so often goes unnamed in Leon's writings (not an insult, but a protective impulse that left her free to be known only to those she chose), remains unnamed in this farewell column. This time, though, it seems like he couldn't yet bear to type it.

WHEN I MET HER, she said she'd go out with me on one condition: if I'd take her to a race at Watkins Glen. It was the first race I'd ever been to, but far from the last and particularly with her. She was the daughter of a Hudson Motor Company VP/engineering (he had started as a draftsman at Franklin and eventually become a Hudson body engineer—not a stylist; never a stylist), and she was absolutely delighted by the MG-TD we drove down from Ithaca.

When she and I crossed the country to live in California, she did more than her share of herding the nasty-handling little Porsche 1500 Normal coupe with her household goods in a rack on top and an Airedale she'd named "Siddeley," for Armstrong/Siddeley, in the back. She got a Morgan Plus 4 in Burlingame, and she and Siddeley would career around the San Francisco Peninsula—she wearing a fore 'n' after, the dog bracing his front paws on the door, his head pointing forward, his ears straight back in the wind, a familiar sight to MG and Healey owners she'd always wave to.

She was such a formidable charger, our friend Rod Carveth offered her a drive in his Aston Martin DB3S in a ladies' race at Salt Lake City; she turned him down graciously, but privately she snorted at the idea of "ladies" races in general—if she couldn't drive with the men she wouldn't drive at all.

But she crewed at Cotati and she sat on a timing stand at Buchanan Field when she was so far gone her ob/gyn—who had his

342

Olivia's wedding portrait. *Mandel Family Archive*

MGA entered—flew over in his single engine Piper, just in case.

She read every line of *ComPress*; then signed on in exasperation at
the shabby job of proofreading even after it became *Competition Press
and Autoweek* (no cap "W"). She looked after a slightly seedy Charlie
Fox, later an immaculate David Abrahamson and the energetic Steve

343

Thompson. (And even after that, at *Car and Driver*, she conspired with Caroline Hadley to keep track of the lot of us, including Pat Bedard and Bob Brown, a source of gentle concern to her up to and including the moment of his departure for *S.I.*)

After the TD and the Porsche and the Morgan, she drove the C-Type around Belmont and San Carlos, occasionally forgetting herself and pumping raw gas into the Webers and onto a hot intake manifold so that the local fire departments soon learned to ignore the

Olivia and Leon. When CART raced in the streets of Detroit, *AutoWeek* had a hospitality tent in the paddock and hosted a party for the racers during the week. *Mandel Family Archive*

alarms about the funny green car that kept catching on fire in the supermarket parking lot.

She polished her share of Lotuses and Rileys and TCs. Later, wearing a headset, she stood out on windswept corners at woebegone airfields once more looking after people who didn't have the sense to look out for themselves.

She went off adventuring at the tinkle of an ice cube to Reno and Santa Barbara and Kent in pickups and banana-boat convertibles and cranky old Rovers with as gay a giggle as a teenager, of which she still reminded many even into her 30s.

She knew everybody and everybody knew her and everyone who met her was enchanted.

She trusted Peter to keep me on track, even though she knew he was McLaren's womanizer of world renown. When he burned at Kyalami, she cried her eyes out for a week.

She took Danny in when he came back from England, suffered with him early and then let me go off on a Can-Am summer and not just me, but her son as well.

"Without pettiness, without artifice," Denise said about her when she died in June, too young by far. Denise was right, of course, but not right enough by half.

Friends I Haven't Met Yet

Dec. 30, 1996

ON FEB. 1, A PERSONAGE OF the Leukemia Society Michigan Chapter will draw a name out of a hat to award a brand-new Porsche Boxster to someone who has entered its raffle.

We have a number of raffles advertised in our classified section each year. The Leukemia Society Porsche Boxster Raffle is not one of them. It stands separate and distinct as a personal cause, contributed to by Porsche Cars of North America from the first shipment to the United States, and initiated by me.

Two years ago I was diagnosed with leukemia. It was not one of the happiest moments of my life. In the time that has passed since that grim announcement, I have learned a great deal not only about leukemia, but about a variety of attendant matters.

Let me begin with what I have discovered about my friends.

Despite the occasional opening into my life through this Jaundiced Eye, I am not the most forthcoming person you know. The current vogue of unburdening oneself about matters small and smaller has always struck me as unseemly. I have never much wanted to know about my neighbor's troubles; I certainly didn't want him knowing about mine.

It wasn't easy to keep things to myself during the early months of my illness. First of all, I couldn't do any work, much less appear in the office, so there were reasons that had to be given, people in whom to confide.

That was my first discovery: If you give them the chance, your friends will be astonishingly protective of your dignity.

In time it became possible for me to rejoin the world. While there is no cure for my leukemia, the Mayo Clinic called my reaction to a drug called Interferon "spectacular." In other words, as I was beginning to understand, I was incredibly lucky. Nobody in the medical world knows quite how or why Interferon works, all they know is that sometimes it slays the disease remarkably. For me, it was magic.

346

Racer Robbie Buhl at the wheel of the Boxster donated by Porsche Cars of North America for the Leukemia Foundation. Standing are PCNA PR rep Bob Carlson and longtime Mandel family friend Lisa Gandelot. *AutoWeek Archives*

So gradually, first to my professional community, then to the Indy car racing world, I came out of the leukemia closet. As I made personal progress, I began to discover how progress was being made with other leukemias, with other blood diseases, with other cancers. My wife urged me to begin to make an effort, not just to rejoin the world of *AutoWeek*, but to devote time to trying to make it possible for others with blood cancers to benefit as I had. I agreed to try and raise awareness and money for my local group, the Leukemia Society Michigan Chapter. My wife was not so lucky as I, and with her death from cancer, I became the more determined to work against the disease.

347

Which is when I discovered even more about my friends.

As I went about the land asking for help, more people stepped up to my side than I would ever have believed possible. From the magazine world, but way beyond that—from the racing world, from past lives, most particularly from the community of car company colleagues and associates, from Ford to Chevy, from Range Rover to Jaguar, from Toyota to Mercedes-Benz; the outpouring of support was overwhelming.

Which brings me to Porsche, their heartfelt and immediate response of the donation of a new Boxster, and my shamelessness in promoting a raffle to take advantage of it. This is my deal, and no apologies. These are my friends, and bless them. I'd be grateful if you'd step up. And I want to shake the hand of the guy who wins it.

And tell him how much it means that he—with all the others—was there.

A Lesson Learned at the Slave Marts of Monterey

Jan. 20, 1997

FOR 35 YEARS I'VE MANAGED TO AVOID contaminating much of what the car world finds important.

I've let the Solo people find solitude.

I've left cosmetology to the buffers and polishers of the concours world.

I've often rallied behind those who wished to rally—quite far behind, so I never actually threatened to be a part of any of it.

A fine antiseptic stance, I told myself. Journalists have no right to be involved, I assured anyone who asked; they are required to be dispassionate observers.

Last summer, I fell, seduced by a fluttery lashed charmer in Monterey, the very manifestation of a fantasy: a Salmson drophead MG in lovely condition as though ready for a full-dress ball, put up for public auction, displayed in front of just anyone to paw and stroke. It was too much for even me, sworn long since to keeping my distance from the hawking, screeching, huckledebuck shell games of the increasingly popular public classic car auction.

Auction proprietors, in my mind, are slave traders. Their audiences are studded with shifty-eyed middlemen, lurking in the crowd for bargains to chain together and march across the desert to be sold in a more civilized place to less-aware buyers at full retail.

So what choice did I have with the delicate, innocent, virginal TA drophead?

Still, ache as I did to rescue the TA from a life on the auction circuit, pushed from one platform to another and forced to expose its charms to cold-hearted profiteers, I thought I knew better than to rush in and bid uncontrollably.

The first thing I did was to enlist the help of a shrewd auction veteran, a connoisseur of the automobile slave marts, quiet and immensely knowledgeable, a man with an encyclopedic knowledge not only of the cars up for auction, but of the carnivores who dwell in the land of auctions.

His name was Jack Flaherty. Tough enough to have been the sprint car champion of California when sprint car drivers picked their teeth with railroad spikes. Later, factory road racing driver of the likes of Lister-Jaguar. Shrewd enough to run a whole handful of dealerships for the legendary British car importer, Kjell Qvale. Known and widely consulted oracle in a variety of marques, including Rolls-Royce, Jaguar and MG. Collector and pilot/racer of World War II fighter planes, and, as someone else once said of him, a man with gunfighter's eyes.

If I were going to abandon my principles and become involved in an auction, I wasn't going to go stupidly into the night. I stayed away in favor of Jack Flaherty as my agent when the TA went across the block. Inevitably, necessarily, it brought an outrageous price. The auctioneers smacked their lips, Flaherty turned away in disgust.

So now comes confession time: All the while I stayed carefully away that auction night, my heart beat faster, and on the news the charmer went to somebody else, it broke into little pieces.

My friend Flaherty stood in my shoes trying to insulate me from the evils of the auction, but thereby a longtime car lesson went ignored: Cars can betray you, they can break your heart, but when a car thing happens, if you're a car guy, it is your obligation to be involved right up to your eyebrows. Had I been there and if I'd gotten the TA, it would have lifted my heart; had I been there and lost it, I would have been crushed. But in either case, it would have been my deal, which is the whole car thing point. Whatever you do with cars, you do yourself. Everything else is for *spectators*. Worse still, *journalists*.

The AC Bristol

Jan. 10, 1994

THERE ISN'T A FATHER ALIVE who doesn't cringe whenever he hears Harry Chapin's song about the man who is so busy providing for his family he ignores his son until it is far too late.

Because I am who I am and do what I do, I have always tried to avoid the fate of the man in the song by bringing my son into my life with cars. I have done this with stories about cars, and with field trips to watch them being made and, of course, with my friends who race cars. Most of all with cars that have taken up residence in the family, and of them all, particularly with an AC Ace Bristol.

For almost 20 years, ever since he was just old enough to peer over a license, he and I lived with that car and the dream of its restoration.

When we drove down to the San Francisco Peninsula to get it, my son and I, manhandling its carcass onto a flatbed and hauling it back up the hill toward Reno, we got as far as Blue Canyon when a CHP black & white blasted up on the port quarter and from its loud hailer came a question that set the tone for the long relationship to come: "Where in hell did you manage to find that?"

For almost two decades thereafter, the AC evoked the same response. The right people demonstrated their rightness by remembering ACs, and remembering them both fondly and with respect.

Eight years ago, my son married a lovely young woman and while his mother made the new couple's sideboard whole, I could think of nothing more precious to give them than the pink slip to the AC.

At about the same time, I gathered my resources together and, having unearthed the name of a well-respected AC expert, importuned him to resuscitate (what I still thought of as) our car. It would cost—he hemmed and hawed and to his credit said it was absolutely impossible to get very close to an accurate figure—about $25,000 to bring it back alive. I swallowed hard. Agreed. Paid half. Then further agreed that there could be no practical time limit placed on a project of this kind.

Three years later, a long-distance inquiry (piqued by detailed letters and Polaroids—mostly of biopsies) revealed no great progress, and not a much better-formed sense of estimated time of completion.

It did, however, result in a revised cost estimate. Another $15,000 would be required. And not much later, more again.

Now $25,000 we could afford. Not easily, and it would have to be paid in stages, but it was possible. Even the additional $15,000 could somehow be managed. But if it were going to be a matter of even more than that . . .

There would have to be a plan. A limit. A deadline. To which the AC expert replied that I could plan all I chose, but the world was not susceptible to control by mere men and what we were dealing with here was . . . art. And the total would be $60,000. I said I couldn't afford it. Stop the work. He said—besides the 20-plus thousand he'd already been paid—there'd be storage and stowage and cartage, and if not there'd be a lawsuit and . . . why go on?

It's been 18 months and some of the humiliation has gone away. As I have told this story, sadly and with chagrin, I've increasingly discovered that almost everybody has one just like it.

The words to the song linger in my mind these days as I watch my son with his sons, two of them babies still, but the elder almost old enough to understand. He went on a business trip with his daddy last month; I remember those trips and the bond they formed, and I ache.

These days there are expenses in life that have to be given priority according to the needs of those concerned. But the more I think of that song and the lost AC, the more I assign a priority to replacing that car with something far more modest but with the gravity to become the center of our multigenerational lives, filled with charm and the capacity for apportioning affection among us. Like others, we have few enough things that bring us together instead of driving us apart. In our family, a car is one of those things: not a mere luxury or even just a necessity, but an essential part of life.

The E at the End of the Rainbow

Oct. 11, 1999

WENT TO PEBBLE BEACH—the auctions, concours, paddock haggling—to watch the fools parted from their money. Of course, I was parted from mine.

Nothing could have made me happier. I bought the other half of the marvelous E-type I owned with Harley Cluxton and which I had been trying to pry away from him for four years. With my son, the editor, I'd road-tested it over three Copperstates. Ever heard of a bulletproof Jag? This one is. Anyway, I insist that cars exist in two incarnations: The first is as a commodity—Escorts, Neons and such, for people who see life as commoditized. Go to work, go home, lie on the couch, have a beer. The second is as something very special, with a distinct flavor, scent and soul. Such cars draw you as your partner did, with an intoxicating allure.

That has to come from context, and context, in turn, must lie in experience.

So the E-type and its elder siblings had been my objects of infinite desire forever.

Now, having gone on record as loathing the dowager Jags, Mk Vs, Mk VIIs and their ilk, I have to be careful to make a distinction. The big cars always seemed like poseurs to me. They were not Bentleys, they were not, even after they put out a car with a Daimler badge on it, fit inheritors of the name. They were cheap, albeit convincing, imitations—which was, of course, their *raison d'etre*. They were hard to embrace.

The sports cars slept on the other side of the blanket. They were conceived in passion; they entered the world rubbing their hands in glee. I didn't make the acquaintance of the prewar cars, the SS90s and 100s, until after I became intimate with their descendants, but when

I saw them first I knew immediately what they were.

I first laid eyes on an XK120 not long after it was introduced. We were both in Paris when suddenly the Jag simply appeared. It was so stunning, its effect 50 years later is hard to convey. It absolutely took one's breath away; what was there like it?

The car that clubbed me between the eyes was parked nose-in at the curb of the Hotel Continental (now Intercontinental). It was late in the evening. I had spent the earlier hours in conviviality. Did I say I was thunderstruck? I sat down on the curb in front of the grille and just stared.

Not long after I enlisted in the colonial Jaguar legions, signed up as a Kjell Qvale helot and was posted to a distant place by the name of Burlingame. In the years that passed, my affection for Jaguar sports cars did not dim a very great deal through the progression from 120 to 140 to 150. The glorious moment I set eyes on the 120 for the first time remained warm in my memory.

Perhaps not so coincidentally, I had acquired a C-type to race. I didn't and neither did it, a rod went through the block when it was revved to 7,000, cold. After the fact, somebody said never do that. The C-type remains the car of memory. My wife drove it to the grocery store. My son, the now-editor, sat in the driver's seat making racing noises though he couldn't even reach the sides of the steering wheel. And by the light of the moon, I went in the C to visit my almost neighbor, Jack Flaherty, who had a Lister-Jag in his garage.

Not much later Jaguar introduced the E. It had never occurred to me I would again be swept away as I had been by the 120. But I was, and it was the E that did it.

Now I own one. Did I mention context? In addition to memories and experiences, Jaguar has brought me dear friends: Mike Dale, Terry Larson (who revived my old C-type and loaned it to me for the Copperstate), Jay Oppenheimer, originator—with his wife, Kay—of the Old Jags dinner in Monterey but who's moved uptown these days with a Cunningham.

On the day the E arrived from Arizona, I called my daughter-in-law and she brought all three grandsons over for a drive. It was a simple obligation. Context for them too.

The Month of Indy

June 11, 1984

You can't hardly keep your membership in the Motor Sport of the Month Club unless you spend all of May bitching about Indy.

The month of May and a good deal of the rest of the year as well.

Does a couple of things for you. Says you spent the month there. Many points on some unseen scoreboard. Says you're hopelessly out of it. Take those points down.

The fact is this: Racing is a community. It is a profession—or, if you must, a craft—but it is also a moving geographic entity. A sort of random, social tectonic plate. Contemplate for a moment that we all live simultaneously in some geographic spot, in some social stratum and in a professional community. Racers almost don't live anywhere. Their geography is determined by a testing and racing schedule. Their social stratum is layered by the people they know and see when they race and test. Likewise with the professional community.

Thus, May at Indy is as close as racers come to having a town of their own. Remember now, racers include crew chiefs, wrenches, gofers, wives, support technicians—even drivers and entrants.

"Word comes from the Championship Auto Racing Auxiliary (CARA) that its style show and luncheon Friday in the Radisson is sold out," wrote the *Indianapolis Star* on May 19. The person who read the item laughed at it. Laughed?

The style show (and what town doesn't have one) was for charity (cancer research). Commentators were to be Paul Page and his wife, Sally. Names on the committee or models include John and Betty Rutherford (CARA president), Mrs. Tony Bettenhausen, Mrs. Pancho Carter and the likes of Steve Chassey, Chrissy Horn (timer and scorer for Bobby Rahal), Mrs. Tom Sneva, Rick and Roger Mears' mother, Skip, Shelly and Al Unser Jr., Kathy Penske, well, why go on?

You and I are damn proud to be asked to serve in a volunteer capacity for a well-known charity in our communities. Likely we work

With Danny Sullivan in pit lane. *AutoWeek Archives*

harder at that sort of thing than we ought. We sure as hell don't laugh at the Good Works being done.

Given that 30 Days in May is as long as anyone in racing spends anywhere, what more logical time or more logical place than Indianapolis to act out all the needs people have to contribute, congregate or plain socialize?

357

These, furthermore, are perfectly splendid people. They live as most of us do not, but they are, by and large, very talented and highly dedicated. They have to be. I cannot tell you the extent to which I value my acquaintanceships and my friendships with a handful of mechanics, a few crew chiefs, some entrants and their families. I wish I knew more of racing's people. Some day, if I continue to be lucky, I will.

Whenever I hear somebody scoff about Indy ("Did I go there this year, are you kidding, there isn't enough money in the world." Or worse: "Yeah, I spent a year last May at the Speedway") I'm in equal part angry and sad. Strike angry. Make that contemptuous. These are outsiders speaking. People who don't have enough regard for racing as a way of life to admire its people—being, for the only time during the year they can, just people.

Nor should it need to be said that May at Indy is more stressful than a decade on the floor of the commodities exchange. May at the Speedway for everyone is grace under pressure time. Year after year there is far more grace than there has any right to be.

The Speedway's top doctor talked a little about this when he said part of his job—and those of his colleagues—was to minister to the needs of the "four or five thousand people who come in at the beginning of the month and stay." To racers, he's a kind of small-town sawbones. And he understands that. And he seems to think it's a pretty nice thing to be.

For him, and for those willing to see and feel, May at Indy is:

. . . A gathering of small hurts and petty illnesses.

. . . Also brutal injury and shocking death.

. . . Not to mention as much pleasure and satisfaction as is to be found anywhere.

No Regrets

RELIVING AUTOMOBILE LIFE
WOULD BE AN EASY CHOICE
Aug. 16, 1993

HOWEVER FILLED WITH MISSED AND MISUSED OPPORTUNITY, I don't regret my car life. Wouldn't change anything. On the contrary, there is much I only wish I could do again.

If I could, I'd drive an almost-new MG-TD from Greenwich Village to Vinita, Okla., nonstop, starting off at 1 a.m. not having had even an inkling that the urge would come upon me until about six minutes earlier. It's the way road trips should come about, without reason or point, just an overwhelming need to be out alone in a car on a trip with real reach to it. It couldn't have the feel of exploration now as it did then—uncovering fresh, marvelous new places—but it could still carry the intoxicating sensation of suddenly cutting free of schedules and a tomorrow filled with obligations. A wonderful lightness of spirit that's become as rare as a diamond lorgnette these days.

Alternatively, I'd take a '59 Twincam across the country on the Southern Route, heading up the California coast to San Francisco. An all-business drive—tough and unrelenting, an over-the-road, fast run to get there but also to domesticate the car, learn it, make it comfortable to live with. Sleep by the road. Eat where it comes. Shower when you get there.

Most of all, on the subject of MGs, I'd want the moment I saw the first one that stopped me cold: a Tickford drophead in Paris just after the war. Somehow it had been sheltered away, and there it was, waiting for me around a corner somewhere, I had no idea what it was, but it went straight from my eyes to my heart, and it has been there ever since. The thought of the Tickford still brings a glorious feeling of utterly unexpected discovery. It has a taste to it, like a special kind of sugary/tart hard candy that melts and suddenly disappears, leaving only its memory behind.

A mug shot used with his column, regarded as "the classic" by those who worked for Leon, who often peered over the top of his glasses at you when delivering advice. *AutoWeek Archives*

If I could, I would drive Bill Harrah's Jerrari again. I'd go to driving school at Zandvoort in a Mercedes with John Fitch as a classmate. I'd try my best to keep up at the Range Rover off-road school, then use what I'd learned on a drive over and through the Welsh countryside.

It would be lovely to revisit the old French fortress town of Carcassonne, but only if I could once again drive there from Geneva in a ZR-1. However cosmopolitan any of us professes to be, the fierce pleasure that comes from bringing superior arms to bear against an enemy or even an ally—perhaps in this case especially against an ally—is rare and delicious. In some ways it's the fulfillment of the going-to-your-high-school-reunion-the-week-you're-on-the-cover-of-*Sports Illustrated* fantasy.

I'd like to have breakfast on race morning in the HoJo in Speedway with my friend, Peter, again; I'd like to do Mulholland riding right seat with Danny in the week between Riverside and Laguna. It would be wonderful to cover a Can-Am with Charlie Fox.

Most of all, I'd like—just once more—the wonder of discovery that accompanies that first moment inside an MG, sensing—but not being absolutely sure—an undreamed-of world lay waiting beyond.

If you enjoyed this book, spread the word.

Go to www.amazon.com and write a review on the book's page.

Visit the book's home page (www.autoweek.com/jaundicedeye).

Become a fan on the book's Facebook page
and suggest it to your friends.

Email info@671press.com and tell us directly.

* * *

671 Press is an independent publishing company,
created and operated by enthusiasts like you.

We encourage your suggestions, ideas, and even corrections.
Your input helps us improve our publications and make better ones
in the future. Please send any feedback to info@671press.com.

Become a fan of 671 Press on Facebook
(www.facebook.com/671press) or check us out at www.671press.com.

Send an email to info@671press.com to receive information about our
upcoming publications and other news from 671 Press.